Poetry and Criticism Before Plato

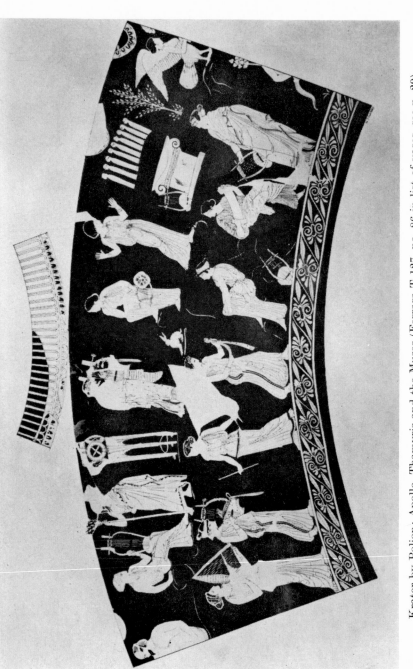

Krater by Polion: Apollo, Thamyris and the Muses (Ferrara T 127, no. 86 in list of vases, see p. 29) From *Scavi di Spina* I. Reproduced by courtesy of "L'Erma" di Bretschneider.

Poetry and Criticism Before Plato

ROSEMARY HARRIOTT

Lecturer in Classics
Royal Holloway College
University of London

METHUEN & CO LTD
11 NEW FETTER LANE
LONDON E.C.4

First published 1969 by
Methuen & Co Ltd,
11 New Fetter Lane,
London, EC4
© *1969 Rosemary Harriott*
Printed in Great Britain by
Butler & Tanner Ltd, Frome and London

Distributed in the U.S.A. by Barnes & Noble Inc.

To my Mother

Contents

Foreword

The literary contest between Aeschylus and Euripides in Aristophanes' *Frogs*, discussed in the last chapter, was, in fact, the starting-point of this book. It suggested lines of enquiry stretching back from the work of the fifth-century sophists and dramatists through the lyric poets to Homer and forward to Plato's writings on poetic inspiration. The material accumulated as a result of these enquiries illustrated the Greek poet's attitude to the Muses, to his audience and to his own art, and it seemed worth while to try to present it in a form accessible to the Greekless reader: accordingly, almost all of the Greek passages quoted have been translated or paraphrased and points of linguistic interpretation have been considered briefly, usually in footnotes.

My thanks are due to Professor T. B. L. Webster and Mr D. A. Campbell, both of whom have read the entire manuscript and given much encouragement, practical help and valuable advice; to Mr J. G. MacQueen, for his comments on the early chapters; to Professor Hugh Tredennick, for reading the proofs, and to Mrs A. C. Gardner, for expert typing. I should like to record here my deep gratitude to Professor A. M. Webster (Miss A. M. Dale) for her unfailing kindness and wise counsel during the five years when I was her pupil and later when this book was in its initial stages.

Abbreviations

In the list below will be found details of works to which frequent reference has been made, together with the abbreviations used, except that those dealing with vase-painting are named, for convenience, at the head of the list of vases following Chapter 1. Verse translations of Hesiod and Pindar are those of Professor Richmond Lattimore (published by the University of Michigan and the University of Chicago respectively).

G.L.P.   M. Bowra, *Greek Lyric Poetry*[2], Oxford, 1961.
Problems: M. Bowra, *Problems in Greek Poetry*, Oxford, 1953.
E. Diehl, *Anthologia Lyrica Graeca*[3], Leipzig, 1949–52.
D.-K.   H. Diels and W. Kranz, *Die Fragmente der Vorsokratiker*[6], 3 vols, Berlin, 1951–2.
Grenfell-Hunt: *Oxyrhynchus Papyri*, ed. B. P. Grenfell and A. S. Hunt *et al.*, London, 1898.
Philosophy: W. K. C. Guthrie, *A History of Greek Philosophy*, Cambridge, vol. 1, 1962, vol. 2, 1965.
Jebb-Pearson: *Sophocles' fragments*, edited with additional notes from the papers of R. C. Jebb and A. C. Pearson, Cambridge, 1917.
G. Kinkel, *Epicorum Graecorum fragmenta*, Leipzig, 1877.
T. Kock, *Comicorum Atticorum fragmenta*, 3 vols, Leipzig, 1880–8.
L.-P.   E. Lobel and D. Page, *Poetarum Lesbiorum fragmenta*, Oxford, 1955.
M.-W.   R. Merkelbach and M. L. West, *Fragmenta Hesiodea*, Oxford, 1967.
A. Nauck, *Tragicorum Graecorum fragmenta*[2], 3 vols, Leipzig, 1889.
P.M.G.   D. Page, *Poetae melici Graeci*, Oxford, 1962.
D.T.C.[2]   A. W. Pickard-Cambridge, *Dithyramb, tragedy and comedy*[2] (rev. by T. B. L. Webster), Oxford, 1962.
Rz.   A. Rzach, *Hesiodus: Carmina*, Leipzig, 1958.

B. Snell, *Bacchylidis carmina cum fragmentis*[8], Leipzig, 1961.
J. Taillardat, *Les images d'Aristofane*, Paris, 1965.
A. Turyn, *Pindari carmina cum fragmentis*, Oxford, 1952.

JOURNALS

Aeg.	*Aegyptus*
A.J.A.	*American Journal of Archaeology*
A.J.P.	*American Journal of Philology*
A. und A.	*Antike und Abendland*
Arch. class.	*Archeologia classica*
A.B.G.	*Archiv für Begriffsgeschichte*
B.C.H.	*Bulletin de correspondance hellénique*
B.I.C.S.	*Bulletin of the Institute of Classical Studies* (London)
C.J.	*Classical Journal*
C.P.	*Classical Philology*
C.R.	*Classical Review*
H.S.C.P.	*Harvard Studies in Classical Philology*
Hermath.	*Hermathena*
J.H.S.	*Journal of Hellenic Studies*
Mnem.	*Mnemosyne*
R.E.	Pauly-Wissowa, *Realenzyklopädie der classischen Altertumswissenschaft*
R.E.G.	*Revue des études grecques*
T.A.P.A.	*Transactions and Proceedings of the American Philological Association*

Chronological Table

Before 700	Homer, Eumelus of Corinth, Hesiod
700–650	Archilochus, Callinus, Aristeas
650–600	Tyrtaeus, Semonides, Alcman, Mimnermus
600–550	Solon, Stesichorus, Sappho, Alcaeus, Cleitias
550–500	Ibycus, Anacreon, Xenophanes, Pherecydes, Theognis, Heraclitus, Hipponax, Simonides
500–450	Parmenides, Pratinas, Timocreon, Pindar, Bacchylides, Aeschylus, Anaxagoras, Empedocles, Herodotus, Protagoras, Gorgias, Socrates, Democritus
450–400	Sophocles, Euripides, Critias, Cratinus, Crates, Achilles painter, Phiale painter, Clio painter, Calliope painter, Telecleides, Pherecrates, Eupolis, Aristophanes, Polion, Pothos painter, Meidias painter, Timotheus, Cinesias

INTRODUCTION

The Background to Criticism

Aristotle is justly famed as the founder of literary criticism, since his are the first works in the genre which have come down to us and are still valued and studied for themselves; but he was not its inventor. It is the purpose of this book to show that the river of Aristotelian criticism was fed by a number of streams. The source of the river is that critical instinct which is innate, if undiscovered, in each of us; and the period of Greek literature from Homer to the advent of the sophists represents a stage in which the channels of water flow for the most part underground and unseen. If we can trace only a little of their course, the process will still be valuable both for its intrinsic interest and for the contribution it can make to our understanding of criticism proper. Aristotle's influence on later critics has been immense, but Aristotle's own criticism was shaped, not only by the ideas newly current in the fourth century, but also by the whole inheritance of literature, and critical attitudes and language, which had come down to him. As we look for the hidden streams, we shall want to discover, if we can, why criticism emerged when it did, in fourth-century Greece and not in some other civilization in which literature was important, and what were the factors which shaped its course.

In using the analogy of channels of water flowing mainly underground I have meant to convey two things, the isolated nature of the evidence and the continuity of tradition. The evidence is found scattered through the works of Homer, Hesiod, the lyric and elegiac poets and the dramatists, who all present information and ideas about literature in the course of their work. Thus there is no poem specifically and entirely about poetry, but a large quantity of long or short extracts from larger works, together with some very short fragments whose context (and sometimes authorship) is unknown. On the other

1

hand, almost every type of poem may contain relevant information. It is not to be expected that material of this kind should form a consistent whole or display signs of progress in the same direction; the poets differ too much in personality and aim, and, moreover, three centuries separate Homer from Euripides. Nevertheless a sort of continuity is to be found. The poetry which has survived was disseminated widely enough to be known by all the writers we are studying, where this is chronologically possible, and it seems not to have been subject to fashion. A fifth-century poet like Aristophanes knew intimately not only Homer but lyric and the plays of his predecessors as well. We may guess that Aristophanes' knowledge was wider and deeper than that of the ordinary run of citizen but we cannot prove it, and the evidence of the comedies, intended to please everyone, suggests that our guess would not be entirely correct. Therefore, for example, Pindar's statements on the function of the poet are to be interpreted in the light of earlier material, to see where he rejects and where he accepts the views of his predecessors.

The work of the fifth-century theorists is difficult to assess because so little has survived and because we are forced to deduce its nature from Plato and later writers, who are not often impartial witnesses. In spite of these difficulties, it is clear that there were separate streams each contributing something to fully-developed criticism. We know that there were handbooks devoted to the theory and practice of particular arts, music and painting for example, and that the sophists began linguistic studies and continued the teaching of oratory begun in Sicily. Treatises of these three kinds, technical, linguistic and rhetorical, established terminology which was to be useful to later writers, and presented theories which they were to criticize or expand.

Material from the pre-Platonic period needs a point of reference if we are to evaluate it correctly: it would have been possible to use Aristotle's critical works as representing such a point, by comparing his theories and language with what had gone before. This procedure seemed to have two disadvantages. Great as the achievements of Aristotle were, his critical work was in a sense more limited than the unorganized utterances of his predecessors; for instance, he tells us nothing of what it was like to be a poet. Indeed it is an important part of his success to have defined and circumscribed the critic's task by his analytical and didactic method. Secondly, the *Poetics* of Aristotle, if not the *Rhetoric*, is written in language so compressed that almost every word has needed exposition, and even where the Greek is clear to us the ideas are often strange and unfamiliar. It has seemed more likely to be useful therefore to introduce the book with a summary of present-day critical attitudes and techniques, so that the beginnings may be viewed in the light of the assumptions we commonly make today.

T. S. Eliot defines criticism as 'that department of thought which either seeks to find out what poetry is, what its use is, what desires it satisfies, why it is written and why read, or recited; or which, making some conscious or unconscious assumption that we do know these things, assesses actual poetry.' And later, 'there are these two theoretical limits of criticism: at one of which we attempt to answer the question "what is poetry?" and at the other "is this a good poem?"'[1] The modern critic has had three lines of approach; he has either tried to theorize about the nature and use of literature in general or of particular forms, or to prescribe methods and aims for others to follow, or to write descriptive analyses of the works of individual authors. These three methods, which may be called the aesthetic, the legislative and the descriptive, are not completely independent of one another, since, for example, the description of a poem may well involve generalization about poetic principle; but they deserve to be separated in our minds because they stem from different attitudes on the part of their authors. At present the third method is most highly valued (although modern criticism is not free from didacticism), but it is hardly to be found at all in Greek and Roman criticism. Critical work appears in many forms, ranging in size from the review or scholarly article through the explanatory or apologetic preface to the book which studies a particular author or literary genre. Literary histories and biographies contain varying amounts of criticism proper, but all criticism needs both historical and comparative methods to be acceptable today. Aristotle was the first to demonstrate the historical method of criticism, although there are slight traces of it earlier, but the comparison of two

[1] *The Use of Poetry and the Use of Criticism* (London, 1964), 16.

national literatures begins with the Romans, and is then rarely more than superficial. The range of the modern critic is immense: there is possible interaction between his studies and those of the sociologist, philosopher, anthropologist, historian and psychologist, and his interest in music, architecture or painting can enrich his appreciation of a poem or play and the critical vocabulary in which he discusses it. If he combines the task of editor with that of critic, his needs are greater still, since he must be able to prepare a text and explain his author's meaning, as well as evaluating the work in detail and as a whole. Some of these lines of approach were impossible for the ancient critics, some were not demanded of them, and they could get little help from related disciplines. What ancient and modern critics have in common is a need for a language in which to discuss literature, and in this respect Plato and Aristotle were almost as well equipped as their successors.

This question of critical language is a vital one. Classical scholars have paid far more attention to the critic's meaning than to the ways in which it is expressed, and there is no general study of the development of critical terminology in Greece. To begin at the lowest level, hymns cannot be commissioned nor plays rehearsed without certain basic terms: words are necessary to differentiate types of literature by metre, form or function, or to distinguish one part of a work from another. These are practical needs: the more stringent requirements of literary discussion include both terms of this sort and ways of talking about subject-matter, style, plot and diction. E. M. Forster preserves an illuminating remark made by an elderly lady: 'How do I know what I'm going to say until I hear myself saying it?' Did the conceptual distinction between form and style, for example, precede or follow the critical terms? When Xenophanes talks about μῦθοι and λόγοι is he contrasting them, and if so, is the contrast between matter and diction, or between fiction and history, or between story and theme? At this second level, vocabulary needs careful study to reveal underlying concepts. The highest, most 'literary', level of critical language is reached with metaphor. The great and enduring questions about the source and nature of poetry were first treated only in metaphor, which is even today almost indispensable in any discussion of

4

poetic inspiration. Such metaphor is not ornamental: the metaphor is the meaning. Our habit of regarding metaphors as mere figures of speech has led to our underestimating their significance in early criticism. It is true that the living metaphor died and became entombed as cliché, but we are concerned with the period of its adolescence and maturity.

We shall see that the metaphors used in discussing poetry spring in the main from two fundamental attitudes to it, which are sometimes complementary and at others difficult to reconcile: one metaphorical complex has its source in beliefs about the Muses and knowledge of their cults and culminates in the splendour of Pindar's victory odes, while the other results from seeing the poet as craftsman and comparing his skill with that of the mason or painter, and this sort of metaphor permeates Aristophanes' criticism. Non-metaphorical language was created in two ways. Words could be coined for a specific purpose, or existing words could be modified in sense to become technical terms. Both types can present difficulties of interpretation as their meaning changes or crystallizes in some quite arbitrary way, but what Saintsbury calls 'the disease of technical jargon, in that specially dangerous form, the form of giving wantonly new meanings to common words' causes most problems, since we cannot always be sure whether the word is being used in its technical significance. To make matters worse, a word like λόγος may have more than one technical sense in addition to its wide range of ordinary meanings.

Critical language may be divided into the essential and the fashionable, and so in part depends on current theories. In Elizabethan England rhetorical terms prevailed in criticism, while at present the critic's vocabulary is more that of everyday speech, though not always free from the tiresome repetition of vogue-words. It would probably be true to say that where a literary passage can be quoted in full and then described in detail, a specialized terminology is least necessary, but for generalizing, defining or creating a system of aesthetics the resources of ordinary language are inadequate or too imprecise.

The literary critic today has a vocabulary adequate for his needs. If we turn aside for a moment to consider the problems facing the writer on music, we shall be better able to imagine the situation of the first poets who discussed their art. The author of a programme note, for example, has words for the basic ingredients of music, pitch, time, rhythm, and the like (though these are rarely logical or self-explanatory since their meaning has changed with the centuries), and for the organization of these ingredients into sections, movements and whole works. He can therefore analyse the work performed and be understood by anyone who has troubled to learn the basic musical and critical language. Nor has the writer any difficulty in communicating his views about the composer's place in history, or the place of this symphony in his total output; but when he wants to convey the meaning and emotional power of the work, words literally fail him. He falls back on metaphor or analogy, noting Dionysiac energy in a Beethoven symphony or pointilliste technique in Debussy. But the greatest challenge to his skill is presented by new works in an unfamiliar idiom which cannot yet be assessed historically. The analogy between these two critical arts is not exact, since interpreting music in the medium of words poses problems which do not face the literary critic, but to see the music critic groping for words and descriptive techniques can increase our awareness of the difficulties the Greek poets encountered when they tried to convey the emotional power of their art. I suspect that some of the notorious problems in interpreting the *Poetics* arise because even the critical techniques of Aristotle were not equal to the demands made on them, and that if we had an expanded version of his catharsis theory, we should still not find it able to endure rigorous scrutiny.

We have seen so far that there are some aspects of our subject in which comparison between modern criticism and the earliest beginnings of Greek criticism are both possible and helpful, but it is now necessary to describe the one major difference between the fully-developed form and its infancy. The modern critic intervenes between author and reader: the earliest Greek critic was the poet. It is true that poets still write criticism, but the prefaces of Dryden and T. S. Eliot and the latter's essays are written by the author in his capacity as critic of his own and others' works, and not as poet and dramatist. If the modern critic is sometimes despised as an author manqué or as interposing his self-conceit and literary pretensions between the author and his reader, or if he is valued as building a bridge between them, it remains true that the author is to some extent an isolated figure, whether he has retired of his own will to an ivory tower or has been prevented by the circumstances of modern life from an interchange of communication with his chosen audience.

In the poetry which we shall study first in this book the relationship between writer (in the modern sense of the word) and audience is close and immediate; there was interaction between the singer of tales and his hearers, there were elegiac drinking-songs produced for particular occasions, hymns commissioned for a specific festival. Paradoxically, this situation made the critical intermediary unnecessary, and provided the soil in which criticism could grow. Where poetry is performed at a gathering, small or large, it is discussed, and the poet feels free to comment in his work on his attitude to poetry. The process grows and develops, acquiring its own way of speaking, until it is making value-judgments based on general principles and theories. This is perhaps an over-simplification of the position, since, as I shall show, the relationship between poet and audience is made up of several strands, according to whether we think of him as teacher or entertainer, statesman or priest; but the communal aspect of Greek poetry needs to be continually stressed, partly because it is foreign to us, and partly so that we may remain aware of its implications.

The work of Parry and Lord has made it clear that a similar relationship between bard and hearers has existed at other times and in other places, in which it has not been accompanied by the emergence of articulate, reasoned criticism. But these other cultures have not provided the range of poetic occasions to be found in early Greece, nor have they given the impulse to criticism that was offered by the competitive nature of Greek literary life. There is much dispute about the date of the establishment of poetic contests of various sorts, but none about their importance. The poet might himself be a competitor, or he might write in praise of a winner in some form of athletic contest, but the agonistic spirit was engrained in society. In consequence, there was an emphasis on choosing the best which

7

was not entirely beneficial to the course of criticism. Ranking authors and their works in an order of merit is a satisfying occupation, but sterile, and it is not made much more useful when the award is accompanied by one or two laudatory epithets. Among the Romans Quintilian was particularly prone to this fault.

It is now possible to make some generalizations about the probable nature of early criticism. Graham Hough has defined the germs of criticism as 'a lively reaction to something we have read, and the desire to share it with another'. He finds this critical genesis in an elementary form in the marginal comments often seen in library books, and notes that these make judgments of a bare and elementary kind whose meaning 'could be reduced without much loss to two terms – "boo" and "hurrah" '. If we apply this proposition to Greece, *mutatis mutandis*, we should expect to find traces of the simple apportionment of praise and blame and no more. And there are judgments of this nature, even as late as the fifth century. One of Aristophanes' characters, for example, pronounces the tragedian Theognis a bore. But even early writers were capable of making fuller statements than these, sometimes actually backing them by reasoned argument. Their subject is more often the role of the poet in the community than the individual poem, and this is natural when we remember what has already been said about the communal characteristics of poetry at this period, and the Greek love of enquiry into basic principles which developed into philosophy. Thus criticism tended to ask and answer the first of Eliot's two questions, and to consider the merits of an individual poem as part of the wider issue, the true nature of poetry.

The sort of processes outlined above belong to what Eliot has called the pre-critical stage, which may be said to have ended in Greece when the influence of the sophists became widespread. The sophists themselves might be called early critics, since in attitude they are different from their predecessors, though living and working during the pre-critical period. The simple term 'critic' cannot properly be applied before the age of Plato, and even then is not strictly justifiable, since his literary criticism is often incidental or subordinated to a philosophical or didactic

8

purpose. Eliot has said that 'the important moment for the appearance of criticism seems to be the time when poetry ceases to be the expression of the mind of a whole people'. External factors usually bring about this change: in Athens they were the defeat by Sparta at the end of a protracted war and the moral upheaval caused partly by this national disaster and partly by the sophists, who were thus doubly responsible for the appearance of criticism, practising the new craft themselves, and upsetting traditional values. With the death of Old Comedy at the end of the fifth century, the ancient quarrel between poetry and philosophy had been temporarily settled – in philosophy's favour.

1. The Muses

No other culture has had deities of poetry comparable with the Muses of the Greeks, and Greek literature, from the earliest time, is concerned with the relationship between the Muse and the poet. The Muses flourished in the centuries from Homer to Plato, but in our era withered into convention, died, and were finally entombed as cliché, their epitaph three words of Byron: 'Hail Muse, etc.' Before we can begin to understand what they meant to early poets we need to imagine them as they were at that period, forgetting the trite guise in which we so often meet them. And so in this chapter I shall try to give a composite picture of the Muses, drawn from literature and vase-painting, in the belief that some such picture was part of the cultural background of the Greeks and affected their views of literature. Our picture cannot be complete since so many works of epic and lyric poetry and drama have failed to survive, but it may not be misleading.[1]

Hesiod's account of the lives and activities of the Muse is the fullest we have. Later poets were more interested in describing their relationship with the Muse than the Muses' own independent actions. In the proem to the *Theogony* Hesiod says that they were children of Zeus and Mnemosyne (Memory) and describes their birth and life:

> Mnemosyne, queen of the Eleutherian hills,
>   bore them
> in Pieria, when she had lain
>   with the Kronian Father;
> they bring forgetfulness of sorrows,
>   and rest from anxieties.
> For nine nights Zeus of the counsels
>   lay with her, going

[1] I exclude information about cults of the Muses which is not drawn from the literature of the period. For cults of the Muses in philosophical schools see P. Boyancé, *Le culte des Muses chez les philosophes grecs* (Paris, 1937).

10

up into her sacred bed, far away
    from the other immortals.
But when it was a year,
    after the seasons' turning
and the months had waned away, and many days
    were accomplished,
she bore her nine daughters, concordant
    of heart, and singing
is all the thought that is in them,
    and no care troubles their spirits.
She bore them a little way off
    from the highest snowy summit
of Olympos; there are their shining
    dancing places, their handsome
houses, and the Graces and Desire live there
    beside them
in festivity.[1]

Hesiod's account of the parentage and birth of the Muses became the dominant one, although there are traces of other versions in the literature of our period. Alcman in one fragment says that he will sing the Muse who is daughter of Zeus,[2] but the papyrus commentary states that he also made the Muses daughters of Ge.[3] According to Pausanias, Mimnermus spoke of two generations of Muses, the elder the daughters of Uranus and Gaia and the younger the children of Zeus.[4] For these poets the Muses were among the most ancient powers. Hesiod expresses their importance by making them children of the reigning deity, Zeus, but he links them with the former generation of gods by making their mother, Mnemosyne, herself the daughter of Uranus and Gaia.[5] It seems likely that there were originally three Muses, as is supposed to have been stated by Eumelus of Corinth;[6] but the Hesiodic nine became the accepted number to such an extent that The Nine was a way of referring to the Muses.[7]

[1] *Theog.* 53–65, Richmond Lattimore's translation.   [2] *P.M.G.* 28.
[3] *P.M.G.* 5 fr. 2.28 (P. Oxy. 2390), cf. *P.M.G.* 67.
[4] Pausanias 9.29.4.   [5] *Theog.* 153.
[6] Eumelus fr. 17. Kinkel: there are three Muses, daughters of Apollo; *Cypria* fr. dub. 23 Kinkel: three Muses named Musa, Thea, Hymno.
[7] For other versions see *R.E.* s.v. Musai.

11

Hesiod makes it clear that the chief function of the Muses is to celebrate the Olympian gods.[1] Later he says that they delight the mind of Zeus as they tell of what is, and what is to be, and what was before now.[2] They hymn Uranus and Gaia and their divine progeny and also the race of human kind and the Giants. They sing too of the laws and customs of the immortals.[3] Homer shows the Muses once on Olympus, entertaining the gods, and once on earth meeting Thamyris.[4] The Homeric Hymn to Apollo expands the picture of the heavenly choir:[5] when Apollo went from Delos to Olympus, the Muses sang the joys of gods and the sufferings of men, while the Graces and their companions danced and Apollo played his lyre, all to the delight of Zeus and Hera. Pindar apparently made this heavenly function of the Muses the cause of their birth: according to Aristides,[6] in his Hymn to Zeus the other gods asked Zeus to create divinities to praise him and his works in speech and music.

Exceptionally the Muses might sing in honour of mortals. Already in Homer they mourn Achilles in the company of the Nereids;[7] more often they attend weddings. The François Vase shows all nine Muses, with other gods, visiting Peleus and Thetis after their wedding,[8] and Pindar and Euripides also record their presence. In the third stasimon of the *Iphigenia in Aulis*,[9] the chorus describes how the Muses came to the wedding and sang in honour of Peleus and Thetis, and Pindar made them attend not only this wedding but that of Cadmus and Harmonia. In the third *Pythian* he says that Peleus and Cadmus were given

'blessedness beyond all mortals. They heard on the mountain and at seven-gated Thebes the gold-chapleted Muses singing

[1] *Theog.* 10.21, cf. *Works* 1–2. See also Stesichorus *P.M.G.* 210.
[2] *Theog.* 38.
[3] *Theog.* 44–52, 67–8.
[4] *Il.* 1.603–4, *Il.* 2.594 ff, see p. 28.
[5] 186–206.
[6] II. 142 Dindorf.
[7] *Od.* 24.60 ff., cf. *P.M.G.* 880 (the Linus-song) and Proclus' epitome of the *Aethiopis* (Kinkel 1. 32–4): Thetis came with the Muses and her sisters and mourned her son. This passage is used by Minton as evidence for his theory of the association of the Muses in the Homeric poems with ultimate defeat – with death, in fact (W. Minton, *T.A.P.A.* 1960, 292–309). This theory is discussed below, p. 45. See also Duchemin, *Pindare, Poète et Prophète*, 269–96.
[8] No. 1 in List of Vases.   [9] *I.A.* 1040.

when one married ox-eyed Harmonia, and the other wise
Nereus' legendary daughter, Thetis.[1]

Theognis has given the song sung by the Muses at Cadmus'
wedding:

'ὅττι καλόν, φίλον ἐστί · τὸ δ'οὐ καλὸν οὐ φίλον ἐστί.'[2]

'The fine is dear: what is not fine is not dear.' Epicharmus'
Marriage of Hebe told of, or possibly presented, seven Muses
among the divine guests at the wedding of Hebe and Heracles.[3]

Two passages in epinician odes show the Muses as givers of
sleep. In the first *Pythian*, Pindar invokes the lyre which
quenches the thunderbolt and soothes Zeus' eagle to sleep; even
Ares and the enemies of Zeus are quelled by its music. The lyre
belongs to Apollo and the Muses and its power is the result of
their skill. Bacchylides, writing in a dithyramb[4] about Io's
escape from the watch set over her by Hera, wonders whether
the Muses made Argos fall asleep. The soothing power of music
is recognized in honouring the Muses as givers of sleep. This idea
is extended when Stesichorus makes them powerful also against
war:

Μοῖσα σὺ μὲν πολέμους ἀπωσαμένα μετ᾽ ἐμοῦ
κλείοισα θεῶν τε γάμους ἀνδρῶν τε δαίτας
καὶ θαλίας μακάρων.[5]

'Muse, with me you repel wars and celebrate the weddings of
gods, the banquets of men and the feasts of the blessed.' The
association of music, feasting and peace was one that appealed
strongly to Aristophanes and he adapted Stesichorus' lines in
the *Peace*.[6] The name of Thaleia suggests feasting and abundance, and Pindar calls his Muse ταμίας κώμων, 'steward of
revels'.[7]

In the *Lysistrata*, the chorus of Laconian envoys invokes first

[1] *P.* 3.89–92.   [2] 15–9, cf. Eur. *Bacch.* 881, 901.
[3] Pickard-Cambridge, *Dithyramb, Tragedy and Comedy*, rev. ed. 260. Epicharmus' Muses bore the names of rivers, and they were represented as chiefly
concerned with food by a pun in their title Pierides and Pimpleides, that is
'Fat' and 'Fill'.
[4] 14.35.   [5] *P.M.G.* 210.
[6] 774–80; cf. e.g. *Birds* 731–4. Muses and peace: Eur. *Suppl.* 489.
[7] *I.* 5.57.

13

a Muse who was present at the battle of Artemisium,[1] and, in their next song, a Laconian Muse, who is to leave the river Taygetus and summon other Spartan deities to help the chorus praise their native city. Aristophanes' words suggest that the Muses of the Spartans were not merely eye-witnesses of battle, as were Homeric Muses, so that they might accurately celebrate heroic exploits afterwards, but that the Spartans, who marched into battle to the music of auloi, came to think of the Muses as something akin to war goddesses.[2] It is possible that Aristophanes knew Spartan choral lyric in which the Muses were invoked as givers of victory, not merely of fame. Professor Page writes: 'For Alcman, too, the Muse whom he invokes is no common spirit. Her temple stands near Athena Chalcioecus; to her the army offers sacrifice before the battle. She is among the oldest goddesses, a blessing and inspiration to all her people, not to her poets only. She is a cosmic power, to be called by Alcman, not vaguely daughter of "Zeus and Memory", but of the Sky and of the Earth.'[3]

When a Muse was invoked she might be honoured with her titles or with a complimentary description. The care which a poet bestowed on such description is some indication of his devotion to a deity. His purpose is not informative: he is not concerned to tell his hearer precisely how the Muse was dressed. However, where the description is strongly visual, it is reasonable to assume that the writer has a mental picture of the Muse as a beautiful goddess, a being whose physical existence was real for him.

Homer tells us nothing of the Muses' appearance, but thereafter poets are lavish with descriptive terms and seem to take delight in inventing fresh compliments. The Muses' hair and eyes, their clothes and hairbands all receive praise in language which was used of mortal women as well, but in addition they were paid the sort of honour usually reserved for deities, particularly in compound words including 'gold'. Hesiod, fol-

[1] *Lys.* 1247, 1296.
[2] Plutarch *Moralia* 238B: Lycurgus sacrificed to the Muses before battle so that the Spartans' military exploits might deserve to be honoured in song. Cf. *de coh. ira* 10: the Spartans sacrified in order that λόγος ἐμμένῃ, and *Lyc.* 21: the Spartans were most musical and most warlike of races.
[3] *Alcman: The Partheneion* 70.

14

lowed by Bacchylides and Pindar, mentions their gold hair-
band, Euripides their gold sandals.

As we might expect, the beauty of their singing and dancing
and their skill in playing musical instruments are extolled by
the poets, sometimes in single words, sometimes in longer
passages. In the *Odyssey*[1] the Muse was λίγεια, 'clear-voiced',
and the Homeric term recurs again and again.[2] In the *Iliad*[3] the
Muses sang 'antiphonally, with fair voice' (ἀμειβόμεναι ὀπὶ καλῇ),
a phrase found also in the Hymn to Apollo.[4] In the proem to the
Theogony Hesiod dwells on the beauty of the Muses' singing,
describing it in a variety of ways, not all of them copied by later
poets. After he has told how the Muses appeared to him, he
appeals to them as singers who delight Zeus by singing of past,
present and future

> with harmonious voices, and the sound
>   that comes sweet from their mouths
> never falters, and all the mansion of Zeus
>   the father
> of the deep thunder is joyful
>   in the light voice of the goddesses
> that scatters through it, and the peaks
>   of snowy Olympus re-echo
> and the homes of the immortals.[5]

There are few instances of more general praise of the Muses.
Hesiod wrote of their unity of thought and feeling,[6] a writer of
Old Comedy called them good-tempered,[7] and Aristophanes in-
voked them as ἀγναί, 'pure', a term more often applied to the
Graces.[8] It is surprising that the Muses are not themselves
called wise.[9]

[1] 24.62.
[2] e.g. *h.Hom.* 14.1, 17.1, 20.1; Alcman, *P.M.G.* 30, Stesichorus, *P.M.G.* 240, 278.
[3] 1.604.　　　　　[4] 186; cf. *Theog.* 68.
[5] *Theog.* 39–43, Lattimore's translation. Hesiod describes the Muses' singing
also at *Theog.* 10, 43–5, 60–1, 65–70.
[6] *Theog.* 60; cf. Servius on *Aen.* 1.8: has Musas Siculus Epicharmus non
Musas sed ὁμονοούσας dicit ('Epicharmus the Sicilian calls these Muses not
Muses but *like-thinking*').
[7] Anon. Com. 22, cf. Bacchylides fr. 21.4.　　　　　[8] *Frogs* 875.
[9] If we read Μοισᾶν instead of Μοιρᾶν at Pindar *N.* 7.1, we have one instance
of Muses as βαθύφρονες, 'deep-minded'; Kenyon conjectured θεμερόφρων
(Hesychius: 'of grave and serious mind') applied to Urania at Bacchylides 16.3.

Homer does not mention any Muse by name but Hesiod lists the names of the nine as the culmination of his account of them. They are: Clio, Euterpe, Thaleia, Melpomene, Terpsichore, Erato, Polymnia, Urania and last, and most important, Calliope:

Κλειώ τ' Εὐτέρπη τε Θάλειά τε Μελπομένη τε
Τερψιχόρη τ' Ἐρατώ τε Πολύμνιά τ' Οὐρανίη τε
Καλλιόπη θ' · ἡ δὲ προφερεστάτη ἐστὶν ἁπασέων.[1]

The complete list does not occur elsewhere in the literature of our period, but there are nine Muses on the François Vase whose names are similar to those of Hesiod, except that Polymnia appears as Polymnis and Terpsichore as Stesichore. There is no complete, clear, regular differentiation of an individual Muse's function in literature at least until Hellenistic times, and even the Romans were inconsistent in their accounts, but the names individually are evocative and taken together cover the chief meanings and associations which music had for the Greeks. Hesiod's names express the union of poetry, song, instrumental music and dance, and their function in spreading the glory of gods and men and in adding to the delights of feasting and festivals.[2] Calliope, who is Hesiod's senior Muse, is mentioned much more often by poets than any of her sisters. She is invoked by Alcman, Sappho, Stesichorus, Bacchylides, who also speaks of her as the giver of fame, and Empedocles.[3]

On red-figure vases Calliope is named several times. She may be shown holding plectrum or lyre (nos. 3, 4 and 6); a vase in New York by the Calliope Painter has Calliope standing before a seated Apollo: each holds a phiale (no. 12).[4] The same painter depicted this Muse on the interior of a cup in London (no. 15). Here Calliope has a phiale for libations and oenochoe and Apollo

[1] *Theog.* 77–9; for different names see p. 11.
[2] For the Hesiodic names see M. L. West, *Theogony, ad loc.*; H. J. Rose, Fondation Hardt, *Entretiens* I, 98; K. Deichgraber, *Die Musen, Nereiden und Okeaninen in Hesiods Theogonie* (Wiesbaden, 1965), 176 ff. If Hesiod invented the Muses' names they need not have been suggested by the preceding description of their character and activities; both description and names may be intended to convey what Hesiod felt about music.
[3] Alcman *P.M.G.* 27, Sappho fr. 124 L.–P., Stesichorus *P.M.G.* 240, Bacchylides 5.176, 19.13, Epicharmus 131.3 D.-K.
[4] For details of these and other vases mentioned here see the list at the end of the chapter.

a lyre. The exterior may also show Muses. Calliope's presence on a vase depicting the murder of Laius is puzzling: if she is the Muse and not a servant named Calliope, she must be 'present as a local deity' (no. 16).[1]

The innovating fifth-century poet Dionysius Chalcus wrote of poetry as Καλλιόπης κραυγήν, 'Calliope's screeching', and was scolded by Aristotle for the bad metaphor.[2] Her position as chief Muse is marked by Plato's epithet for her: βασιλική, 'queenly'.[3] Timotheus called her the mother of Orpheus,[4] and she is named in a monody in Euripides' *Hypsipyle*.[5]

Bacchylides calls on Clio to hymn Demeter, Persephone and Hiero's swift horses at the beginning of his third ode. Later in the poem, in a passage reminiscent of Pindar's First *Olympian*, he suggests that the Muse makes virtue imperishable.[6] Bacchylides was certainly conscious of the connection of the name Clio with κλέος, 'fame', but neither he nor Pindar thought of her as the unique giver of fame, to the exclusion of her sisters. In his twelfth ode Bacchylides prays to Clio, for whom he coins the epithet 'mistress of hymns',[7] to 'direct his thoughts like an experienced steersman'. Clio appears again in the mutilated ending of the thirteenth ode. Bacchylides seems to be writing about his relationship with the victor and his family and says that if Clio, the giver of all bloom, has really instilled this friendship in his heart, his songs will proclaim it to the whole people.

Pindar's Third *Nemean*, which begins with an invocation of the Muse as the Mother of poets, ends with the statement that light has shone for the victor from three cities because Clio wished it. Pindar does not say whether the light is that of victory or fame.

Finally Plutarch[8] preserves a fragment of Simonides[9] in which he addressed Clio as ἀγνᾶν ἐπίσκοπε χερνίβων, 'guardian of the undefiled waters of purification', in the Muses' sanctuary at Delphi.

Clio is named on two red-figured vases, one by the Clio Painter and the other by the Calliope Painter (nos. 8 and 11; see also nos. 7, 9, 17, 18 and 19). The former shows her standing

---

[1] See also nos. 9, 13 and 14 in the list.   [2] *Rhet.* 1405a 31.
[3] *Phaedrus.* 309.   [4] *P.M.G.* 791.223.   [5] Fr. 1. iv. 8. Bond.   [6] 3.90–2.
[7] 12.1–2, ὑμνοάνασσα.   [8] *Pyth. orac.* 17.iii.43.   [9] *P.M.G.* 72(b).

on the right of the picture looking down at her sister Terpsichore who is seated holding a lyre and is looking away from Clio at Apollo who returns her gaze. Clio raises her right hand and may be speaking or singing. The interior of the second vase associates Clio with Musaeus, and she is probably depicted again on one of the exterior scenes.

Literary evidence for Urania is slighter: she is mentioned only by Hesiod and Bacchylides, whose fondness for naming individual Muses distinguishes him from other poets. A fragment of Hesiod names Urania as mother of Linus mourned by all singers and harpers.[1] Bacchylides in his fifth ode speaks of himself as the renowned servant of Urania sending a hymn from Ceos to Hiero; the following ode mentions a hymn of Urania, queen of song, to be sung for the Cean victor, and the invocation of the sixteenth poem mentions Urania in a context which is fragmentary.[2] The Muses Erato, Euterpe, Melpomene and Thaleia are not mentioned individually in poems except in Hesiod's list, and references to Polymnia and Terpsichore are rare. Here the practice of poets differs from that of vase-painters. A lyric fragment speaks of Polymnia as 'giver of all pleasure'; Terpsichore, whose name means 'delight in choral dance', is invoked by Corinna and in Pindar's Second *Isthmian* called 'honey-voiced'.[3]

Although poets more often chose to stress the kinship of Zeus and the Muses, their mother Mnemosyne was not unhonoured. The importance of her symbolic role would be hard to overestimate: Memory, the bride of Zeus, was source of the arts of poetry, song and dance and the repository of all knowledge. For the Greeks she and her daughters had a double significance: they brought about poems by stirring men's memories and emotions and they preserved knowledge of the past. Mnemosyne was both Memory, the accumulated store of inherited knowledge, and the Reminder, who caused κλέα ἀνδρῶν, 'the deeds of men', to be recalled and kept fresh. At the stage when culture was oral she occupied a key position.

When Mnemosyne is associated with the Muses it is often

---

[1] fr. 192; for Linus see *Il.* 18.570 and Aeschylus, *Agamemnon* 121, 139, 160.
[2] 5.13, 6.11, 16.3.
[3] *P.M.G.* 942, ascribed by Blass to Alcman, Corinna *P.M.G.* 655.1, *I.* 2.7–8.

their function of keeping memory alive which is emphasized.[1] Aristotle says[2] that the Muses, daughters of Mnemosyne, will increase the deathless glory of Hermeias. Euripides reveals his reverence in his praise of the Muses and Apollo in the Second Stasimon of the *Hercules Furens*:[3]

> ἔτι τοι γέρων ἀοιδὸς κελαδεῖ Μναμοσύναν ·
> ἔτι τὰν Ἡρακλέους
> καλλίνικον ἀείδω.

'In old age the poet still hymns Mnemosyne; I still sing Heracles' victory song.' The connection between Mnemosyne and Heracles' fame is close. Pindar's Seventh *Nemean* ode established Mnemosyne as giver of fame: she is Memory which mirrors the ages.[4] When Aeschylus' Prometheus recounted the blessings he bestowed on man, he numbered the invention of writing among them:[5]

> καὶ μὴν ἀριθμόν, ἔξοχον σοφισμάτων,
> ἐξηῦρον αὐτοῖς, γραμμάτων τε συνθέσεις,
> μνήμην ἁπάντων, μουσμήτορ' ἐργάτιν.

'I invented for men number, the supreme skill, and writing, which records all things, handmaid and mother of the musical arts'. This is a revolutionary claim, both because Prometheus takes to himself a function not usually regarded as his, and because the importance given to writing is at odds with the traditional importance of oral transmission of knowledge, but the harshness is softened by the introduction of an allusion to the figures of myth. Memory, the abstraction, is followed by words which recall her role as Mother of the Muses and handmaid of poets; here it is the art of writing which is elevated to serve mankind as source of poetry.[6]

---

[1] On a vase in Syracuse (no. 3) Mnemosyne stands holding a roll, while Calliope, seated, plays her lyre. See B. Snell, *A.B.G.* 1964, 19–21, J. Notopoulos, *T.A.P.A.* 1938, 465–93.

[2] *P.M.G.* 842.

[3] 679 ff.

[4] 7.12–16: see p. 128 for text, translation and comment.

[5] *P.V.* 459–61.

[6] Mneme and Mnemosyne are interchangeable names. See *P.M.G.* 133.

When Hermes played his newly-invented lyre 'first in his song he praised the goddess Mnemosyne':

Μναμοσύναν μὲν πρῶτα θεῶν ἐγέραιρεν ἀοιδῇ.[1]

Later poets often associated Mnemosyne with the Muses,[2] and Socrates, imitating the poetic convention, felt that he must invoke the Muses and Mneme to aid his memory.[3]

When poets seek to honour the Muses they may do so by glorifying their appearance and their musical powers or by giving them titles which recall their place on Olympus or their cults at Pieria or Helicon. Homer says little about his Muses, only that they are daughters of Zeus[4] and dwell on Olympus.[5] Hesiod, who varies his titles for the Muses more than Homer, also often refers to their Olympian home.[6] The pattern established by Homer and Hesiod is found repeatedly in other poets[7] and can even be parodied by Hermippus.[8]

It was on Mount Helicon in Boeotia that the Muses appeared to Hesiod, and it is clear from Pausanias' description and from archaeological work that their cult was important there over a long period.[9] Here, Hesiod says, they

> possess the great and holy mountain
>   of Helikon
> and dance there on soft feet
>   by the dark blue water
> of the spring, and by the altar
>   of the powerful son of Kronos;
> who wash their tender bodies in the waters
>   of Permessos
> or Hippokrene, spring of the Horse,
>   or holy Olmeios,

[1] h.Hom. 4.429.

[2] e.g. Alcman, P.M.G. 8.9, the author of P.M.G. 941, Solon 1. Aristophanes invokes her (Lys. 1249).   [3] Euthyd. 275D.

[4] Od. 1.10. The Muses were so often addressed as daughters of Zeus that the phrase θύγατερ Διός by itself denotes the Muse in Aristophanes, Peace 736 (= Simonides 62).

[5] Il. 2.484, 11.218, 14.508, 16.112; cf. 'Ολυμπιάδες at Il. 2.491.

[6] Theog. 25, 52, 966, 1022.

[7] e.g. Alcman (P.M.G. 3. fr. 1.1) and Sappho (58 L.-P.).

[8] fr. 63.

[9] Pausanias 9.29 ff.; Roux, B.C.H. 1954, 22–48.

and on the high places of Helikon
  have ordered their dances
which are handsome and beguiling,
  and light are the feet they move on.[1]

Helicon's springs became the pre-eminent symbol for poetic
inspiration to the Romans and through Latin poetry to the
European tradition, but this symbol was not used by early
Greek writers. Ibycus,[2] Pindar[3] and Euripides[4] are among the
writers who speak of Heliconian Muses. The Boeotian Corinna,
who may be contemporary with Pindar, writes of a musical
contest between the mountains Helicon and Cithaeron; the gods
cast votes to decide the issue and this democratic process was
supervised by the Muses. Cithaeron, surprisingly enough, won,
to Helicon's chagrin.[5]

The Pierian cult of the Muses, about which less is known, is
nevertheless reflected in literature to a greater extent than the
cult at Helicon. At the beginning of the *Works and Days* Hesiod
asks the Muses to come from Pieria, where, as he tells us in the
Theogony, they were conceived. Pieria is in Macedonia, near
Mount Olympus, and the North was traditionally the source of
the shadowy figures of the early poets, among them Orpheus and
Thamyris.

Pindar, Bacchylides and Sappho name the Muses as Pierian;[6]
Pratinas called the Muse herself Pieris:

τὰν ἀοιδὰν κατέστασε Πιερὶς βασίλειαν.

'Pieris made Song queen.'[7] Pausanias[8] preserves a story that
the Muses were the children of Pieros, and there is a trace of this
legend in the Muses' title of Pierides.[9] The *Bacchae* of Euripides,
which he wrote when he was staying at the court of King
Archelaus of Macedonia, honours the cult of Zeus and the Muses
which Archelaus had established at Dion. In the first stasimon
the chorus of Maenads, horrified at Pentheus' impiety, express
their longing to be in Cyprus. In the passage quoted below they

[1] *Theog.* 2–8.   [2] *P.M.G.* 282.24.   [3] Paean 7b.14.
[4] *H.F.* 791.   [5] *P.M.G.* 654.
[6] e.g. Pindar *O.* 10.96, *P.* 6.49; Bacchylides 1.3; Sappho 103 L.-P
[7] *P.M.G.* 708.6.   [8] 9.29.3–4.
[9] For a comic interpretation of this title see p. 13.

21

pray to Bromian Dionysus to take them to 'Pieria, the lovely
haunt of the Muses, the holy slope of Olympus where Graces and
Desire have their homes and where it is lawful for Maenads to
celebrate their rites:'

> οὗ δ' ἁ καλλιστευομένα
> Πιερία μούσειος ἕδρα,
> σεμνὰ κλιτὺς Ὀλύμπου,
> ἐκεῖσ' ἄγε με, Βρόμιε Βρόμιε,
> προβακχ' εὔιε δαῖμον.
> ἐκεῖ Χάριτες,
> ἐκεῖ δὲ Πόθος · ἐκεῖ δὲ βακ-
> χαις θέμις ὀργιάζειν.[1]

The second stasimon also associates Orpheus, whose playing
subdued trees and animals, with Pieria; the chorus' reverence
is summed up in the line μάκαρ ὦ Πιερία, 'O blessed Pieria'.[2]
We have seen that by the time of Homer the Muses were
already established securely as Olympian. Yet traces persist, at
least until the time of Plato, of a belief in the Muses as local
deities, like the various nymphs of streams and mountains, but
having wider powers. Hesiod's description of the Muses' life on
Helicon showed them bathing in the mountain's springs and
streams, but he did not make the association significant: the
springs did not symbolize inspiration for him. Yet for the
Romans the gushing forth of water was the chief symbol of
poetic inspiration and was satirized as such by Juvenal and
Persius. The rejection of the 'inspired' poet's role is made clear
by Persius in his Prologue:

> nec fonte labra prolui caballino
> nec in bicipiti somniasse Parnaso
> memini, ut repente sic poeta prodirem.
> Heliconidasque pallidamque Pirenen
> illis remitto, quorum imagines lambunt
> hederae sequaces: ipse semipaganus
> ad sacra uatum carmen adfero nostrum.[3]

[1] *Bacch.* 409–16; for the cult at Dion, see Diodorus 17.16.3.
[2] *Bacch.* 560–75.
[3] 1–7; cf. Horace, *Ars Poetica*, 295–8.

'I never soused my lips in the Nag's Spring; never, that I can remember, did I dream on the two-topped Parnassus, that I should thus come forth suddenly as a poet. The maidens of Mount Helicon and the blanching waters of Pirene I give up to the gentlemen round whose busts the clinging ivy twines: it is only as a half-member of the community that I bring my lay to the holy feast of the bards.' We cannot now trace the origin and development of this idea which we merely glimpse from time to time,[1] and at this point I shall merely draw attention to the passages of literature which connect the Muses with actual, not metaphorical, streams.

Plutarch[2] tells us that there was a shrine of the Muses at Delphi of which Simonides wrote:[3]

ἔνθα χερνίβεσσιν ἀρύεται τὸ Μοισᾶν
καλλικόμων ὑπένερθεν ἁγνὸν ὕδωρ.

'There the pure water of the Muses with their beautiful hair is drawn up for purifications.' The pure water of the Muses, from the spring Cassotis, seems likely to have been used by them, in a ceremony supervised by Clio, in the worship of Apollo. Pindar connects the Muses with Dirce, the spring of his native Thebes. At the end of the Sixth *Isthmian*[4] he says that the Muses made the waters of Dirce gush forth outside the walls of Thebes.

There were also Muses described as local deities who were not linked with springs or streams and whose significance is not easy to understand. We know that there were many local cults of the Muses in Greece,[5] but the literary evidence which concerns us does not merely refer to local cult. In Bacchylides' second Ode,[6] written to celebrate a victory at Corinth won by a Cean, the poet says that the native (αὐθιγενής) Muse summons the music of flutes. Again Aristophanes' Acharnians,[7] preparing to state their wrongs, invoke the Acharnian Muse. It is an interesting and unique invocation, whose imagery will be discussed later, but it is clear that this Muse represents the essential Acharnian spirit and belongs to them. It looks as though the feeling that Muses were local powers remained strong enough to support innovations of this kind.

[1] See p. 83.   [2] *Pyth. orac.* 17.iii.43 Pohl.-Siev.   [3] *P.M.G.* 577(a).
[4] 74–5.   [5] R.E. s.v. Musai.   [6] Bacchylides 2.11.   [7] *Ach.* 665–75.

The god most frequently associated with the Muses was Apollo. The gods of Olympus after their council were entertained by Apollo and the Muses jointly: Apollo played, the Muses sang.[1] Apollo was Musagetes, the leader of the Muses,[2] although on one occasion he spoke of himself as their follower. In the Homeric Hymn to Hermes, Apollo says:

καὶ γὰρ ἐγὼ Μούσῃσιν ᾿Ολυμπιάδεσσιν ὀπηδός,
τῇσι χοροί τε μέλουσι καὶ ἀγλαὸς οἶμος ἀοιδῆς
καὶ μολπὴ τεθαλυῖα καὶ ἱμερόεις βρόμος αὐλῶν.

'I attend the Olympian Muses, whose concern is with dancing and the bright path of song, with abundant singing and the lovely sound of flutes.'[3] One of the scenes on the shield of Heracles[4] showed Apollo playing his golden lyre among the deathless gods while the divine Pierian Muses were beginning a song, like women who sing with clear voices. Pausanias[5] describes a similar scene depicted on the Chest of Cypselus in which Muses sang and Apollo led the song, with an inscription which emphasizes both the grace of the dancers and the leadership of Apollo.

Simonides too is reported to have written that the Muses who always enjoy song and dance make the whole of Helicon resound when Apollo comes to lead them.[6] The Homeric Hymn to Apollo and the Muses[7] is a re-working of Hesiod's words in the *Theogony*[8]

ἐκ γάρ τοι Μουσέων καὶ ἑκηβόλου ᾿Απόλλωνος
ἄνδρες ἀοιδοὶ ἔασιν ἐπὶ χθόνα καὶ κιθαρισταί.

In these lines Hesiod makes the Muses and Apollo jointly responsible for the existence of bards and cithara-players among men.[9] In the Fifth *Pythian* Pindar lists the blessings bestowed by Apollo on men; 'he provided the lyre, and grants the Muse as

---

[1] *Il.* 1.604.
[2] Sappho 91 L.-P., Pindar fr. 159, the writer of *P.M.G.* 941; Eumelus of Corinth, fr. 17K, is said to have made him father of his three Muses.
[3] *h.Hom.* 4.450.   [4] 'Hesiod', *Shield* 201–6.   [5] 5.18.4.
[6] Himer. or. lxii 54, p. 226 Colonna; *P.M.G.* 578.
[7] *h.Hom.* 25; for evidence of a joint cult of Apollo and the Muses see *P.M.G.* 1027(g).
[8] 94–5.
[9] The lyre is joint possession of Apollo and the Muses at *Pythian* 1. 1–13.

he pleases', and this gift is connected with a peaceful condition of good order in the community.[1]

Groups of Muses are a common subject on red-figure pottery, either alone or with Musaeus or Thamyris. On black-figure, from 515 onwards, they more usually occur as companions of Apollo, a subject which retains its popularity through the red-figure period also. Their association with Apollo resembles that of the maenads with Dionysus; it is not surprising that this should be so: the poets record their own professional link with the Muse, but the vase-painters show Muses as goddesses of the arts of music, song and dance, and not usually in their relationship with a poet, unless that relationship is established in myth.

The most celebrated portrayal of the Muses in art is that on the third band of Kleitias' François Vase (no. 1), painted in about 560. The gods are visiting Peleus and Thetis after their wedding, and among them are the nine Muses. All the Muses are named, and their names coincide with those established by Hesiod, except that Polhymnia appears as Polhymnis and Terpsichore is replaced by Stesichore.[2] The Muses are led by Calliope, as in Hesiod, and she plays the syrinx. All nine Muses are only twice shown again, once on a South Italian red-figure vase in Munich.[3] The scene is perhaps a temple, and the Muses are not named but identified by the possession of musical instruments, a scroll or a box. A bird, possibly a heron, is at the feet of the Muse who plays the flute.

When fewer than nine Muses are shown the number does not reflect variation in mythology; for example, the presence of four Muses does not mean that the artist was referring to a legend which gave the number of Muses as four. In fact, vases whose subject is Apollo and the Muses frequently place Apollo centrally, flanked by single Muses, or a pair of Muses.[4] The number of Muses represented varies from one to ten (if the ten women on no. 22 are indeed Muses).

[1] P. 5.60–9.
[2] If the name Stesichore means 'establisher of the chorus' rather than 'leader of the chorus' we may see an allusion to the growing importance of choral lyric poetry and, in particular, to lyric poetry accompanied by dancing in one place, as apposed to e.g. processional hymns. The only other variations from the accepted names for Muses are Melousa on no. 5 and Choro on no. 17.
[3] No. 9. For the nine on a krater by Polion see p. 25.
[4] e.g. no. 51, Apollo between pairs of Muses; no. 56, Apollo between two Muses.

The location of scenes depicting Muses is usually likely to be Helicon. Once (on no. 23), the mountain is named, more often, indicated by rocks.[1] The early-Italiote volute-krater in Munich (no. 29), which shows nine Muses, is unique in placing them between two columns. Elsewhere an interior scene is suggested when a Muse is shown seated on a stool.[2] In view of the frequency of references to the Muses' chariot in Pindar and Bacchylides, it is disappointing that there is probably no comparable scene in art. A Melian amphora (no. 67) shows Apollo returning to Artemis at Delos. In his chariot, drawn by winged horses, are two female figures, said by Pfuhl to be Hyperborean Maidens, but sometimes, less convincingly, identified as Muses.[3]

The portrayal of Muses with musical instruments and not as singers and dancers partly serves as a means of distinguishing them from nymphs and Graces. Even so, it is often difficult to be sure whether women holding or playing instruments are Muses or mortal musicians, and even more difficult to be sure which of the goddesses who accompany Apollo are to be identified as Muses. During the second half of the fifth century scenes of this type occur more frequently and are no doubt to be associated with occasions of domestic music-making, and in particular with symposia. Often Muses are shown holding or singing from rolls and this may reflect the spread of literacy.[4]

It is not possible to identify an individual Muse by the musical instrument she carries, and we may conclude that there is no consistent differentiation of Muses in our period.[5] For instance, Calliope may play a lyre or hold a box. Muses are shown with various types of lyre (most frequently), with syrinx, with auloi, with castanet, cymbals, tympanon, with branch, flower or garland, with mirror, phiale or oenochoe.[6] Calliope appears rather more often than her sisters and may be thought of as the representative of the Muses, but the evidence is not abundant enough to admit of complete certainty.

There is not a great deal that the study of vase-painting adds

[1] e.g. on nos. 59, 27, 56. [2] e.g. on nos. 4 and 22.

[3] e.g. by Collignon and Couve.

[4] H. Immerwahr, in *Classical, mediaeval and renaissance studies in honour of Berthold Ullman*, vol. 1, 11–48.

[5] M. Wegner, *Die Musensarkophage*, 95.

[6] On no. 6 Terpsichore holds two lighted torches.

to our knowledge of the Muses. It does, I think, show that the Muses were part of the experience of the ordinary Greek, not just of the poet, and this makes it seem less likely that poets' mention of them was mere literary convention. For the ordinary Greek they could be visualized as singing and playing in the company of gods and poets and so glorifying the power of music. Portrayal of the Muses, which began with the François Vase, continues by showing them as a choir singing to delight and honour Apollo, and then, from the mid-fifth century onwards, as instrumentalists as well as singers, with or without Apollo. The evidence of the vases reinforces the belief gained from literature that the Muses had not yet each been assigned a separate sphere and that Calliope was generally held to be their leader and representative. The association of the Muses with Apollo is more frequently exemplified in paintings than in literature; their association with Musaeus is known almost entirely from vases, but that with Thamyris becomes even more puzzling when literary and artistic evidence are placed side by side.

One may usefully distinguish between those vases which merely set out to portray Apollo accompanied by Muses and those which suggest a definite, quasi-dramatic situation. Probably the best-known of the latter is the mid-fifth century kylix in Boston, on the cover of which Apollo is shown revealing himself to a Muse on Mount Helicon (no. 59). The Muse is seated on a rock, resting her chin on her hand, in an attitude several times adopted by Muses, and gazing into the god's eyes. When Musaeus appears, it is usually as a sort of representative musician, so much so that it may be difficult to distinguish him from Apollo (nos. 64 and 57). For example, on a neck-amphora in London, painted about 440, Musaeus is seated between Terpsichore and Melousa (no. 5). All are named. The Meidias pelike, however, adds to our knowledge of Musaeus (no. 13): he is shown in the centre of the picture, dressed in Thracian costume, playing the cithara to an audience which includes his wife, named as Deiope, his child, Eumolpus, the Muses Melpomene, Erato, Calliope and Terpsichore, and the goddess Aphrodite who is accompanied by Eros, Peitho and Harmonia. This vase is fifth-century evidence for Musaeus' Thracian origin

27

and for the names of his wife and son. It is also interesting for
the light it may throw on the portrayal of Thamyris.

Meidias also painted a remarkably similar scene on a lekythos
in which the central figure is not Musaeus but Thamyris (no. 87).
The paintings resemble each other not only in composition but
in the personages they portray; on the lekythos only Thamyris
and Apollo are named, but the identity of Calliope, again with
winged Pothos, and Aphrodite cannot be doubted, and it is
reasonable to assume that at least three of the remaining women
are Muses.

It seems that here Thamyris is waiting to play to an audience
of divinities. The poor preservation of a hydria by a Meidian
painter (no. 88) prevents certainty about its subject, but it
probably depicted a similar scene, as does the krater by Polion,
which may be dated rather earlier than the pictures of Meidias
and his school (no. 86). The late fifth century paintings already
described make no statements about the relationship of Musaeus
or Thamyris with the Muses. The Muses are just an audience.
It was, however, traditional to regard Thamyris as the rival, not
the associate, of the Muses.

Homer, in a digression in the Catalogue of *Iliad* Book Two[1]
caused by the mention of Dorion, says that there 'the Muses met
Thamyris the Thracian as he was on his way from Oechalia and
the home of Oechalian Eurytus. Thamyris had boasted that he
would win in a singing-match with the Muses themselves,
Daughters of aegis-bearing Zeus. This angered them. They
struck him blind; they robbed him of the divine gift of song, and
caused him to forget his harping.' This Homeric episode is not
itself illustrated on vases, since the subject is almost certainly
not found until after the production of Sophocles' *Thamyris*.[2]
Few fragments of this play remain[3] and we know little about it.
We are told that in the Stoa Poikile Sophocles was represented
as playing the lyre in the play, from which it is conjectured that
he himself took the part of Thamyris.[4] Pollux says that
Thamyris' mask had a grey (sightless) eye on one side, and a

[1] *Il.* 2.594–600, E. V. Rieu's translation; cf. *Minyas*, frs. 3, 4 Kinkel. For the
blinding of Thamyris, see p. 115 f. and references there cited.
[2] Sophocles' *Thamyris* cannot be dated, but is usually thought to be early.
[3] Jebb-Pearson 1.176–84.
[4] *Vita Soph.* 5.

28

dark one on the other: if so, the Muses struck him blind while he was on stage.[1] The theme of the play will have been the downfall of the hero through hybris: the course of the plot is much harder to conjecture. This is the only Sophoclean tragedy whose subject is a musician, and in general Sophocles is much less interested than Euripides in the Muses.[2] The fragments make it clear that Thamyris broke his lyre and flung the pieces from him, presumably when the Muses deprived him of his musical skill, and that the overwhelming power of his music was described (? by the Thracian chorus). The material we can suggest (Thamyris' encounter with the Muses, his boast of his superiority, the contest, the punishment) seems both too slight for a complete play and resistant to normal tragic structure.[3] If Thamyris was punished for boasting, there was no need of a contest. If there was a contest, who was the judge? Was the boast made in the presence of a Muse and in knowledge of her identity?

The evidence from vases suggests that Thamyris' mother, Argiope, was a character in Sophocles' play. One of the vases on which she appears is the Polion krater,[4] to which I now return. In the lower portion of the picture seven Muses are shown, two of them seated on a group of rocks. Above are the two remaining Muses, separated by the figures of Apollo and Thamyris, between whom is a large tripod. Thamyris wears Thracian dress and holds a cithara; there is a hare at his feet. On the right, a woman in Thracian dress, who must be Thamyris' mother, is praying before an altar, against which a lyre is propped. Behind the altar is a tree, and above it are nine statuettes.

The remaining portrayals of Thamyris are quite different in spirit and scene from those already studied. The presence of statuettes is a link between the Meidian and the Polion vases and two more on the same subject, a hydria in the Vatican and another in Naples.[5] The Vatican hydria shows Thamyris seated

---

[1] Pollux 4.141.   [2] See p. 71 f.

[3] The scholiast on Euripides' *Rhesus* 916 imputes an erotic motive to Thamyris; this seems unlikely in Sophocles but may be consistent with Meidias' painting.   [4] See frontispiece.

[5] No. 83; no 82 discussed by Miss Richter in G. Richter and L. Hall, *Red-figured Athenian vases in the Metropolitan Museum of Art* (New Haven, 1936) 1.204: 'The little figures have not been recognized as statuettes by any of the

on a rock holding a lyre; to his left are two Muses, to his right, his mother, holding a branch. Schefold shows three statuettes above Thamyris' head and says that they are images of the Muses to demonstrate that the play was set on the Muses' mountain.[1] It seems to be generally accepted that the statues represent divinities and mark the locality as sacred.

There is no sign of hostility between Thamyris and the Muses in any of the paintings already discussed, whether they show the singer with few companions or many. A hydria in Oxford however clearly depicts Thamyris' downfall (no. 84): as he is blinded, the lyre falls from his hand; his mother looks on, tearing her hair in grief and a Muse is present also. This scene may have been painted not long after the production of Sophocles' play.

LIST OF VASES

A.B.V. = Sir J. Beazley, *Attic Black-figure vase-painters* (Oxford, 1956)
A.R.V. = Sir J. Beazley, *Attic Red-figure vase-painters*[2] (Oxford, 1963)
L.C.S. = A. D. Trendall, *Red-figured vases of Lucania, Campania and Sicily* (Oxford, 1967)

A. Vases showing named Muses

Black-Figure
1. The François Vase, *A.B.V.* 76.
   Stesichore, Era(to), Polumnis, Melpomene, Kleio, Euterpe, Thaleia, Orania, Kaliope.
2. A fragment from Athens showing part of two Muses with the inscription O)rania – AP 3491, *A.B.V.* 682.

Red-Figure
3. Syracuse 20542, *A.R.V.* 624 – Kalliope and Mnemosyne.
4. Louvre G 440, *A.R.V.* 633 – Kalliope, Melpomene, Ourania.
5. London E 271, *A.R.V.* 1040 – Terpsichore, Musaeus, Melousa.
6. Paris, Petit Palais 308, *A.R.V.* 1040 – of the five Muses shown Terpsichora, Kalliope and Thaleia are named.

---

commentators but they seem to me to be clearly such.' Thamyris is shown with four Muses on no. 85.

[1] K. Schefold, *Die Bildnisse der antiken Dichter, Redner und Denker* (Basle, 1943), 59.2.

7. Naples 2667 fr., *A.R.V.* 1046 – see *A.J.A.* 1927, 350, No. 12, where Beazley reads the fragmentary inscription as Kl)eo, Te(rpsichore.
8. Berlin 2401, *A.R.V.* 1080 – Apollo with Terpsichore and Klio.
9. London E 805, *A.R.V.* 1080 – Polu(m)nia, Kleo, Euterpe, Thaleia, Era)to, Kalliop(e.
10. Athens, Pnyx 196, *A.R.V.* 1156 – Euterpe.
11. Ferrara T 293, *A.R.V.* 1259 – Interior: Klio and Musaeus; K)leo appears on exterior.
12. New York Metropolitan Museum, 12.229.12, *A.R.V.* 1259 – K)alliope with Apollo.
13. New York 37.11.23, *A.R.V.* 1313 – Erato, Kalliope, Melpomene, Terpsichore and Musaeus.
14. Naples 3235, *A.R.V.* 1316 – Kalliope, Thalia, Marsyas and Olympos.
15. London, Victoria and Albert Museum, 666.1864, *A.R.V.* 1678 – Interior: Kalliope with Apollo. Exterior: four male and four female figures. 'The women are likely to be Muses.' Inscription: kalos Mosais Kalliope.
16. Adria BC 104 fr. – Kalliope.
17. Athens (*B.C.H.* 1962, 644, pl. 23) – Erato, Klio, Melpomene, Terpsichore, Thaleia, Urania, Choro and an unnamed figure.
18. Basle (*Auktion* 14 No. 85, pl. 21) – Klio and Erato with Thamyris.
19. Naples, Betti collection (*A.Z.* 1848, 247) – Klio, Terpsichore Thaleia.

B. Other vases depicting Muses

i) *Muses alone*

20. Acropolis 594, *A.B.V.* 682.
21. Louvre CA482, *A.R.V.* 774.
22. Bologna PU271, *A.R.V.* 825.
23. Lugano, Schoen 80, *A.R.V.* 997.
24. Naples 3194, *A.R.V.* 1011.
25. Agrigento, *A.R.V.* 1017.
26. Vatican, *A.R.V.* 1017.
27. Munich SL483, *A.R.V.* 1080.
28. Louvre C1103 fr.
29. Munich 3268, Trendall 22, 39 pl. 20.

On the following vases Muses *may* be depicted:

30. London E461, *A.R.V.* 601.
31. Leningrad 732, *A.R.V.* 857.
32. Athens 12480, *A.R.V.* 994.
33. New York 23.160.80, *A.R.V.* 1075.
34. Ancona, *A.R.V.* 1076, No. 14.
35. Leipsic T66, *A.R.V.* 1077, cf. a vase now lost (Roman market) *A.R.V.* 1078.

36. Madrid, *A.R.V.* 1163, No. 43.
37. Heidelberg 208, *A.R.V.* 1189.
38. Louvre CA2220.

ii) *Muses with other deities*

Apollo and Muses:

39. ? Louvre F256, *A.B.V.* 371.
40. ? Berlin 1868, *A.B.V.* 372.
41. Carlsruhe (once) *A.B.V.* 372, No. 155.
42. Louvre F253, *A.B.V.* 372.
43. Villa Guilia 760, *A.B.V.* 372.
44. Orvieto, *A.B.V.* 372, No. 162.
45. London B261, *A.B.V.* 373.
46. Würzburg 216, *A.B.V.* 383.
47. Toronto 311, *A.B.V.* 484.
48. Würzburg 225, *A.B.V.* 605.
49. New York 06.1021.47, *A.B.V.* 667.
50. Athens 1241, Collignon and Couve 1533, pl. 47.
51. London B346, Haspels, Appendix 14.72.
52. ? Madrid 10930, Haspels, Appendix 14.73.
53. Louvre MNB 910, Haspels, Appendix 11.7.
54. Berlin 2388, Roscher 3246, fig. 2.
55. Schwerin 1261, *A.R.V.* 618.
56. Oxford 524, *A.R.V.* 620.
57. Vatican, *A.R.V.* 623, No. 70.
58. ? Warsaw 142331, *A.R.V.* 639.
59. Boston 00.356, *A.R.V.* 741.
60. Hanover, *A.R.V.* 1021.
61. Ferrara T303, *A.R.V.* 1171.
62. Erlangen 290, *A.R.V.* 1259.
63. New York 06.1021.47, *A.R.V.* 1259.
64. Cambridge 73, *A.R.V.* 1287.
65. Dresden, Albertinum L331.
66. Stockholm 12, *L.C.S.* pl. 36.4.
67. Apollo, Artemis and Muses: ? Melian amphora, Athens 911, Pfuhl, pl. 24, fig. 108.
68. ? Berlin 1860, *A.B.V.* 372.
69. Apollo, Artemis, Hermes and Muses: Berlin 1905, A.B.V. 322.
70. Apollo, Dionysus, Hermes and Muses: ? London B347, *A.B.V.* 334.
71. Apollo, Marsyas and Muses: Naples 81392.
72. Naples 3231.
73. Taranto 20305, *L.C.S.*, pl. 32.9.
74. Louvre G516, *A.R.V.* 1189.
75. Heidelberg 208, *A.R.V.* 1189.
76. London 1920.6–13, *A.R.V.* 1190.
77. Louvre G490, *A.R.V.* 1190.
78. Zeus, Apollo, Hermes and Muses: Copenhagen 3241, C.V.11H 102, 2b.

32

79. Apollo, Athene, Dionysus, Muse (or Ariadne) and Poseidon: Villa
    Guilia 532, *A.B.V.* 427.

iii) *Muses with Poets*

With ? Archilochus
80. Boston 98.887, *A.R.V.* 774.
81. Palermo, Banco di Sicilia 44, *A.R.V.* 1686.

With Thamyris
82. Naples 3143, *A.R.V.* 1020.
83. Vatican, *A.R.V.* 1020, No. 92.
84. Oxford 530, *A.R.V.* 1061.
85. Leningrad 711, *A.R.V.* 1123.
86. Ferrara T127, *A.R.V.* 1171.
87. Ruvo, Jatta 1538, *A.R.V.* 1314.
88. New York 16.52, *A.R.V.* 1321. See also 18.

With Musaeus
89. Villa Giulia, *A.R.V.* 623, No. 70 bis.
90. Cambridge 73, *A.R.V.* 1287. See also 5, 11, 13.

2. The Poets and the Muses: Homer to Anacreon

The attitude of the individual Greek to the multiplicity of gods and supernatural beings of mythology is one that is always hard for us to determine, since it is completely different from modern ideas of the nature of religious belief and since it varied from place to place as well as changing considerably between, for example, the ages of Homer and Plato. It must not be expected then that the relationship between the poet and the Muse, or any other divinity connected with poetry, will be clear and consistent throughout our period. But if the attitude of individual poets differs widely we are bound to wonder whether the Muse had any objective reality to the poet and his hearers, and if she was not rather the projection of the poet's own feelings about his art. If, on the other hand, the poets' attitude to the Muses reveals only minor differences, we may confidently make generalizations about their beliefs.[1]

The evidence for the relationship of poet and Muse is of three kinds. First, poets often expressed the relationship through metaphor, speaking, for example, of the Muses' gifts or teaching, or of themselves as servants of the Muses. Secondly, their habit of invoking the Muse and the terms in which they couch their invocations imply certain attitudes and beliefs which we can deduce with fair assurance. Thirdly, there are the descriptions of poets meeting the Muses.

In one of his *Olympian* Odes, Pindar speaks of the Muse standing beside him as he tried to find a way of linking words and music for his choir.[2] We have two accounts of actual encounters between Muses and a poet. The first has long been

---

[1] Studies of the relationship between the poets and the Muses have been made by S. Accame, *Riv. di fil.* 1963, 257–81, 385–415, and 1964, 129–56, 257–87, O. Falter, *Der Dichter und sein Gott*, Würzburg, 1934, and W. Otto, *Die Musen*, Darmstadt, 1956.

[2] *O.* 3.4b.

known: in the proem to the *Theogony* Hesiod describes how, when he was looking after his sheep on the slopes of Mount Helicon, the Muses taught him beautiful song. First they spoke to him and his fellow-shepherds:

'Ποιμένες ἄγραυλοι, κάκ' ἐλέγχεα, γαστέρες οἶον,
ἴδμεν ψεύδεα πολλὰ λέγειν ἐτύμοισιν ὁμοῖα,
ἴδμεν δ', εὖτ' ἐθέλωμεν, ἀληθέα γηρύσασθαι.'

'You shepherds of the wilderness, poor fools,
    nothing but bellies,
we know how to say many false things
    that seem like true sayings,
but we know also how to speak the truth
    when we wish to.'[1]

Next the Muses plucked and gave him a wand of laurel, and breathed divine song (or voice) into him so that he might celebrate past and future. Then they told him to hymn the immortal race of the gods and always to sing of themselves, first and last.[2]

I take it that Hesiod is describing what he believes actually to have happened to him: he is not inventing. Dispute about this passage has centred on the interpretation of the Muses' words: this subject I discuss in the general context of truth and lies in poetry.[3] There are other points of interest: the gift of the wand, and the phrases 'taught Hesiod beautiful song' and 'breathed into me divine song'. Hesiod was an oral poet. In what sense did the Muses make him a poet all at once? Perhaps he had listened to singers and amassed material, and was only now to begin to practise the craft himself. Are 'teaching' and 'inspiration' different ways of conveying the same meaning? It is surprising that the metaphor of breathing poetic skill into a poet does not certainly recur in the period we are studying, although 'inspiration' for us has become a dead metaphor.[4] It

---

[1] For a similar beginning see Epimenides, D.-K. 1. Hesiod fr. 197 (= M.-W. 310) again makes the Muses givers of eloquence (Μουσάων αἶτ' ἄνδρα πολυφραδέοντα τιθεῖσι θέσπιον αὐδήεντα).

[2] Hesiod *Theog.* 22–34; see also *Works*, 651–9.

[3] See p. 112 f.

[4] It is unlikely that Clement's quotation of Democritus is verbally accurate when he reports him as saying 'Whatever a poet writes with inspiration of a holy breath is especially fine.' (D.-K. 18) see p. 87.

D

would be misleading to think of the laurel wand as the equivalent of the staff later held by the rhapsodes or of that passed to the speaker at a council in Homer, but the gift of a wand rather than a lyre may signify spoken, not sung, poetry. The wand is much more likely to be that associated with Apollo δαφνηφόρος and to signify Hesiod's relationship with Apollo, which is alluded to briefly later in the proem.[1]

Sir John Beazley originally suggested that a white-ground pyxis cover in Boston, painted c. 460–450 (no. 80),[2] depicted the encounter of Hesiod and the Muses. The painting shows a cowherd and six women. There are three groups of figures: the first has the cowherd, a cow and a woman who is differently dressed from her companions; the second, three women with lyre, cithara and syrinx respectively; the third, two women, one with flute and the other with cithara. The women are clearly Muses, and the male figure is likely to be a poet. Beazley also suggests that a similar encounter may be depicted on a vase by the Pothos Painter in Palermo (no. 81). The vase shows 'a youth in travelling dress and four women, one of whom holds writing-tablets, the second a lyre, the third a flute, the fourth a basket. The women must be Muses; and the one with tablets is a replica of the left-hand Muse on Heidelberg 208.' Is the youth Archilochus?[3]

In 1954, a new inscription from the Monumentum Archilochi in Paros was published which includes a traditional story of Archilochus' meeting with the Muses.[4] It appears that when the young Archilochus, on his father Telesicles' orders, was taking a cow to the market very early one morning, a group of women appeared, teased him and offered him a fair price for the cow. At once they and the cow vanished but Archilochus found a lyre at his feet. When Archilochus recovered his wits he realized that the women were Muses and returned and told his father, who started an unsuccessful enquiry into the cow's

---

[1] *Theog.* 94–5. See M. L. West, *ad loc.*

[2] Boston 98.887, *A.R.V.* 774. See L. Caskey and J. Beazley, *Attic Vase paintings in the Museum of Fine Arts Boston* (Boston, 1931–63). 34–7 and Plate XV.

[3] No. 75, also by the Pothos Painter, depicts Apollo and Marsyas with three Muses, one of whom holds a box.

[4] See W. Peek, *Philologus* 1955, 186 ff. N. Kontoleon, *Philologus* 1956, 29 ff.

whereabouts. Finally the Delphic oracle was consulted and replied that a son of Telesicles would be deathless and celebrated.[1] If this story was originally told by Archilochus himself in a poem, it is possible that his mention of the 'Muses' lovely gift'[2] may be an allusion to the lyre he found. If the Boston pyxis represents Archilochus, not Hesiod, the story must have been well-known in Athens in the mid-fifth century and this is most likely if it was preserved in a poem.[3] The Monument however does not ascribe the story to Archilochus and it has some rather puzzling associations which make it hard to take completely seriously. First it sounds rather like gentle mockery of the Hesiodic encounter and is reminiscent also of the meeting of Thamyris with the Muses while he was travelling from Thrace. Secondly, the tone of the story is like that of the Homeric Hymn to Hermes where again cows and lyre and trickery are associated. It may be that Archilochus himself wrote about this event, but I do not feel that he can have been relating a genuine and deeply-felt experience like that of Hesiod.[4]

We deduce Homer's relationship with the Muses partly by analysing his invocations and partly by observing what he says in the *Odyssey* about bards, who must to some extent be a reflection of himself. Besides mentioning their love for Demodocus Homer tells us that the Muses teach bards and that they give them song. Both metaphors recur frequently in the work of later poets.

When Odysseus is replying to Euryalus' insults he says that the gods do not grant pleasing gifts to all men, not physique and intelligence and eloquence.[5] If it was natural to regard eloquence as a gift of the gods, poetic skill may easily be accounted for in this way too. And this is what we find. King Alcinous summons the bard Demodocus to sing at the banquet he is giving for Odysseus in these words: 'Call the god-like bard Demodocus, for a god has given him exceptional power as a poet to give pleasure in whatever way his spirit rouses him to

[1] Mon. Arch. E, col. II, 20–52 in, e.g., M. Treu, *Archilochus*, Munich 1959, 42–4.   [2] fr. 1.
[3] Archilochus was the subject of a comedy by Cratinus (frs. 1–14).
[4] On the resemblance to *H. Herm*, see Fondation Hardt, *Entretiens* 10, 48.
[5] *Od*. 8.167 ff.; cf. *Il*. 4.320.

sing'.[1] When Demodocus appears, a few lines later, Homer tells
us more about him, saying that the Muse loved him dearly but
gave him a mixture of good and evil; she deprived him of his
sight but gave him delightful song.[2] It is clear that the god of
Alcinous' remarks is to be identified with the Muse mentioned
later. The use of the imperfect tense (δίδου) alongside the aorist
(ἐφίλησε, ἄμερσε) shows that the gift of song is closely connected
with the blinding.[3] When the Muse blinded Demodocus she
gave him, by way of compensation, poetic skill to be his lasting
possession. It is worth noting too that the gift is the expression
of the Muses' love and that its purpose is to spread enjoyment;
moreover, the poem cannot come into being until the poet's
spirit is moved.

Since the profession of rhapsode normally passed from father
to son it would be natural for Greeks to think of the gift of song
as inborn, as an inherited talent, but there is little evidence for
this belief, possibly only a couplet of Theognis writing about
the Muses:

αὗται γὰρ τάδ' ἔδωκαν ἔχειν κεχαρισμένα δῶρα
    σοὶ καὶ ἐμοί.[4]

'For it was they who bestowed these generous gifts on us both.'
It seems likely that Theognis is confident of having the gift of
poetry as a permanent possession, an endowment at birth. There
is a fragment, attributed to Bacchylides by Blass, which may
imply that poets are born, not made:

οὐ γὰρ ἐν μέσοισι κεῖται
δῶρα δυσμάχητα Μοισᾶν
τῶπιτυχόντι φέρειν.

'The gifts of the Muses, ? fought over in vain, do not lie before
all for the chance comer to bear away.'[5] Interpretation is not
easy: firstly the passage states that the gifts of the Muses do
not lie about for all and sundry to pick up. The image suggests
a pile of goods, perhaps of booty, left unguarded and available
to all comers,[6] and I believe that the poet has in mind separate

[1] *Od.* 8.44 f. [2] *Od.* 8.62–4.
[3] For this use of the imperfect see Chantraine, *Grammaire Homérique* II, 193.
[4] Theognis 1057–8. [5] *P.M.G.* 959. [6] cf. e.g. *Il.* 18.507.

poems rather than poetic ability when he speaks of the Muses' gifts. A second point is added by δυσμάχητα which might mean 'keenly contested', as Jebb takes it, or 'fought over in vain'. If the latter, the writer is saying both that the writing of poetry is the prerogative of few, and that the gift is not to be acquired by the poet's own exertions. The metaphor of the Muses' gift is in fact used by Archilochus to speak of his combined career as soldier and poet:

εἰμὶ δ'ἐγὼ θεράπων μὲν 'Ενναλίοιο ἄνακτος
καὶ Μουσέων ἐρατὸν δῶρον ἐπιστάμενος.[1]

'I am servant of Lord Ares and the Muses, and am skilled in using their lovely gift.' The poet's career is denoted in similar terms in Solon's Muse elegy:

ἄλλος 'Ολυμπιάδων Μουσέων πάρα δῶρα διδαχθείς,
ἱμερτῆς σοφίης μέτρον ἐπιστάμενος.[2]

Another important use of the metaphor is as a synonym for 'this poem' or for 'poetry in general', a concept for which no single word existed at this period. Thus the metaphor is not primarily decorative, although, particularly when an adjective like 'lovely' is added, the effect is to add colour to the statement. Pindar, who usually avoids the conventional in speaking of his relationship with the Muse, employs this metaphor almost as a simplification of the complex beginning of an Olympian ode, when he says that he sends poured nectar, the Muses' gift, to the victor.[3] Theognis, writing to Cyrnus, assures him that the glorious gifts of the violet-wreathed Muses will convey him to fame, and in spite of the plural, he is referring chiefly to the present poem.[4] Anacreon expresses his disapproval of those who tell stories of wars at symposia, at which the gifts of the Muses and Aphrodite should be mentioned. For Anacreon the metaphor means all that the Greeks understood by the word 'music'.[5]

[1] Archilochus 1; on the combination of soldier and poet see Prof. Page in Fondation Hardt, *Entretiens* 10, 134.
[2] Solon 1.51–2: 'Another man has learned the gifts of the Olympian Muses and understands the measure of the lovely art.'   [3] *O.* 7.7.
[4] Theognis 250; cf. Alcman *P.M.G.* 59(b), Anacreon *P.M.G.* 346, frr. 11+3+6. 7–9.   [5] Anacreon 96D.

39

Solon believed that the poet learnt the Muses' gifts, and Archilochus uses ἐπίσταμαι, 'I am skilled', in the same connection. The teaching of the Muses was a Homeric metaphor stemming from Homer's belief in the Muses as a source of knowledge. This belief is fully stated in the *Iliad* and reflected in one passage of the *Odyssey*. Homer gives his reasons for invoking the Muses as follows:

> ὑμεῖς γὰρ θεαί ἐστε, πάρεστέ τε, ἴστε τε πάντα,
> ἡμεῖς δὲ κλέος οἶον ἀκούομεν οὐδέ τι ἴδμεν · ...
> πληθὺν δ' οὐκ ἂν ἐγὼ μυθήσομαι οὐδ' ὀνομήνω,
> οὐδ' εἴ μοι δέκα μὲν γλῶσσαι, δέκα δὲ στόματ' εἶεν,
> φωνὴ δ' ἄρρηκτος, χάλκεον δέ μοι ἦτορ ἐνείη,
> εἰ μὴ 'Ολυμπιάδες Μοῦσαι, Διὸς αἰγιόχοιο
> θυγατέρες, μνησαίαθ' ὅσοι ὑπὸ "Ιλιον ἦλθον.[1]

Homer is saying here that the Muses are eye-witnesses of events; men depend on hearsay. Homer could not tell how many individuals were engaged in the war, not if he had ten tongues and mouths, an unwearying voice, and a spirit as hard and enduring as brass, unless the Muses acted as reminders for him.[2] The striking thing about this passage is the inappropriateness of the central lines. Homer speaks as if his physical strength will not be equal to the long task of recounting the participants in the war and gives us a vivid picture of the strain which all bards must have felt, but I do not think we are meant to infer that the Muses supplied his physical needs, only perhaps that he was as apprehensive about his stamina as about possible lapses of memory when he was embarking on the catalogue. For Homer, the Muses' teaching is the imparting of knowledge, and two passages of Pindar express the same belief.[3] Generally speaking, the lyric poets do not employ the metaphor of the Muses' teaching, and this suggests that teaching meant primarily giving information.

There are other metaphors expressing the poet's relationship with the Muse more directly. In the *Birds*,[4] Aristophanes makes

---

[1] *Il.* 2.485–92; cf. *Od.* 8.487–91.

[2] Empedocles expresses the same idea when he calls the Muse πολυμνηστή, 'much-remembering' (D.-K. 174).

[3] Paean 6.38–43, 7b.1–10.   [4] 914 ff.

fun of the most hackneyed of these: his impecunious but self-important poet arrives in the Birds' new city proclaiming himself the servant of the Muses, a term first occurring in Hesiod.[1] Bacchylides describes Hesiod as the Muses' servant and himself as Urania's, but Pindar avoids this metaphor.[2] The words for servant, θεράπων and πρόπολος, have no menial implications but suggest a close association between the Muse and the attendant poet. With θεράπων Theognis combines ἄγγελος, 'messenger'.[3] When poets speak of themselves as messengers or heralds of the Muses, another frequent image, they must see themselves entirely as intermediaries, but although this metaphor might seem to diminish their position it stressed the truth of their words. For the Greeks poetry was always communication, never merely self-expression.

The facts about Homeric invocations of the Muse can be simply stated. As is well-known, both *Iliad* and *Odyssey* begin with an invocation: in the *Iliad* the poet calls on the goddess to sing the wrath of Achilles from the time when he and Agamemnon first quarrelled, and goes on to ask 'Which god brought about the quarrel?' The next line gives the answer 'Apollo', and introduces the personal motives expressed in the heroes' antagonism. The beginning of the *Odyssey* is similar in that it too commands the Muse and mentions the starting point of the narrative, but its emphasis is on the man, Odysseus, rather than the emotion of wrath: ἄνδρα μοι ἔννεπε, Μοῦσα. Homer in the next few lines summarizes the wanderings and sufferings of Odysseus and his comrades, without however revealing their outcome for Odysseus, and then appeals again to the goddess:

τῶν ἁμόθεν γε, θεά, θύγατερ Διός, εἶπε καὶ ἡμῖν.

'Of these events, from some point at least, tell us also now.' Both epics therefore begin with invocations which state their general

[1] *Theog.* 100, cf. Archilochus 10, *Margites* 2, Sappho 109 L.-P., Choerilus fr. 1 Kinkel.
[2] Bacchylides 5.14, 192. Euripides extends the metaphor: the flute is Μουσᾶν θεράπων (*El.* 717), and the swan Μούσας θεραπεύει. (*I.T.* 1105).
[3] Theognis 769. For the poet as herald, see e.g. Bacchylides 13.228. Pindar speaks of himself as messenger (e.g. *P.* 2.4.) but not as messenger of the Muses.

41

theme and provide a precise starting-point, and both are silent about the end of the story.[1]

Although the *Odyssey* has no other invocation two passages in Book Eight are concerned with the impulse to song. In the first[2] Homer says that, after the banquet, Μοῦσ᾽ ἄρ᾽ ἀοιδὸν ἀνῆκεν ἀειδέμεναι κλέα ἀνδρῶν ('the Muse stirred Demodocus to sing the deeds of men'). Later in the book, after receiving Odysseus' compliments, Demodocus takes up the tale again: ὁ δ᾽ ὁρμηθεὶς θεοῦ ἄρχετο, φαῖνε δ᾽ ἀοιδήν.[3] It is possible that on both occasions Homer is describing the same situation, the moment at which the Muse, as it were, releases the words pent up within the bard. If so, the second passage must be translated 'he, set in motion by the goddess, began'.[4] This translation finds support from a passage in Plato's *Ion* which seems to reflect Homer.[5] Socrates is defending his argument that inspiration, not *technē*, is the cause of poetic ability, by observing that each writer can only do well in that one genre (dithyramb, epic and so on) to which the Muse has impelled him (ἐφ᾽ ὃ ἡ Μοῦσα αὐτὸν ὥρμησεν).

The *Iliad* contains five invocations after the proem, four of them beginning with the formula ἔσπετε νῦν μοι, Μοῦσαι Ὀλύμπια δώματ᾽ ἔχουσαι and continuing with an interrogative. Three of the four contain the word πρῶτος, 'first'.[6] The fifth is less elaborate but basically similar:

τίς τ᾽ ἄρ τῶν ὄχ᾽ ἄριστος ἔην, σύ μοι ἔννεπε, Μοῦσα.[7]

'Tell me, Muse, who was best of them.' The first of the invocations of Book Two precedes the Catalogue of Ships and contains the statement contrasting the omniscience of the Muses with the poet's powerlessness which we have already studied.[8] Homer says: 'Tell me who were the leaders of the Danaans.' The second invocation eases the passage between the Catalogue and the resumption of the narrative: the poet asks the Muse

[1] I take εἶπε καὶ ἡμῖν to mean 'tell us, i.e. bard and audience, the story you have told to others on previous occasions'.
[2] 8.73–4; cf. Pindar fr. 169.   [3] 8.499.
[4] In this translation ὁρμηθεὶς θεοῦ is taken together (see Chantraine, ii. 61 and 65); if θεοῦ is taken with ἄρχετο ('began with the goddess') we have a reference to an invocation.
[5] 534C.   [6] *Il.* 2.484 ff., 11. 218–19, 14. 508–9, 16. 112–13.
[7] *Il.* 2.761.   [8] p. 40.

which were best of the Greek men and horses, and moves, via a mention of Admetus' horses and of Telamonian Ajax, back to Achilles and the present situation. The invocation of Book Eleven occurs after Hector has rallied the Trojans, when Homer calls upon the goddesses to say which Trojan first fought Agamemnon. It 'may be intended to mark the introduction of a critical moment, the last phase of the Achaean offensive and the retreat of Agamemnon'.[1] In Book Fourteen, when the Achaeans appear momentarily to be victorious, there is an appeal to the Muses to say which of the Achaeans first won spoils, and finally, in Book Sixteen, the Muses are asked how first fire was cast into the Achaean ships.

This is the material on which theories about Homer and the Muses have been based. These theories, some of which I shall examine, have sought to answer two questions: Why did Homer invoke the Muses? Why are the invocations placed where they are? The sort of answer given to these questions is conditioned by the writer's beliefs about the nature of the epic in general and about Homer. Because of the research into the nature of oral epic instituted by Milman Parry there has been a resurgence of interest in Homer's attitude to his craft and new answers have been sought for the two questions.

Ancient writers were chiefly concerned with the second question. Most of them answer it from the point of view of the poet's relationship with his audience, saying that he uses invocations to focus their attention on something important to come, to gain their goodwill, or to emphasize a summary.[2] Servius however stresses the poet's personal need; it should be noticed, he says, that the divinity is not invoked in all poems but when we need 'aliquid ultra humanam possibilitatem', 'something beyond human power'.[3] Servius gives as an example Vergil's need to be informed about the thoughts and plans of the gods who influence the epic, but there is no evidence that this was the motive underlying any Homeric invocation except perhaps that of the *Iliad* proem. The difficulty with both classes of ancient solution is that, though they can be made to account

---

[1] Calhoun, 'The Poet and the Muses in Homer', *C.P.* 1938, 157–66.
[2] See *scholia* AB and Eustathius on *Il.* 2.484; Quintilian 4 proem and 10.1.48.   [3] Servius on *Aeneid* 1.8.

for the presence of invocations, they do not deal with their absence in places where they might be expected, many of the crises of action in the *Iliad*, for example, and more remarkable, throughout the narrative of the *Odyssey*.

In an article entitled 'Homer's Invocations of the Muses: Traditional Patterns', W. W. Minton has summarized modern theories before advancing his own.[1] 'First of all, the invocations are essentially *questions*, appeals to the Muse for specific information to which the poet clearly expects an *answer*. Secondly, the information for which the poet asks and which is reflected, however vestigially, in the following "answer" is that of an *ordered enumeration* or catalogue.'[2] Minton adds[3] that this phenomenon was first pointed out by Falter, whose ideas were developed by Otto, although the association betweeen invocations and catalogue material had been noticed in ancient times; 'the perception that the association is an essential one, that a basic function of the Muses, as "daughters of Memory"[4] was to supply the poet with such quantity of factual information as would not be easy for him to muster without some external assistance, remained to be stated by Gilbert Murray'.[5] If the belief about the importance of memory in oral poetry is accepted in its widest form then this theory is even more persuasive. Notopoulos has argued[6] that the oral poet is dependent on memory not only for factual information obviously difficult to memorize, but for the formulae which constitute much of epic material and for the organization of larger recurrent units such as descriptions of arming a warrior or launching a boat. If we

---

[1] *T.A.P.A.* 1960, 292–309. [2] Minton's italics.
[3] Note 3. [4] i.e. of Mnemosyne.
[5] O. Falter, *Der Dichter und sein Gott bei den Griechen und Römern* 4–5, 55–6; W. F. Otto, *Die Musen* 33–4 and Part 3 *passim*; Murray, *The Rise of the Greek Epic* (Oxford, 1907), 96. It should be noted that Murray's theory requires the intervention of 'a traditional book' between the Muse and the poet and thus debases the importance of memory. Murray's theory was attacked by G. M. Calhoun, 'The Poet and the Muses in Homer', *C.P.* 1938, 157–66, for its failure to account for invocations which precede passages where memory is unimportant. Calhoun's attack was in turn challenged by Minton who seems to have missed part of Calhoun's case against Murray (the 'book') and to have assumed that Murray could have developed his theory in such a way as to meet Calhoun's objections. In fact, it is unlikely that any one who believes in oral epic as both Minton and Calhoun appear to believe, could accept Murray entire.
[6] *T.A.P.A.* 1938, 465–73.

accept this argument we are freed from the search for 'vestigial catalogues' after all invocations and we can understand *why* poets appealed to the daughters of Memory: what still remains puzzling is Homer's motive for placing invocations precisely where he does in the body of the *Iliad*.

At this point, we must return from the poet's needs *qua* poet to his relationship with his audience. Minton[1] develops the ancient view that invocations were employed 'in contexts of special importance' to focus the hearers' attention. He points out that it is more useful to speak of *critical* points in the action and examines the distribution and content of all Homeric invocations, which he sees as preludes to a sequence of *crisis-struggle – defeat*; 'this defeat, furthermore, always falls on the . . . protagonists'. Minton's association of the Muses with 'ultimate defeat' is a hypothesis unsupported by later evidence and contradicted by their more usual appearance at scenes of rejoicing on Olympus and on earth, and he fails to convince me that the proem-invocations of *Iliad* and *Odyssey* fit into his pattern. He deals with the problem of the absence of invocations at points of crisis by pressing into service to fill the gaps 'formulaic questions' which are 'faded invocations'.[2]

I have now briefly reviewed the Homeric invocations and the major theories that have been advanced to account for them. Each theory has been seen to tackle the problem either of the poet *vis-à-vis* his audience or of the poet *vis-à-vis* his Muse. In my opinion no single theory is likely to account for all examples of invocations in all their aspects. Calhoun[3] is right to approach the question by examining what Homer says about his bards. I accept his re-definition of the purpose of an invocation, since it avoids the difficulties of the narrower 'appeal for knowledge' and is supported by the practice of later poets. 'When the singer invoked the Muses, addressing to them an imperative, he desired them to do something.' The Muse whom he addressed loved the bard and gave him the gift of song; the good bard, taught by the Muse or Apollo, could sing events accurately and as vividly as if he had been present at them. The 'gift of song',

---

[1] *op. cit.*, 293.
[2] *Il.* 5.703–4, 8.273, 11.299–300, 16.692–3.
[3] *op. cit.*, 163–66.

poetic ability, complements the knowledge of fact and formula obtained through Memory. Both are essential.

As we approach each invocation we must bear in mind the whole picture Homer had of the Muses (as far as we can discover it): their singing for the gods, their anger with Thamyris, their affection for Demodocus, all their varied powers. Then we may look for a reason for a particular invocation, but it must be consistent with this picture. It is wrong to expect one theory to account for the placing of all invocations: there are too many unknown factors: the nature of the inherited material, the interaction between bard and hearers from moment to moment during the telling, his feeling for pause and stress. The most we can do is to say what may be the chief motive among several for an individual invocation, and what we say must neglect neither Homer's beliefs about the Muses nor his relationship with his audience.

The next poet whose work provides enough material for a detailed study of his relationship with the Muse is Pindar, but before I turn to his work (and that of Bacchylides) something should be said about the intervening centuries. It is certain that the poetry of Homer and other writers of epic was central to the literary experience of the Greeks of this time and certain also that these centuries saw the rise of choral lyric poetry and solo lyric and that elegiac and iambic verse were practised. Poetry was part of life on religious and secular occasions, but we cannot trace the development of poets' attitudes to their work for lack of evidence. For epic we have fragments of a variety of poems, dealing with the Trojan and other stories, usually of uncertain authorship. These poems were later put together to form a historical cycle and their beginnings therefore lost. What is left suggests that some began with invocations to the Muse, while others had only a declaration of subject, like the *Little Iliad*:

"Ἴλιον ἀείδω καὶ Δαρδανίην εὔπωλον

'My theme is Ilium . . .' It must be remembered that this sort of proem might be *followed* by an invocation, in the pattern used by Virgil in the *Aeneid*.[1] Muse invocations remain for the

---

[1] *Aeneid* 1, statement of theme; 8, prayers to the Muse.

Thebais and the *Epigoni* and it seems certain that writers of epic continued to use them, though whether as mere convention we cannot say.[1] The Homeric Hymns exhibit the same variety, although here the problem is complicated by our ignorance of their date of composition. Of those certainly early the Hymn to Hermes has an invocation[2] while that to Apollo begins with the formula

μνήσομαι οὐδὲ λάθωμαι ᾿Απόλλωνος

'I shall remember and shall not forget Apollo.' When the Muse is invoked, it is in terms familiar from Homer: she is clear-voiced, goddess, daughter of Zeus. It is interesting that the writers of the Hymns nowhere appeal to the Muse for knowlege or poetic power.[3]

Of the early elegiac writers only Mimnermus and Solon are known to have invoked the Muse, but since we have few demonstrably complete poems it would be misleading to argue from silence.[4] Solon begins his reflections on prosperity with a unique prayer to the Muses:

Μνημοσύνης καὶ Ζηνὸς ᾿Ολυμπίου ἀγλαὰ τέκνα
Μοῦσαι Πιερίδες, κλῦτέ μοι εὐχομένῳ ·
ὄλβον μοι πρὸς θεῶν μακάρων δότε καὶ πρὸς ἁπάντων
ἀνθρώπων ἀεὶ δόξαν ἔχειν ἀγαθήν.

'Splendid children of Mnemosyne and Olympian Zeus, Pierian Muses, listen as I pray. Grant me prosperity from the blessed gods, and grant that I ever receive fair fame among all men.'[5] Solon later expresses the customary view of the Muses' powers when he says that the poet, taught the Muses' gifts, knows the measure of the lovely gift of poetry.[6] A. W. Allen[7] has argued

[1] e.g. Choerilus fr. 1 Kinkel, Antimachus fr. 1 Kinkel.
[2] ῾Ερμῆν ὕμνει, Μοῦσα . . .᾿; 'Muse, hymn Hermes'.
[3] The Hymn to Selene which speaks of the Muses as ἵστορες ᾠδῆς, 'discoverers of song', is accepted as late.
[4] Pausanias (9.29.4) says that Mimnermus in the prelude to his elegiac lines makes the original Muses daughters of Uranus and the younger ones children of Zeus. Presumably Mimnermus began by invoking both generations of Muses. Theognis has a near invocation in 1055–8. Where we have a complete elegy it is often addressed to a human recipient.
[5] Solon 1.1–4.
[6] 1.51–2. I accept the wider sense of ὄλβος proposed by Allen.
[7] *T.A.P.A.* 1949, 50–65.

that the Muses, as source of wisdom, give Solon the ability so to use his intellect as to obtain a prosperity which Fate will not destroy. I am not convinced by Allen's argument that the γνωμοσύνη, 'wisdom', of fr. 16 is the key to the understanding of the poem, nor that it underlies the thought of the final lines, and I doubt whether the poem is so constructed as to make the understanding of the opening prayers dependent on grasping the implications of the elegy's end.[1] The case for the Muses as givers of wisdom in this sense is shaky, and is not proved by examples which show their omniscience. If we are to find any links between this unparalleled appeal to the Muses and their usual functions, I suggest that we should bear in mind Hesiod's remarks at the end of the proem of the *Theogony*, where the eloquence (and consequently the influence and reputation) of a king is attributed to the Muses' favour.[2] For Solon, who was both statesman and poet, this passage would have had a special significance.

Many invocations to the Muse by the lyric poets have survived, though often in isolation, and we can see in them the beginnings of the outpouring of praise which was to reach its climax in the poetry of Pindar. Alcman and Stesichorus[3] seem often to have begun their poems with invocations, Sappho less often, but none of the lyric poets fails to mention the Muses somewhere. What is difficult is to make a precise statement about the relationship between any one of these poets and the Muses. It is unlikely that any of the poets defined the relationship in detail, but the lyric fragments that remain do not permit even inferences about its nature. The frequency of appeals to the Muse probably demonstrates the poet's sense of dependence upon her, but may be partly a matter of convention. It would be tempting to suppose that some of the metaphors in which Pindar and Bacchylides spoke about the Muses originated with Alcman or Stesichorus, but it is unlikely that the earlier poets' invocations were more than brief and undeveloped. A fragment which Wilamowitz attributed to Stesichorus makes clear the extent of the Muse's task, using imagery we shall find again

---

[1] For the structure of the poem see R. Lattimore, *A.J.P.* 1947, 161–79.

[2] *Theog.* 81–97, quoted on p. 117.

[3] Alcman: e.g. *P.M.G.* 3, 14(a), 27; Stesichorus: e.g. *P.M.G.* 193, 210, 240, 250.

later: ἁ Μοῦσα γὰρ οὐκ ἀπόρως γεύει τὸ παρὸν μόνον ἀλλ᾽ ἐπέρχεται
πάντα θεριζομένα. 'The Muse does not taste only what lies at
hand, lacking resourcefulness, but goes forward, culling everything.'[1] This sounds like the defence of a poet who has enlarged
the conventional domain of poetry, or perhaps of one as dis-
cursive as Pindar. The opening of one of Sappho's poems suggests a longer invocation than usual:

δεῦρο δηὖτε Μοῖσαι χρύσιον λίποισαι[2] ...

The tone of Ibycus' only surviving mention of the Muses is
hard to assess. His address to Polycrates, at whose court he
was living, presents a sketchy account of some of the *Iliad*
material, including what is undoubtedly an allusion to the great
invocation preceding the Catalogue of Ships. 'On such particu-
lars the Muses of Helicon might well embark, learned as they
are, but no man living could relate all the facts about the ships
...'[3] Whereas Homer vouches for the detailed accuracy of his
Catalogue by appealing to omniscient Muses, Ibycus justifies
his perfunctory treatment by contrasting the ordinary man's
information with that of the Muses: the epithet 'learned'
(σεσοφισμέναι), with its reference to the poet's *sophia*, surely
suggests in this context that the Muses' expertise is unwanted:
Ibycus will skim over the legends at speed to reach his goal, the
glorification of Polycrates.[4]

It is usually said that the Muses' function was to 'inspire' the
poet. It is worth examining the connotations this word has for
us to see if its use is appropriate to the material discussed in
this chapter. One of the qualities of inspiration is its suddenness:
Auden's *Hymn to St. Cecilia*, which has in its ancestry Greek
appeals to the Muse, puts this in a forceful series of images:

In a garden shady this holy lady
With reverent cadence and subtle psalm,
Like a black swan as death came on

[1] *P.M.G.* 947.
[2] Sappho 127 L.-P. The line quoted ('Hither once more, Muses, leaving your golden ...') suggests that the poem followed the pattern of an invocatory hymn.
[3] *P.M.G.* 282.23–7; cf. *Il.* 2.484–92, quoted on p. 40.
[4] 46–8; see p. 127.

Poured forth her song in perfect calm:
And by ocean's margin this innocent virgin
Constructed an organ to enlarge her prayer,
And notes tremendous from her great engine
Thundered out on the Roman air.

Blessed Cecilia, appear in visions
To all musicians, appear and inspire:
Translated daughter, come down and startle
Composing mortals with immortal fire.

Auden's 'startle' is paralleled by the colloquial use of 'inspiration' to mean a sudden bright idea, an apparently instantaneous answer to a problem. If Greek poets experienced the flash of inspiration, they did not say so. The creative artist's self-awareness is implied in this view of inspiration: the poet feels 'inspired'; he is conscious that his own abilities are being stretched to meet what comes, both as a challenge and as a gift, from outside himself. Poets may compare this creative experience to that felt by a mystic or induced by a drug. This sort of experience was known to the Greeks, and for Plato was made manifest in poets as well as in seers and magical healers.[1] It is extremely unlikely that the majority of Greek poets would have agreed with Plato about the nature of the poetic experience or that they would have thought their emotions during the act of creation worth noting. The notion that the artist is uniquely interesting in himself had fortunately not yet occurred to the Greeks.

Is there then any way in which the word 'inspiration' may properly be used of the Greek experience? If we remove the ideas of suddenness and possession from inspiration, what is left? The evidence of Greek poets from Homer to Anacreon which I have surveyed demonstrates two attitudes to poetry. The first is to regard it as a gift, usually the Muses', sometimes Apollo's. By this metaphor the Greeks expressed the belief that poetry is in some mysterious way 'given', that it comes from a source external to the poet and is other than he is. This view of inspiration is still current, although partly replaced by psycho-

---

[1] *Phaedrus* 245A; see p. 82.

logical theories in which poetry is held to emanate from the unconscious mind. The second Greek attitude to the creation of poetry is exemplified by the appeal to the Muses for knowledge. As I have tried to show, this is to some extent a plea that the oral poet's memory may not fail him, but it is also a way of expressing the certainty and inner conviction which the 'inspired' poet feels. The Muses know all things, past, present and future, and he, sharing their knowledge, will say what is precisely right, and deserve to be heard. This certainty that the poem, in its final form, could not be other than it is, still remains an essential feature of belief.

The Greek ways of talking about the sources of poetry magnify the poet's importance, not as an individual, but as an authority in the community. His relationship with the Muse is not one-sided; he does more than passively receive her gifts, as if in a trance.[1] Yet no Greek poet could have written, as Auden writes:

It is true that, when he is writing a poem, it seems to a poet as if there were two people involved, his conscious self and a Muse whom he has to woo or an angel with whom he has to wrestle, but, as in an ordinary wooing or wrestling match, his role is as important as Hers. The Muse, like Beatrice in *Much Ado*, is a spirited girl who has as little use for an abject suitor as she has for a vulgar brute. She appreciates chivalry and good manners, but she despises those who will not stand up to her and takes a cruel delight in telling them nonsense and lies which the poor little things obediently write down as 'inspired ' truth.[2]

[1] See p. 81 f.
[2] W. H. Auden, *The Dyer's Hand* (London, 1963) 16.

E

51

3. The Poets and the Muses:
Pindar, Bacchylides and the Dramatists

This chapter will continue the account of the poets' attitude
to the Muses and study some of the metaphorical ways in which
they talked about their art. Since much of their imagery was
traditional in origin we need to ask whether it still had a living
force, and this leads us on to the wider question of belief in the
Muses, its nature and extent. In the fifth century the validity
of established belief was often questioned, and one might take
the extreme view that belief in the Muses was no longer possible, their presence in so many poems being a matter of orna-
ment or convention. The Greeks continued to use the word *musa*
to mean the art of music (that is, poetry-plus-music), or to
denote an individual poem:[1] it would be easier for us if we
could make the distinction between *musa* and *Musa* simply that
between music and the Muse (or a Muse). But there are more
possibilities than these two, even if the context makes an
editor's decision between upper- and lower-case *m* straightforward. The word can mean music, Music, the Muse, a Muse
or the Muses. In come cases where *musa* is printed there may
still be a trace of the mythological associations, or at least a
vestigial feeling of the Muse portrayed in woman's form; even
when *Musa* is printed the degree of personification is not always
obvious: the poet may be writing about a goddess in whose
physical existence he firmly believes; he may be sceptical of her
existence but value her as myth; he may, with the legendary
figure in the back of his mind, be personifying, and as it were
sanctifying, the art of music.

In the introduction to his edition of Bacchylides Bruno Snell
wrote: 'Bacchylidem eo a Pindaro differre, quod non tam sen-
tentias nouas inuenerit quam acceptas mutauerit, a uiris doctis

---

[1] e.g. *Od.* 24.62, *h.Hom.* 4.447, Eur. *Ion* 757 (music); *Ion* 1097, *Tro.* 120
(individual poem); both uses are common in Euripides.

statim intellegebatur.'[1] In his attitude to the Muses and to his art Bacchylides' debt to his predecessors is obvious and his modification of tradition interesting. I shall therefore consider him in some detail and try to show by comparison how Pindar's more startling innovations are themselves rooted, though less conspicuously, in tradition. To show that these two poets used conventional material does not in itself prove that they shared the beliefs of their predecessors, since they may have been chiefly concerned to demonstrate that they were part of a long poetic tradition, but a reading of their poems does suggest that the Muses were not for them an empty convention, just a convenient and picturesque way of beginning a poem.

Bacchylides' normal practice is to mention the Muses at, or near, the beginning and end of the poem, while Pindar, beginning often with a maxim or an apostrophe to a city or divinity connected with the occasion of the poem, is particularly likely to address them or refer to them before or after the central myth.[2]

To take invocations first; two passages of Bacchylides contain an appeal to the Muses reminiscent of an invocatory hymn. Of the first epinician enough remains to show that the poet asked the Muses to come and celebrate an Isthmian victory: he perhaps sees them as singing and dancing themselves.

κλυτοφόρμιγγες Διὸς ὑ-
ψιμέδοντος παρθένοι,
δεῦρ᾽ ἴτε Πιερίδες
ἐνυφαίνετε δ᾽ ὕμνους.

'Maidens, famed lyre-players, daughters of heaven's ruler, Zeus, come hither, Pierians, and weave your patterned hymns.'[3] The second passage is very similar in tone and may also form

---

[1] Intro. 22.

[2] Bacchylides invokes or mentions the Muses or a Muse at 1.3, 2.11, 3.3,71,92, 4.8, 5.4,13,176, 6.11, 9.3,87, 10.11, 12.2, 13.9,222,228, 15.47, 16.3, 19.4,13,35, fr. 20B.4, fr. 20C.3, fr. 21.5, fr. 55.2, fr. 63.1, Epigram 1.3.

Pindar: *Olympians*: 1.112, 3.4, 6.21,91, 7.7, 9.5,87, 10.3,14,100, 11.17, 13.21b,92; *Pythians*: 1.2,12,14,58, 3.90, 4.3,67,279, 5.65,114, 6.49, 10.37,65, 11.41; *Nemeans*: 1.12, 3.1,27,79, 4.3, 5.23, 6.28,33, 7.12,15,77, 8.47, 9.1,55, 10.26; *Isthmians*: 1.65, 2.2,6,34, 3+4,61, 6.2,54,72, 7.23, 8.5c,57,62; Paeans: 6.4,41,42,134, 7b.11,14, 8.18, 9.39; fr. 1.6, 86.20, 89.14, 150, 152.3, 168, 169, 170, 234, 238, 309. [3] 1.1–5.

the beginning of an epinician.[1] The Muses summoned to leave Helicon were addressed as 'daughters of Zeus of the thunderbolt, leaders of choral dance, gold-crowned maidens'. These two examples show the poet's fondness for piling up compound adjectives,[2] adjectives which describe the Muses' appearance, their divine status and their musical talents: this is not a Pindaric technique. The closest Pindaric parallel, and indeed his only traditional invocation, occurs at the beginning of the Third *Nemean*, probably written about 475: 'Lady Muse, our mother, I beseech you, in the month of Nemean festival, come to the hospitable Dorian island, Aegina; by the water of Asopus the boys' choir whose work is honey-voiced revel-songs stands waiting for your voice.'

> ὦ πότνια Μοῖσα, μᾶτερ ἀμετέρα, λίσσομαι,
> τὰν πολυξέναν ἐν ἱερομηνίᾳ Νεμεάδι
> ἵκεο Δωρίδα νᾶσον Αἴγιναν · ὕδατι γὰρ
> μένοντ' ἐπ' Ἀσωπίῳ μελιγαρύων τέκτονες
> κώμων νεανίαι, σέθεν ὄπα μαιόμενοι.[3]

There is an adaptation of traditional beginnings in the Ninth *Nemean*: 'We shall lead the revel-song from Apollo's shrine in Sicyon, Muses, to newly-founded Aetna . . . now accomplish a sweet hymn in verse,'[4] and the Pindaric tone is unmistakable in the quasi-invocation of the Fourth *Pythian*: σάμερον μὲν χρή σε παρ' ἀνδρὶ φίλῳ στᾶμεν . . . Μοῖσα. 'To-day it is your duty, Muse, to stand by a man who is my friend.'[5]

Both poets use convention deliberately when they echo the Homeric 'Muse, who first . . . ?' as an introductory formula. One such occurs in a dithyramb by Bacchylides ('Muse, who first began the just pleas?'),[6] and another in Pindar's Fourth *Pythian* ('What was the beginning of their sea-faring?').[7] Where Bacchylides differs from his predecessors (as far as we can tell) is in his fondness for addressing a single Muse by name, Urania,

---

[1] fr. 65.11–14; cf. Sappho 127 L.-P. This poem was written for Argeius of Ceos, possibly about 456.

[2] e.g. ἰοβλέφαρος ('violet-eyed') 9.3, φοινικοκράδεμνος ('with crimson kerchief') 13.222, ἀναξίμολπος ('queen of song') 6.10, ὑμνοάνασσα 12.1.

[3] N. 3.1–5.   [4] N. 9.1–3.

[5] P. 4.1–3; cf. O. 10.3b.

[6] 15.47, cf. 19.15.   [7] P. 4.70–1.

Calliope or Clio.[1] It is hard to see significance in his choice of individual Muse, although perhaps Clio is invoked in the third ode as giver of fame, whereas Pindar's naming of Clio, Terpsichore and their mother in each case enriches the meaning of its context. We shall see that Bacchylides uses the Homeric metaphors of the 'path of song' and of 'weaving' hymns;[2] he is traditional too in speaking of himself as the servant of the Muses and of poetry as their gift,[3] but he has a few more ornate ways of alluding to a poem which are probably not inherited. Although both poets may refer to their works simply as hymns and the like,[4] they often use instead, or in addition, a periphrasis designed to enrich, or to harmonize with, its context. Pindar uses this technique with great elaboration, for example when in the Third *Nemean* he speaks of sending the victor 'this mixture of honey and white milk',[5] but Bacchylides prefers greater concision. His favourite word for poetry is *agalma*, which has the basic meaning 'what someone delights in'; since gods delight particularly in statues it comes to mean 'statue' also;[6] both meanings are present in the address to Hiero at the beginning of the fifth epinician, an unusually rich passage:
'Blest war-lord of Syracuse, city of whirling chariots, thou, if any mortal, wilt rightly estimate the sweet gift brought in thy honour by the Muses of violet crown.'

Εὔμοιρε Συρακοσίων
  ἱπποδινήτων στραταγέ,
γνώσηι μὲν ἰοστεφάνων
  Μοισᾶν γλυκύδωρον ἄγαλμα, τῶν γε νῦν
αἴ τις ἐπιχθονίων,
  ὀρθῶς.[7]

---

[1] Bacchylides: Urania 4.8, 5.13, 6.11, 16.3; Calliope 5.176; Clio 3.3, 12.2, 13.9,228.

Pindar: Clio *N*. 3.79 (the victor's name is Aristocleides); Terpsichore *I*. 2.7; Mnemosyne *N*. 7.15, *I*. 6.72.   [2] See pp. 57, 67.

[3] Servant of the Muses: 5.9 (Urania), 191 (Hesiod is their servant), fr. 63. 'Gift of song': 3.3, 5.4, 12.179, 19.4, fr. 55.2. For Bacchylides as the Muses' 'interpreter' see p. 88; he also calls himself a bee (10.10) and a nightingale (3.95), cf. Eur. fr. 588 (about Palamedes).

[4] *ἀοιδά, μέλος, μολπά, ὕμνος, ᾠδή.*

[5] *N*. 3.73–7; cf. the 'Lydian crown' of *N*. 8.15.

[6] 1.184, 5.4, 10.11, fr. 20B.5, fr. 65.23. Pindar's single comparable use occurs in a poem which may be late, *N*. 8.16.   [7] 5.1–6.

The *agalma* delights Hiero and the Muses, and has, by implication, the enduring qualities of a statue (elsewhere the Muses' *agalma* is actually called 'deathless ').[1] In a passage explaining how song immortalizes achievement Bacchylides speaks of the Muses' *athyrma*, 'plaything', again expressing the idea that what the Muses enjoy is of permanent value to men.[2]

The sense of poetic abundance which is conveyed at the beginning of Bacchylides' Io-dithyramb (19.1–8) and in the metaphor of the Heracles-dithyramb (probably a late poem) in which Urania is said to have sent from Pieria 'a golden cargo-boat laden with famous hymns' is common in both Pindar and Bacchylides,[3] but there is some evidence that Bacchylides was also conscious of the difficulties of writing poetry. Pindar must have felt differently: his problems did not arise from a fear that his invention would dry up but from the need to wrestle with a tendency to over-copiousness and to find the appropriate tone of voice. Bacchylides' fifth epinician, written in 476, contains his only statement of the need to limit the myth;[4] his feeling that poetry is a rare gift is expressed in a fragment of a paean, imperfectly preserved: 'As of old, so now, poet is heir of poet, (for it is not easy) to discover the gates of verse before unspoken.'[5] A similar idea is found in the fragment, reasonably attributed to Bacchylides, which says that the Muses' gifts are not for all.[6]

As we have seen, Bacchylides does not usually feel the need to dilate on the exact nature of his relationship with his Muse but is content with familiar modes of expression: there are two passages however in which he breaks new ground. At the beginning of the twelfth ode he prays to Clio:

ὡσεὶ κυβερνήτας σοφός, ὑμνοάνασ-
σ᾽ εὔθυνε Κλεοῖ
νῦν φρένας ἁμετέρας
εἰ δή ποτε καὶ πάρος.

[1] 10.11, cf. 1.84. For Simonides' comparison of song and statue, see p. 95.
[2] 9.87, cf. Epigram 1.3; Pindar (*P.* 5.22) calls the victory-choir Apollo's *athyrma*.
[3] 16.1–4; the use of 'cargo-boat' (ὅλκας) here is a rather bold extension of an image occurring in *N.* 5.3–5: Pindar's ode is bidden to travel by cargo-boat to announce Pytheas' victory. [4] 5.176–8.
[5] fr. 5; Bacchylides seems to be picturing a storehouse of new song.
[6] fr. 55, quoted on p. 38.

PINDAR, BACCHYLIDES AND THE DRAMATISTS

'Like an expert helmsman, Clio, mistress of hymns, steer my
thoughts, now if ever before.'[1] The poem is seen as a voyage, and
the poet as needing guidance in the ordering of his material.
A fuller account of his task is given in the difficult concluding
lines of the thirteenth ode, difficult because the precise sequence
of thought cannot now be recovered:

> τᾶι καὶ ἐγὼ πίσυνος
> φοινικοκραδέμνοις τε Μούσαις
> ὕμνων τινὰ τάνδε νεόπλοκον δόσιν
> φαίνω, ξενίαν τε φιλά-
> 225 γλαον γεραίρω,
> τὰν ἐμοὶ Λάμπων[
> βληχρὰν ἐπαθρήσαιστ[
> τὰν εἰκ ἐτύμως ἄρα Κλειὼ
> πανθαλὴς ἐμαῖς ἐνέσταξεν φρασίν,
> 230 τερψιεπεῖς νιν ἀοιδαὶ
> παντὶ καρύξοντι λαῶι.[2]

The first part is clear: 'in this hope, I too, trusting in the Muses
of crimson scarf, am now displaying a newly-woven gift of
hymns; so I honour the illustrious friendship of Lampon ...'
The two incomplete lines cannot be satisfactorily restored, but
should contain an antecedent for the relative which begins 228:
'If Clio truly instilled this (?grace)[3] in my heart, my songs
which proclaim him to the whole people shall be delightful.'
Bacchylides must here be saying both that he feels able to
address his patron because of his trust in the Muses and that the
sweetness of his poetry is the direct result of the Muses' effect on
his mind.

The incomplete fourth ode for Hiero is original in its coupling
of Apollo and Urania and, apparently, in metaphor. Bacchylides is demonstrating Apollo's continued goodwill towards
Syracuse and refers to him as 'sweet-voiced consort of Urania,
mistress of the lyre'. He goes on (if the supplement is accepted):
'with willing mind he shook down new hymns upon the old'

[1] 12.1–4.
[2] 13.221–31.
[3] cf. I. 3+4.90; σὺν Ὀρσέᾳ δέ νιν κωμάξομαι τερπνὰν ἐπιστάζων (ἀποστ άζων
B: ἐπιστοχάζων D) χάριν; I. 3+4, if written in 475, may be about ten years later
than Bacchylides 13.

(ἑκόντι νόωι | καὶ νέους ἐπέσεισεν ὕμνους). Snell suggests that the image is that of casting leaves and branches in the victor's honour: if so, the poet is not so much making Apollo the guardian of a tree of poetry as emphasizing that the heaping up of honours for Hiero and Syracuse is by his will.[1]

It is obvious that the writer of epinician and of some other lyric poetry was expected to include some mention of the individual poem or of his art in general; in Bacchylides' case, as we have seen, such material is often linked with the Muses and is sometimes concerned with problems of originality or construction. Bacchylides does not tell us about the genesis of any poem or about his emotional state when composing: what he does make plain is that he is aiming at a truthful, lasting ennoblement of his subject which will glorify the poet also. Pindar certainly tells us rather more than Bacchylides and his manner of telling is both fuller and more veiled, but when Bowra writes that of all Greek poets he 'alone speaks of the creative process from the inside',[2] his words can be accepted only with some reservations. Pindar does not reveal himself in the way that a modern poet may in his letters, notebooks or explanatory prefaces; he does not, I think, expect us to be interested in him as a man. If Pindar's purpose is not primarily self-revelation of the sort practised by the Romantic poet we need to find if we can why he says so much about poetry in all the genres in which he writes. The answer lies partly in his need to establish his authority *qua* poet: although we no longer condemn commissioned poetry as 'insincere', it is still true that an understanding of Pindar's attitude to his art depends on an insight into, and acceptance of, the conditions of epinician, the immortalizing by a poet of a particular athletic victory, this carried out both by relating it to the heroic tradition of the victor's family and city and by a glorification of poetry. When Pindar wrote that the Muse stood by him as he was composing it was more an assurance to the recipient of the ode's authority than a personal touch.

For the purposes of this study it is necessary to isolate from

---

[1] 4.7–10; cf. Pindar fr. 170, where the Muses are associated with the golden apples of the Hesperides.
[2] *Pindar* 2.

their context Pindar's statements about the poetic art. If such statements merely formed a detachable prelude to each song the process would be less misleading: in fact, and not only because they are placed in the body of the ode, they are part of its material, form and texture. Their structural function is like that of a bridge passage in music when they mark the transition from prelude to myth, or from myth to maxim, but their effect is quite different, since we are more often startled by the change of course than eased into the new section. This abruptness of Pindar's is deliberate, not a failure in technique, and stems, I believe, from a desire to give his poem the immediacy of improvization; he writes as if impulse alone dictated his course and so disguises the fact that he was bound both by the terms of his commission and by the principles of his art. One result of the insertion of statements about the poetic art into the body of the ode is that its hearers are invited to contemplate the poem rather than experience it as participants in the myth, or at least that they are sometimes jolted out of their absorption.

It may be significant that it is in Paeans, associated with Apollo, that Pindar follows Homeric tradition in ascribing knowledge to the Muses. We have seen that for the Homeric bard knowledge could cover both the ability to remember and present vividly the material of his lay, and the technical skill he needed. Pindar's Paeans were known only in isolated quotations until the beginning of this century: now we have considerable portions of six, and fragments, some fairly substantial, of others. Two are important for us: Paean Six, written for the people of Delphi, and Seven (b), which is less well preserved. Six begins with Pindar's prayer to be received at Delphi as the 'interpreter of the Pierians in song' (ἀοίδιμον Πιερίδων προφάταν).[1] Later, after a lacuna, it looks as though we have a traditional appeal to the Muse for knowledge (e.g. 'tell me the source of strife among the immortals') followed immediately by the grounds of the appeal. (The text is uncertain.) 'The gods can persuade wise men of these things; for mortals it is impossible to discover them: come maidens, Muses, you know all things; with Zeus, hidden in dark cloud, and with Mnemosyne you

---

[1] Paean 6.4; I agree with Bowra's interpretation of ἀοίδιμον (*Pindar* 3). See also p. 88.

have this portion; hear me then, for my tongue longs to pay this sweetest honey-tribute.'[1] This sounds like an attribution to the Muses, as children of Memory and the Father of Gods, of the power, and perhaps the duty, of revealing truth to poets, revealing it in such a way as to gain credence. In Seven (b) the prayer is similar:

> ... δ' Οὐρανου τ' εὐπέπλῳ θυγατρὶ
> Μναμοσύνᾳ κόραισί τ' εὐ-
> μαχανίαν διδόμεν.
> τυφλαὶ γὰρ ἀνδρῶν φρένες
> ὅστις ἄνευθ' Ἑλικωνιάδων
> βαθεῖαν ἐλθόντων ἐρευνᾶι σοφίαις ὁδόν.

'(I pray) to Mnemosyne in her fine robe, daughter of Uranus, and to her daughters, to grant me fullness of resource: for men's minds are blind, if any of them, without the Heliconian Muses, seeks the steep path of those who walked it by their wise skill. This deathless task they (? the Muses) have given me . . .'[2] The difficulties here are not only textual but due to combining the metaphor of blindness with that of the poet as traveller. The connection of thought may be that 'fullness of resource' is allied to inventiveness, the poet's own effort of discovery; such discovery, though made by his mental ingenuity, is nevertheless ultimately derived from the Muses, and he will see nothing as he goes unless they are with him. Blindness in this case will not be simply ignorance but a failure of perception.

Pindar repeatedly makes it clear that he is a joint worker with the Muses: there is no evidence that he was a passive recipient of their gifts nor that he could compose only in the excitement of inspiration.[3] His usual word for his part in their work is *heurisko*, 'discover' or 'invent',[4] and his plainest description of the shared task occurs when he says: 'The Muse

---

[1] 38–45.

[2] 7b.10–17; I accept the rendering suggested by Grenfell-Hunt (*P. Oxy.* V.101), although ἐλθόντων (Snell suggests ἐμπατῶν) remains worrying and the reference to former poets seems out of place here.

[3] In Paean 9 (33–40), written for the Thebans, there is an incomplete allusion to a *daimon*, but since immediately after Pindar speaks of composing a lament 'with subtlety of mind' he cannot be stating complete dependence on a deity.

[4] See p. 101 f.

stood by my side as I was inventing a new-shining way of harnessing the bright voice of praise to the Dorian chariot.'

Μοῖσα δ' οὕτω ποι παρέστα μοι νεοσίγαλον εὑρόντι τρόπον
Δωρίῳ φωνὰν ἐναρμόξαι πεδίλῳ
ἀγλαόκωμον.[1]

Sometimes he speaks with confidence, as when he describes himself as 'willing helper of the Muses'; elsewhere he prays to be dear to them or that they may be well-disposed to him.[2] In describing their relationship he tends to steer clear of the hackneyed 'son' or 'servant' of the Muses, perhaps by expressing the idea in a different way, in the address to the Muse as 'our Mother', for example. The less common 'herald' is found in his boast 'The Muse has raised me up as her chosen herald of words of wisdom'.[3] There is an interesting development of the picture of the poet as the Muses' messenger in the Fourth *Pythian*. Pindar is writing to Arcesilas, king of Cyrene, who had banished Damophilus for his part in a disturbance. Pindar has probably already interceded with the king for the exile in private: the plea is repeated tactfully and allusively after the Fourth *Pythian's* long myth. The topic is introduced by an adaptation of Homer: 'Homer declared that a good messenger brings the greatest honour to any deed: even the Muse is made greater as a result of good reporting.'[4] This means, I think, that Arcesilas' clemency will shine more brightly in Pindar's verse and that the poet who is a successful intermediary honours his art and his Muse. Pindar is not here talking about verisimilitude or truth, as Norwood seems to imply with his comment 'even inspiration cannot dispense with accuracy'.[5]

Of the impulse to poetry he can write quite simply that Apollo, leader of the Muses, is bidding him sing and dance: *ὁ Μοισαγέτας με καλεῖ χορεῦσαι,*[6] or he can echo Homer, as in fr. 169 (*Μοῖσ' ἀνέηκέ με*).[7] At other times he is spurred on by

---

[1] *O.* 3.4b–6; cf. fr. 130.11.
[2] *O.* 13.92–3, fr. 150, *I.* 3+4.61; cf. the slightly peremptory request of *P.* 1.58.
[3] fr. 86.18–20.
[4] *P.* 4.276–9; Burton 170–1.
[5] *Pindar* 166.
[6] fr. 159; for Apollo and dancing cf. fr. 157.
[7] *Od.* 8.73–4, discussed on p. 42.

desire to emulate a predecessor; hearing the melody invented by the Locrian Xenocritus he is roused to song like the sea-dolphin who is moved by a lovely flute-tune.[1] On one occasion he pays tribute to the part played by his native Thebes in his musical development: 'the son whom famed Thebes reared was no stranger, ignorant of the Muses.'[2]

As we have seen in the Fourth *Pythian*, Pindar thinks of the Muse in connection with his relationship with his patron; the two passages dealing with the financial aspect of his commission will be discussed in Chapter 6: here, we look at the proem to the Tenth *Olympian*, where he makes the Muse a party to the contract he has with his patron, Agesidamus, and apologizes for his delay in writing the ode: 'I owed him a sweet song and forgot. O Muse, you and Zeus' daughter, Truth, come, with upraised arm ward off the reproach of broken promises, the sin against friendship.'[3]

Many of the passages already quoted have illustrated the fact that both poets, like their predecessors but to an even greater extent, talk about their work in metaphorical language.[4] The interpretation of Pindaric metaphor in particular is not easy. Much of the splendour of his poetry results from his use of elaborate complexes of metaphor, and difficulties arise if one tries to paraphrase his meaning in non-figurative language, partly because his images may develop during their course an independent life, and partly because he mixes metaphors and revives dead ones. Of dead metaphors William Empson writes: 'Among metaphors effective from several points of view one may include, by no great extension, those metaphors which are partly recognized as such and partly received simply as words in their acquired sense. All languages are composed of dead metaphors as the soil of corpses, but English is perhaps uniquely full of metaphors of this sort, which are not dead but sleeping, and while making a direct statement, colour it with an implied comparison. The school rule against mixed metaphor, which in itself is so powerful a weapon, is largely necessary because of

[1] fr. 222.
[2] fr. 234.
[3] *O.* 10.3–6; cf. *O.* 6.19-21, where Pindar speaks of the Muses enjoining (or permitting or perhaps sharing in) his performance of his oath to Agesias.
[4] See A. Sperduti, *T.A.P.A.* 1950, 209 ff., K. Svoboda, *Aeg.* 1952, 108–20.

the presence of these sleepers, who must be treated with
respect; they are harder to use than either plain word or metaphor because if you mix them you must show you are conscious
of their meaning, and not merely insensitive to the possibilities
of the language.'[1]

I take first one of Pindar's most striking metaphors, that of
the Muses' chariot, which was probably his own invention. It
occurs in his earliest surviving ode, the Tenth *Pythian* written
in 498, where he tells us about his patron: 'I trust Thorax' kind
friendship, who, labouring for my sake, yoked this four-horsed
chariot of the Pierides.'[2] The present poem is the vehicle which,
as it were, conveys the Muses. This is not the only connotation
of the metaphor: the poet may see himself as privileged to ride
in the Muses' chariot as when Pindar, writing between 490 and
476, alluded to lyric poets as 'the men of old who mounted the
chariot of the golden-banded Muses with the ringing lyre in
their hands'.[3] In 478 he produced a further variation when he
spoke of the Muses' chariot rushing to honour the victor.[4]
Bacchylides' single instance of the metaphor is not a dull copy:
in the eloquent fifth ode, written for Hiero, he breaks off the
long myth: 'Fair-armed Calliope, stay here your well-made
chariot.'

λευκώλενε Καλλιόπα,
    στᾶσον εὐποίητον ἅρμα
αὐτοῦ.[5]

Bacchylides is riding in the Muses' chariot; the control of the
poem's course is shared by him and his deities.[6] Finally we must
consider the more difficult passage of the Sixth *Olympian* in
which the chariot is primarily that of the victor, not the Muses.
Pindar was writing for Agesias of Syracuse; the occasion was

[1] *Seven Types of Ambiguity* (London, 1947) 25.
[2] *P*. 10.64–6; cf. fr. 127 (about 490), where Pindar sends 'a waggon-load of
lovely songs' to Thrasybulus, the recipient of *I*. 2. Simonides (790) had spoken
of Victory's chariot.
[3] *I*. 2.1–2; cf. *O*. 9.86–7 (after 466).
[4] *I*. 8.59–62.
[5] 5.176–8.
[6] Bowra (*Pindar* 39) thinks the chariot is external to the poet.

victory in a mule-chariot race. After an introductory passage of praise Pindar addresses the charioteer:

'Up then Phintis, yoke me the strength of the mules
with speed, let me mount the chariot, drive a clean
highway to the source of these men's race.
They understand, and will guide us better than others.'

ὦ Φίντις, ἀλλὰ ζεῦξον ἤδη μοι σθένος ἡμιόνων
ἇ τάχος, ὄφρα κελεύθῳ τ᾽ἐν καθαρᾷ
βάσομεν ὄκχον, ἵκωμαί τε πρὸς ἀνδρῶν
καὶ γένος · κεῖναι γὰρ ἐξ ἀλλᾶν ὁδὸν ἁγεμονεῦσαι
ταύταν ἐπίστανται.[1]

The poet's destination is the birth of Iamus, son of Apollo and ancestor of the family of seers to which Agesias belongs. The imagery of this passage can be understood in purely literary terms and metaphysical interpretation is unnecessary: Pindar's goal is to be attained most directly by borrowing the swiftness of Agesias' mules.[2] In general meaning this passage is not very different from one in the Sixth *Nemean*, where Pindar uses the metaphor of the 'path of song' from which the chariot image no doubt developed.[3] Writing for an Aeginetan victor Pindar says 'on all sides there are broad ways by which a poet may glorify this island' since the exploits of Aeacus' descendants have provided much material for story-tellers; 'even early poets had found the highway'.[4]

When Alcinous was giving the feast for Odysseus, 'the Muse impelled the bard Demodocus to sing the deeds of men, and

[1] O. 6.22–6 (472 or 468).

[2] The metaphysical interpretation (Bowra, *Problems* 45 ff., *Pindar* 39) rests partly on the supposed influence of Parmenides, discussed below, and partly on phrases like κελεύθῳ ἐν καθαρᾷ (translated by Lattimore as 'clear highway'), which Bowra takes to mean 'a road through the air': probably the primary meaning of καθαρός here is 'broad', 'open', with a secondary connotation of brightness; cf. ἀγλαὸς οἶμος, 'bright path of song' (h.Herm. 451).

[3] Words for path are οἴμη (Od. 8.74,480; 22.347), οἶμος (h.Hom. 4.451), κέλευθος (I. 4.1), τρίβος (h.Hom. 4.448). See O. Becker, 'Das Bild des Weges' (Hermes Einzelschriften, Heft 4, 1937), A. Kambylis, *Die Dichterweihe und ihre Symbolik* (Heidelberg, 1965).

[4] N. 6.47–8, 55–6, of unknown date but unlikely to be earlier than the Sixth *Olympian*.

the fame of that song reached the broad heaven'.[1] Later,
Odysseus remarks on the esteem in which bards are held, since
the Muse has taught them the paths of song (οἴμας) in her love
for them.[2] Finally Phemius claimed that the Muse had implanted in him paths of song of every kind.[3] These three passages make it clear that the metaphor is already dead by
Homer's time and that it may sometimes be translated merely
by 'song'.[4] Professor W. B. Stanford writes: 'in selecting his
material (the bard) had to find a clear and continuous path of
song through the mass of heroic legends which lay like a thick
and tangled wood before him'.[5] In my opinion the metaphor
alludes to more than the narrative element in epic and includes
what we should call the structural and stylistic aspects of the
poet's task.[6]

There is no doubt that ultimately Homer is the source of all
occurrences of the 'path' metaphor. However, by the time of
Parmenides the metaphor had developed a specialized meaning
which we must now consider; this development has sometimes
been attributed to the Shaman-poet Aristeas of Proconnesus.
Professor Guthrie has this to say about Parmenides: 'The equation "road or journey = quest for knowledge = lay or narrative
conveying the results of that quest" was not his own, but
already present in the shamanistic practices of which his poem
contains distinct though far-off echoes'.[7] Parmenides is now
generally agreed to have been born 515–510, but we do not
know when his work was written and disseminated. The Proem
of his work on the Nature of Being contains an extended treatment of the metaphor and is written in the metre and manner

[1] *Od.* 8.73–4 (οἴμης).   [2] *Od.* 8.479–81.
[3] *Od.* 22.347.
[4] cf. *O.* 9.51 ἔγειρ᾽ ἐπέων σφιν οἶμον λιγύν, 'awaken for them a clear-voiced
path of song'.
[5] *Odyssey* intro. xvi. Bowra (*Heroic Poetry* 220), writing on *Od.* 22.347, seems
to interpret the metaphor along the same lines when he says that 'οἶμαι . . .
means literally "ways" or "approaches" and suggests that (the bard) can
approach any theme'.
[6] In the Hymn to Hermes (451–2) the Muses are said to be concerned with
'dancing and the glorious path of song (οἶμος ἀοιδῆς), with flourishing song
(μολπή) and the lovely deep-toned flute'. Here the author is distinguishing epic
from other types of song.
[7] Guthrie, *Philosophy* ii, 12; for Aristeas see J. Bolton, *Aristeas* (Oxford,
1962).

of epic: 'The mares that carry me as far as my heart ever desires were escorting me when they had brought and set me on the resounding road of the goddess, which bears the man of knowledge over all cities. On that road was I carried; on it the wise horses took me, pulling at the chariot, and the maidens led the way . . . the daughters of the Sun, having left the house of Night, hastened to bring me to the light, when they had thrown back the veils from their heads with their hands.

'There are the gates of the paths of Night and Day, set between a lintel and a threshold of stone.'

Parmenides goes on to describe how the maidens appeased Dike, who was in charge of the doors between the gates, and how she opened the gates for them: 'through the gates the maidens kept the chariot and horses straight on the highway.

'And the goddess welcomed me graciously, took my right hand in hers, and addressed me with these words:

"Young man, who comest to my house accompanied by immortal charioteers, together with the horses which carry thee, I give thee welcome. It is by no means an evil lot that has sent thee forth on this road (far from the paths of men) but Right and Justice." '[1]

The problems presented by this passage are formidable and it is as difficult to follow the philosopher's journey as it is to explain his imagery.[2] Although it is natural to equate darkness with ignorance and light with knowledge, consistent identification of the other images is so tenuous that the passage can hardly be called allegorical in the strict sense. Parmenides had a new task, that of bringing his hearers to understand a rigorous exposition of logic, and his Proem had not only to present his poetic credentials and establish his links with tradition but to prepare their minds to follow a new mode of thought. Whereas Homer and Hesiod had invoked the Muses, Parmenides begins by demonstrating that his Goddess has received him in her own realm. It is interesting that although Parmenides vividly

---

[1] Parmenides, *D.-K.* 1.1–28, tr. Guthrie.
[2] See Bowra, *Problems* 38–53, E. F. Dolin, *H.S.C.P.* 1962, 93–9, J. Mansfeld, *Die Offenbarung des Parmenides und die menschliche Welt* (Assen, 1964), especially chap. 4, G. E. L. Owen, *C.A.* 1960, 84–102, F. M. Cornford, *Principium Sapientiae* 88–106, L. Tarán, *Parmenides* (Princeton, 1965) 24–31.

depicted features of the journey his Goddess is only a voice, not a figure whom we see. Hesiod's Muses with their power to tell truth and lies and Homer's Muses who impart knowledge must form the background of Parmenides' images, but he cannot have wanted them in the forefront of his hearers' attention. Similarly there is familiar myth behind his claim to be transported in the Sun's chariot: what is new is that he seems to have access to this chariot *qua* poet.

The Sicilian philosopher Empedocles, a younger contemporary of Parmenides, again used the image of the way as a recurrent motif; near the beginning of his poem on Nature he wrote: 'I beseech you, much-remembering, white-armed, maiden Muse, as far as it is lawful for mortals to hear, escort me, driving from the house of Reverence your chariot obedient to the reins.'[1] Later he writes: 'But now I shall come again to the path of hymns I spoke before, marking off one channel of speech from another.'[2] Like Pindar, Empedocles is using the image not just as a periphrasis for poem, nor to describe the philosophical quest, but as a formal, structural device.

In Pindar and Bacchylides the 'path of song' metaphor is used in a variety of ways. As often with genitive-link metaphors the terms may be related grammatically in two ways: sometimes the genitive defines, so that song is, or is in many ways like, a path; sometimes a particular path may be thought of as belonging to a poem.[3] In the latter case we picture the poem as proceeding continuously but with manifold changes of direction and level. There are numerous occasions on which the metaphor illustrates poetic abundance of one sort or another. 'I have through the gods' grace on all sides a far-reaching path, Melissus, since you have shown me at the Isthmian games plentiful ways along which to follow your family's *aretē*.'[4] Pindar's goal here is the adequate celebration of his subject's *aretē*, but this *aretē* is also what inspires his journey.[5] A similar

[1] D.-K. 3.3–5; πολυμνήστε is sometimes translated as 'much-wooed', not 'much-remembering'.

[2] D.-K. 35.1–3; cf. 17.15,24.

[3] See Christine Brooke-Rose, *A Grammar of Metaphor* (London, 1958) 146–205.

[4] *I.* 3+4.19.

[5] cf. *N.* 6.47–8, 55–6, 58–9.

F

passage in a dithyramb of Bacchylides lays more stress on the
resources of the poet himself:

πάρεστι μυρία κέλευθος
ἀμβροσίων μελέων,
ὃς ἂν παρὰ Πιερίδων λά-
χῃσι δῶρα Μουσᾶν,
ἰοβλέφαροί τε† καὶ
φερεστέφανοι Χάριτες
βάλωσιν ἀμφὶ τιμὰν
ὕμνοισιν.

'Innumerable are the paths of song available for the man blessed
with the gifts of the Pierian Muses, whose hymns the dark-eyed,
garlanded Graces clothe in glory.'[1]

A further recurrent theme in Pindar which develops the same
image is his sense that he must keep within limits.[2] Sometimes
these are technical: the poet must not be carried away so that
his poem, or part of it, becomes unwieldy; sometimes they are
moral: he must not boast or be overbold. It is easy to see that
skill in choosing the right course in a chariot race could suggest
that song too must not deviate from the best route: so Bacchylides concludes a passage on the blessings of human life: 'Why
have I turned my voice so far from the course?'

τί μακρὰν γλῶσσαν ἰθύσας ἐλαύνω
ἐκτὸς ὁδοῦ;[3]

The structural use of this theme is seen very clearly in
Pindar's Eleventh *Pythian,* an ode in which the myth appears
abruptly and deals with a subject not obviously relevant to the
occasion. At the conclusion of the myth Pindar addresses his
audience: 'My friends, at the crossroads where the paths diverge
I have been whirled about, though I had trodden the right path
before: has some gale blown my ship from its course?'[4]

Pindar's most striking expressions of this idea are put in

[1] 19.1–14; it is not certain that Bacchylides knew *I.* 3, but this dithyramb
may be late.
[2] In this context Pindar often uses the word καιρός (e.g. *N.* 1.18, *O.* 13.47).
See R. B. Onians, *The Origins of European Thought* (Cambridge, 1951), 343–8,
Burton, 45–9, W. S. Barrett on Euripides' *Hippolytus* 386–7.
[3] 10.51–2.
[4] *P.* 11.38–40.

geographical terms, as when he breaks off the myth about the family of Peleus in the Fourth *Nemean* by saying:

Γαδείρων τὸ πρὸς ζόφον οὐ περατόν · ἀπότρεπε
αὖτις Εὐρώπαν ποτὶ χέρσον ἔντεα ναός.

'One must not voyage into the darkness beyond Gadeira: turn back again your ship to the mainland of Europe.'[1] Similarly he recommends moderation both to his recipient, Theron, and to himself in the characteristic epilogue of the Third *Olympian*:

εἰ δ' ἀριστεύει μὲν ὕδωρ, κτεάνων δὲ χρυσὸς αἰδοιέστατος,
νῦν γε πρὸς ἐσχατίαν Θήρων ἀρεταῖσιν ἱκάνων ἅπτεται
οἴκοθεν Ἡρακλέος σταλᾶν · τὸ πόρσω δ' ἐστὶ σοφοῖς ἄβατον
κἀσόφοις. οὔ μιν διώξω · κεινὸς εἴην.

'But if water is best, and gold the most prized of possessions, yet still by his virtues Theron has reached and touched the furthest limit, Hercules' pillars. Further can no man go, wise or foolish. I shall go no further. I should be a fool.'[2]

The two ideas of abundance and limit are frequently expressed by Pindar in another image as old as Homer. The epic phrase 'winged words' (ἔπεα πτερόεντα) probably meant that speech, like a winged arrow, flies straight to its mark, but it may also easily suggest that words once uttered fly beyond recall; and indeed it may be used as a 'faded' metaphor, one not intended to create a picture in the mind.[3] Pindar uses weapon-metaphors in prayers that he may aim his song successfully.

ἄνδρα δ' ἐγὼ κεῖνον
αἰνῆσαι μενοινῶν, ἔλπομαι
μὴ χαλκοπάραον ἄκονθ' ὡσείτ' ἀγῶνος βαλεῖν ἔξω παλάμᾳ
δονέων,
μακρὰ δὲ ῥίψαις ἀμεύσασθ' ἀντίους.

'In my intention of praising that man (Hiero), I trust that I shall not, like one who whirls the bronze-sided javelin, cast it

---

[1] *N.* 4.69–72.   [2] *O.* 3.44–8.

[3] The Homeric phrase is discussed by G. H. Calhoun, *C.P.* 1935, 215–27, J. A. K. Thomson *C.Q.* 1936, 1–3, Milman Parry *C.P.* 1937, 59–63, R. B. Onians, *Origins* 469.

outside the arena, but throw it a great distance to outstrip my
rivals.'[1] He speaks too of the many arrows of his ready tongue,[2]
and of the arrows he has in his quiver which 'speak to the intelligent'.[3] A few lines later in the same poem the image is picked
up again in epic reminiscence:

ἔπεχε νῦν σκοπῷ τόξον, ἄγε θυμέ · τίνα βάλλομεν
ἐκ μαλθακᾶς αὖτε φρενὸς εὐκλέας ὀϊστοὺς ἱέντες;

'Come, my heart, aim your bow at a target: at whom am I
shooting, releasing from a kindly mind arrows which bring fame?'

At the moment when Odysseus was preparing his great bow
for use against the suitors Homer compares him with a bard
who is 'skilled in playing the lyre and singing and easily
stretches the string round the new peg, making fast the pliant
sheep gut at each end'. Later the bow-string 'sings' like a
swallow as Odysseus checks its tension.[4] When Pindar equates
the bow and the lyre he may be remembering this passage but
the equation is in any case made easy by the fact that these are
Apollo's emblems, and may be borrowed by the Muses. Eros
too must be mentioned since the lover conventionally darts
glances from his eyes and these are sometimes said to enchant
the beloved.[5] With these associations in mind the mixed metaphor of the Second *Isthmian* is easily acceptable: 'The men of
old, Thrasybulus, who mounted the chariot of the golden-
filleted Muses in company with the famous lyre, lightly aimed
their honey-voiced love poems.'[6] The splendid opening of the
First *Pythian* describes the lyre which Apollo and the Muses
share as having arrows which cast a spell on gods as well as
men, lulling Zeus and Ares to sleep.[7]

Although Pindar and Aeschylus were contemporaries, at first
sight the world of tragedy seems to have no connection with
that of choral lyric. The Muses who bestowed epinician and
other odes on their composers are nowhere suggested to have

[1] *P.* 1.42–5, Burton 100.   [2] *I.* 5.51.
[3] *O.* 2.91, 98–100; for other weapon-metaphors see *O.* 1.111–13, *O.* 9.5, *N.*
7.70–2, *N.* 9.54–5; Plato, *Prot.* 342D, *Theaet.* 180A.
[4] *Od.* 21.404–11.
[5] e.g. Aeschylus, *Supp.* 1005; 'Anyone who passes their (the Danaids') garden
shoots arrows which can enchant out of desire for them.'
[6] *I.* 2.1–3.   [7] *P.* 1.1–12.

70

been responsible for the tragic gift, nor is there much evidence of an association between the Muses and Dionysus, the god of drama. The chorus of Sophocles' *Antigone* recall how Lycurgus was imprisoned when he fought against the worship of Dionysus and quarrelled with the Muses.[1] Aeschylus' Lycurgus-tetralogy however points to hostility between Dionysus and the Muses: we are told that in the second play, the *Bassarae*, the Muses collected and buried the mutilated remains of Orpheus when he had been punished for his rejection of Dionysus.[2]

Some aspect of the Muses' story was also dramatized in Sophocles' *Thamyris*, as we have seen, and in the *Rhesus*, which may be the work of Euripides. This is the only surviving play in which a Muse is among the *dramatis personae*. Rhesus was the son of the river Strymon and a Muse, unnamed by Euripides but traditionally Terpsichore. When he is killed by Odysseus his mother appears as *dea ex machina*, laments him and takes his body for burial. As part of her lament she relates how she encountered Strymon as she and her sisters were on their way to Pangaeum for the 'great contest of song with the Thracian sophist' in which they blinded Thamyris, who had 'greatly insulted their art'. She goes on to blame Athena for sending Rhesus to his death at Troy, but exempts Athens from reproach. (It would be interesting to know which details of her narrative, if any, were invented by Euripides.)[3]

The majority of the references to the Muses in drama occur in lyric, particularly in the choral odes of Euripides (and his monodies) and Aristophanes. The dramatists have little to say directly about the Muses' function: a fragment of Sophocles makes them the source of fame and solace:

λάθα Πιερίδων στυγερὰ
κἀνάρατος · ἁ δὲ μνᾶστις
θνατοῖς εὐποτμοτάτα μελέων,
ἀνέχουσα βίου βραχὺν ἰσθμόν.

---

[1] *Ant.* 955–65.
[2] Eratosth. *Catast.* 24.140, quoted on Aesch. fr. 9N². Aeschylus has no other direct mention of the Muses: he uses *musa* to mean music at *Supp.* 695, *Eum.* 308.
[3] *Rhesus* 890–949, 962–82. The Muses were also a subject for Comedy, perhaps in mythological burlesque. The following titles are recorded: *The Muses* of

'It is hateful and accursed to be forgotten by the Muses; the memory given by songs is most joyful for men, sustaining life's short path.'[1]

We have seen that Pindar and Bacchylides took pains to use traditional devices in their poems: a similar archaizing tendency is often found in the lyrics of Euripides and Aristophanes. The clearest example is the invocation of the *Trojan Women*: 'Sing Ilion, Muse, I pray you, with new hymns, sing Ilion in dirge of tearful lamentation. Now shall I cry my song aloud to Troy.'

ἀμφί μοι ᾿Ίλιον, ὦ
Μοῦσα, καίνων ὕμνων
ἄεισον ἐν δακρύοις
ᾠδὰν ἐπικήδειον·
νῦν γὰρ μέλος ἐς Τροίαν ἰαχήσω.[2]

The antode of the *Birds'* parabasis is less obviously traditional but certainly gains some of its power from earlier descriptions of music-making on Olympus. The chorus tell how the swans by the river Hebrus sang to honour Apollo; animals cowered in fear and the sea was stilled; the music reached the gods and 'awe seized the princes. The Graces of Olympus and the Muses joined in the lament they heard.'

εἷλε δὲ θάμβος ἄνακτας· ᾿Ολυμπιά-
δες δὲ μέλος Χάριτες Μοῦ-   ·
σαί τ᾿ ἐπωλόλυξαν,
τιοτιοτιοτιγξ.[3]

There is a good deal of variety in Aristophanes' treatment of invocations, ranging from the brevity of the θύγατερ Διός ('Zeus' daughter'), slipped into the parabasis of the *Peace*, to the con-

---

Phrynichus (frs. 31–4), produced in 405, *The Birth of the Muses* of Polyzelus (frs. 7–9); Ophelion is also said to have written a comedy called *The Muses*.

[1] fr. 145N²; cf. the Muses' power to assuage grief at Euripides, *Helen* 1341–5. Muses are shown on two white-ground kalyx-kraters by the Phiale-painter (c. 450 B.C.) on which the *Andromeda* and the *Dionysiskos* of Sophocles are also respectively illustrated (*A.R.V.* 1017).

[2] *Tro.* 511–14; cf. *h.Hom.* 19.13; ὕμνων ... ᾠδάν recalls the Homeric ἀοιδῆς ὕμνον (*Od.* 8.429) as does Aristophanes' *Birds* 905.

[3] *Birds* 769–83.

scious originality of Agathon's appeal in the *Thesmophoriazusae*.[1]
It is not always poets who need the Muses' help: the crone
in the *Ecclesiazusae*, singing to herself while waiting for
custom, prays 'Come here to my lips, Muses, and invent a little
love-song for me' (Μοῦσαι δεῦρ᾽ ἴτ᾽ ἐπὶ τοὐμὸν στόμα, μελύδριον
εὑροῦσαί τι τῶν Ἰωνικῶν).[2] The quasi-invocation by the Herald
at the end of the *Birds* when he commands the Muses' utterance
is a poetic, pious-sounding substitute for the simple observation
that it's time for the chorus to sing, and earlier in the play a
similar feeling is created by the fortune-seeking poet's epinician
pastiche:

Νεφελοκοκκυγίαν τὰν εὐδαίμονα
κλῇσον ὦ Μοῦσα τεαῖς ἐν ὕμνων ἀοιδαῖς.

' "Cloud-cuckoo-land the blest", sing, Muse, in hymns of praise.'[3]
It is probably Pindaric associations, rather than those derived
from Homer or Hesiod, which enrich Euripides' hymn in praise
of music in the difficult second stasimon of the *Madness of
Hercules*. The chorus of old men wish to honour Hercules' out-
standing *aretē*, and for this song is indispensable:

οὐ παύσομαι τὰς Χάριτας
    Μούσαις συγκαταμειγνύς,
ἁδίσταν συζυγίαν.
μὴ ζῴην μετ᾽ ἀμουσίας,
αἰεὶ δ᾽ ἐν στεφάνοισιν εἴ –
ην · ἔτι τοι γέρων ἀοι –
δὸς κελαδεῖ Μναμοσύναν ·
    ἔτι τὰν Ἡρακλέους
    καλλίνικον ἀείδω
παρά τε Βρόμιον οἰνοδόταν
παρά τε χέλυος ἑπτατόνου
μολπὰν καὶ Λίβυν αὐλόν ·
οὔπω καταπαύσομεν
Μούσας, αἵ μ᾽ ἐχόρευσαν.

'I shall always yoke together Graces and Muses, a union of
delight. I should not wish to live without music. I long for

[1] *Peace* 736; cf. Simonides 62D; *Thesm.* 107–10.
[2] *Eccl.* 882–3.　　　　　　　[3] *Birds* 1718–19, 904–5.

continual garlands. The singer, although he is old, does not cease to praise Mnemosyne. Nor do I cease to sing Hercules' victory-song (with Bromius, wine-giver, the seven-string lyre's melody and Libyan flute). Not yet shall we silence the Muses: they set me dancing.'[1]

Pindar is probably the source of the imagery in two interesting passages of Aristophanes. In the parabasis of the *Wasps* Aristophanes wants to find fault with his audience for their rejection of the *Clouds* the previous year: he alludes to his earlier practice of entrusting the production of his plays to men of greater experience and praises his daring in finally accepting responsibility for the *Clouds* as his own. The metaphor he uses twice in this highly allusive passage is a development of the 'chariot of song': his play is a chariot entered for competition and he is the driver. In the second occurrence of the metaphor Aristophanes speaks of the damage he caused the chariot in his efforts to outstrip his rivals, meaning that the *Clouds* failed because it was too ambitious.[2] The details of comparison cannot be pressed in these lines, nor can they in the earlier occurrence of the chariot-image where he describes himself as 'guiding the mouths of Muses, not another's but his own' (οὐκ ἀλλοτρίων ἀλλ᾿ οἰκείων Μουσῶν στόμαθ᾿ ἡνιοχήσας).[3] If the chariot is the finished play the Muses who are guided by Aristophanes must be the performers, spoken of as belonging to himself now, no longer to another producer.

The other passage, from the *Acharnians*, is more straightforward, and shows Aristophanes' power of transforming what he borrows. The chorus of elderly charcoal-burners needs inspiration and calls on the Muse who lives in Acharnae and whose nature is suggested by their occupation.

δεῦρο Μοῦσ᾿ ἐλθὲ φλεγυρὰ πυρὸς ἔχουσα μένος, ἔντονος
᾿Αχαρνική.
οἷον ἐξ ἀνθράκων πρινίνων φέψαλος ἀνήλατ᾿, ἐρεθιζόμενος οὐρίᾳ
ῥιπίδι,
ἡνίκ᾿ ἂν ἐπανθρακίδες ὦσι παρακείμεναι,

---

[1] *H.F.* 637–700; the stanza quoted is 673–86. See the persuasive interpretation of this ode by H. Parry, *A.J.P.* 1965, 363–74.
[2] 1049–50. [3] 1022.

οἱ δὲ Θασίαν ἀνακυκῶσι λιπαράμπυκα
οἱ δὲ μάττωσιν, οὕτω σοβαρὸν ἐλθὲ μέλος, ἔντονον, ἀγροικότονον,
ὡς ἐμὲ λαβοῦσα τὸν δημότην.

'Come, Acharnian Muse, brilliant, sturdy, come with powerful
fire. As a spark leaps up from burning oak at a blast from the
bellows, when the small fish are lying ready (people are stirring
the marinade "of gleaming crown" or kneading the bread), so
come to me your demesman and bring a tempestuous, strong,
country song.'[1] This is the first appearance of the 'Muse of
fire' who later came to exemplify the consuming vigour of
inspiration. Pindar had seen his odes as a flame which could
make city or victor blaze like a beacon, conspicuous from afar,
and when Bacchylides wrote 'boys' hymns are blazing' he was
probably thinking of the vitality of fire, as well as its illumina-
tion, but neither poet described the fire of inspiration.[2]

It seems that the dramatists value the Muses for the emotional enhancement they bring to poetry: in particular they
often mention the Muses when they want to glorify a city or
district. This was not altogether a new technique, since Pindar
could write of a place that the Muse lived there, but it does
become more frequent and elaborate.[3] Euripides' Medea, for
example, announces her intention of making her home in Athens
after she has murdered her children; the chorus deplore this
plan since Athens is the home of love and wisdom: 'There
they say that the nine Pierian Muses brought forth golden
Harmony.'[4] In Comedy, Muses may even be said to have
made their home with a specific poet, as with Agathon in
the *Thesmophoriazusae*, or with Aristophanes himself: 'Thou
shalt not invoke Muses of curling locks; thou shalt not call
Olympian Graces to the dance. They're here: thus saith our
poet.'[5]

[1] 665-75.
[2] Pindar *O.* 9.21-2, *P.* 5.45, *N.* 10.2-3, *I.* 7.23; Bacchylides fr. 4.80.
[3] e.g. *P.* 10.37.
[4] *Medea* 830-1; Euripides here borrows the Pythagorean connection of the
Muses with Harmonia: see D. L. Page *ad loc.* See also *Rhesus* 41-8 and Sophocles: *O.C.* 691-3.
[5] *Thesm.* 40-2, fr. 334; cf. Cratinus fr. 222 (in the same Cretic metre) where
the Muse is chided for her late arrival. According to the *Life* (6), Sophocles
honoured the Muses: see p. 138.

75

While it is impossible to draw any conclusions about the attitude of Sophocles and Aeschylus to the Muse for lack of evidence (except in so far as lack of evidence is an indication) Euripides and Aristophanes at least provide an abundance of material.[1] From what Euripides says one forms the impression that writing about the Muses was one way in which he could express his feelings about poetry and music. Aristophanes on the other hand presents the Muse in so many guises that it is impossible to do more than further illustrate their variety. The *Frogs* is particularly rich. At one extreme it has the ugly hag of a castanet-player who personifies the lyric art of Euripides.[2] A different comic technique is evident in the choral ode which begins the parabasis, where charming lyrical language, both in the address to the Muse and later, almost disguises the purpose of insulting Cleophon.[3] Another lyrical invocation to the 'nine holy maidens of Zeus' precedes the contest between Aeschylus and Euripides and is remarkable for its skill in modernizing the Muses, who are to be expert in the new sophistries of argument.[4] Finally each chorus quite seriously establishes its association with the Muses: the Frogs claim that they are loved by the Muses, Pan and Apollo, and the Mystics forbid participation in their ceremonies to anyone 'who has not seen nor danced in the rites of the noble Muses'.[5]

At the beginning of this chapter I mentioned the difficulty of deciding exactly what the poet means when he writes the word 'Muse'. Is the 'woodland Muse' whom the Birds summon just the nightingale, or is she also the embodiment of music?[6] There is probably some degree of personification when the Knights flatter the spectators as experts in every branch of Music (ὦ παντοίας ἤδη Μούσης πειραθέντες καθ᾽ ἑαυτούς).[7] But to say that the flexibility of Aristophanes' attitude to the Muses

---

[1] In addition to the *Rhesus* and to the passages already quoted Euripides mentions the Muses at *Androm.* 476–8, *H.F.* 791, *Med.* 1085–6, frs. 184, 588.

[2] 1306–8. The Muse plays the castanets because Euripides' lyrics did not deserve anything better and because he had represented Hypsipyle as playing them (fr. 769N² with von Arnim 49, fr. 1.2,9). Dionysus' insult ('This Muse certainly never played the Lesbian') has been variously explained: see Radermacher and Stanford *ad loc.* and Taillardat, 428; cf. *Wasps* 1028.

[3] 675–85.   [4] 875–84.
[5] 229–31, 356.   [6] *Birds* 737.
[7] *Knights* 505–6; cf. *Clouds* 313, 972, 1030.

demonstrates scepticism or cynicism would be misleading. Just as the Clouds represent a lovely and beneficent force of nature as well as vaporous intellectual pretensions, so the Muses stand for the art of music at its holiest or most degraded.

4. Plato and the 'Inspired' Poet

It is beyond the scope of this book to discuss Plato's views about the place of poetry and the arts in society as revealed in the *Republic*. But the story of the Greek poet's dependence on the Muse would not be complete without Plato's contribution, which is essentially different from what had gone before and was destined to have a widespread and lasting influence. Plato once spoke of the 'ancient quarrel between poetry and philosophy'[1] and it must always be remembered that they were at war within himself;[2] since he valued the old beliefs about the Muses we find them given a place in philosophy and we find gentle and humorous mention of them, often in traditional terms, but we also find, whenever Plato discusses poetic inspiration, that they are incorporated in a doctrine which devalues poetry.

The important dialogues for our purposes are the *Ion*, the *Phaedrus* and the *Laws*, the first two purporting to recount conversations between Socrates and a friend, and the last, written at the end of Plato's life, being a discussion about good government between an Athenian, a Spartan and a Cretan. It is in the *Phaedrus* that we find a new legend about the Muses, one probably invented by Plato.[3] Phaedrus has never heard of the blessing bestowed by the cicadas and Socrates explains it to him in a short myth. 'The story is that once upon a time these creatures were men – men of an age before there were any Muses: and that when the latter came into the world, and music

---

[1] *Rep.* 607B.

[2] 'And truely, even *Plato*, whosoever well considereth, shall find that in the body of his work, though the inside and strength were philosophy, the skinne as it were and beautie depended most of Poetrie: for all standeth upon Dialogues, wherein he faineth many honest Burgesses of Athens ... Besides, his poetical describing the circumstances of their meetings, as the well ordering of a banquet, the delicacie of a walk with enterlacing meere tales, as *Giges* Ring, and others, which who knoweth not to be flowers of Poetrie did never walke into *Apollos* Garden.' (Sidney, *The Defence of Poesie*.)

[3] *Phaedrus* 258E–259E.

78

made its appearance, some of the people of those days were so thrilled with pleasure that they went on singing, and quite forgot to eat and drink until they actually died without noticing it. From them in due course sprang the race of cicadas, to which the Muses have granted the boon of needing no sustenance right from their birth, but of singing from the very first, without food or drink, until the day of their death: after which they go and report to the Muses how they severally are paid honour amongst mankind, and by whom. So for those whom they report as having honoured Terpsichore in the dance they win that Muse's favour; for those that have worshipped in the rites of love the favour of Erato; and so with all the others, according to the nature of the worship paid to each. To the eldest, Calliope, and to her next sister Urania, they tell of those who live a life of philosophy and so do honour to the music of those twain whose theme is the heavens and all the story of gods and men, and whose song is the noblest of them all.' A further allusion to the cicadas speaks of them as these 'interpreters of the Muses, the singers above our heads', who perhaps have breathed into Socrates the ability to analyse Lysias' speech.[1]

In this dialogue, to which I shall return later in the chapter, Socrates represents himself as becoming more and more inspired, whether by the deities of the stream by which they were walking or by the Muses, and he prefaces one of his speeches with a mock-serious, conventional, 'learned' appeal: ἄγετε δή, ὦ Μοῦσαι, εἴτε δι᾽ ᾠδῆς εἶδος λίγειαι, εἴτε διὰ γένος μουσικὸν τὸ Λιγύων ταύτην ἔσχετ᾽ ἐπωνυμίαν, ᾽ξύμ μοι λάβεσθε᾽ τοῦ μύθου, ὅν με ἀναγκάζει ὁ βέλτιστος οὑτοσὶ λέγειν, ἵν᾽ ὁ ἑταῖρος αὐτοῦ, καὶ πρότερον δοκῶν τούτῳ σοφὸς εἶναι, νῦν ἔτι μᾶλλον δόξῃ.

'Come then, ye clear-voiced Muses, whether it be from the nature of your song, or from the musical people of Liguria that ye came to be so styled, "assist the tale I tell" under compulsion by my good friend here, to the end that he may think yet more highly of one dear to him, whom he already accounts a man of wisdom.'[2]

Conventional material is found too in the *Laws*, first when

---

[1] 262D; at *Il.* 3.151 Homer had described them as 'lily-voiced', a description applied to the Muses' singing by Hesiod (*Theog.* 41).

[2] *Phaedrus* 237B.

the Athenian Stranger tells his companions that the gods established festivals on earth as a respite from toil and gave men the Muses, Apollo Musagetes and Dionysus as their fellow-celebrants.[1] Again the Athenian follows a quotation from the *Iliad* by remarking that Homer 'speaks in accordance with God and nature, for the inspiration of poets is divine, and in many of their songs, helped by the Graces and Muses, they often attain truth.'[2] Even more striking to the reader of the *Republic* than this defence of the truth of poetry is the passage in which music is called in aid to control and diminish the natural appetites.[3] On two occasions in earlier dialogues Plato had drawn the Muses into the context of pure philosophy rather than social ethics, once in the *Phaedo* where Socrates calls philosophy ἡ μεγίστη μουσική, 'the greatest of the Muses' arts', and again in the *Theaetetus* when the philosopher's memory is the gift of Mnemosyne, mother of the Muses.[4]

So far Plato has appeared the inheritor of tradition. When we examine the *Ion* and *Phaedrus* a different picture emerges, one that is foreshadowed as early as the *Apology*. There Socrates had described how he went to see politicians, poets and craftsmen in an attempt to discover whether the Delphic oracle was right in saying that no man was wiser than he. He visited writers of tragedy and dithyramb and others and found them unable to answer him. He concluded that their works were not the result of knowledge but of natural endowment and possession by god, and that in this they resembled seers and tellers of oracles who have no true knowledge of what they are saying.[5] In the *Meno* we first find the distinction between true knowledge (*epistēmē*) and right opinion (*orthē doxa*). Socrates persuades Meno that politicians succeed through the possession of right opinion which is not based on real knowledge, and again compares them with seers and the like, who are justly called 'divine' (*theios*) as are all writers of poetry.[6] Here Plato is by implication denying that the poet had access to true knowledge.

The *Ion* approaches the same goal by a different contrast: Socrates attempts to show that the *technē* of the rhapsode in

---

[1] 653D; cf. 665A, 670A, 672D and 796E (where musical training is spoken of as 'the gift of Apollo and the Muses').   [2] 682A.   [3] 783A.
[4] *Phaedo* 61A, *Theaet.* 191D.   [5] *Apology* 22B-C.   [6] *Meno* 99D.

interpreting Homer and the other poets is not truly *technē* but again divine possession. Plato develops his picture of inspiration through a series of images. When Ion interprets Homer his activity is the result of divine influence emanating from the Muse and extending via poet and interpreter to the audience: 'There is a divine power which stirs you to action, like the power in the stone which Euripides called Magnetic. . . . This stone not only attracts iron rings to itself but endows them with a power like its own to attract other rings. Sometimes in the end quite a long chain of iron rings is formed. In the same way the Muse inspires men who in turn inspire others until a chain is formed.'[1] This image, no doubt Plato's own, conveys in terms of a phenomenon not then understood the mysterious cohesion felt by poet and audience.

The idea of an inexplicable force is amplified in the images which follow. 'For all good poets, epic as well as lyric, compose their beautiful poems not by art, but because they are inspired and possessed. And as the Corybantic revellers when they dance are not in their right mind, so the lyric poets are not in their right mind when they are composing their beautiful strains: but when falling under the power of music and metre they are inspired and possessed; like Bacchic maidens who draw milk and honey from the rivers, when they are under the influence of Dionysus, but not when they are in their right mind. And the soul of the lyric poet does the same, as they themselves say; for they tell us that they bring songs from honeyed fountains, culling them out of the gardens and dells of the Muses; they, like the bees, winging their way from flower to flower. And this is true. For the poet is a light and winged and holy thing, and there is no invention in him until he has been inspired and is out of his senses, and reason is no longer in him: no man, while he retains that faculty, has the oracular gift of poetry.'[2] Before discussing this passage in detail it will be useful to look at the section of the *Phaedrus* myth in which Socrates describes poetic madness. Socrates, recanting his earlier condemnation of the

---

[1] *Ion* 533D-E; Wilamowitz (*Platon* II, 45) suggests that Plato invented the magnet image. The power of attraction is linked with musical skill in the legends of Orpheus and of the Sirens.

[2] *Ion* 533E–534C (Jowett's translation, slightly adapted).

god of Love, speaks of four kinds of divine madness, those of divination, ritual healing, poetry, love. 'The third possession and madness comes from the Muses and seizes the tender and inexperienced soul and rouses it and fills it with Dionysiac excitement to write lyric and other poetry, and by glorifying countless deeds of the ancients it educates generations to come. If anyone comes to the gates of poetry without the madness of the Muses, believing that he will be an adequate poet as a result of *technē* alone, he is refused admission and his poetry of sanity is brought to nothing by the poetry of the mad.'[1]

If we were required to construct a Platonic doctrine of inspiration on the basis of these passages we should be hard put to it: we should not be certain, for example, whether to say that inspiration was recurrent or an outright gift (and we should probably feel like applying Plato's view to the genesis of brief, lyric poems only). In fact, we have no positive theory of inspiration here. This is not to deny the immense importance of Plato's words, which evoke, for the first time, one aspect of the creative experience, an aspect which was supremely important for subsequent poets and philosophers.[2] While Plato seems to give a new and exalted conception of the poet we should not be blind to what he has taken away. He has disposed of the belief that the poet transmitted knowledge, the gift of the Muses with whom he had a personal relationship, that he was in control of his material,[3] that he was concerned to communicate with an audience. The matter-of-fact acceptance of poetry conspicuous previously has vanished, without a single destructive word being spoken. For Plato, if anyone, literature must have brought powerful emotional experience, but his intellectual attitude is a continuation of earlier attacks on poetry. Where Xenophanes or Heraclitus had censured poetry with direct reproof as untrue or unedifying Plato attacks more subtly from

[1] *Phaedrus* 245A.

[2] The 'inspirational' view has a modern champion in Robert Graves; e.g. *Poetic Craft and Principle* (London, 1967). For accounts of inspiration see John Press, *The Fire and the Fountain* (Oxford, 1955) and R. Harding, *An Anatomy of Inspiration* (Cambridge, 1948).

[3] cf. Charles Lamb, 'On the Sanity of True Genius' (*Last Essays of Elia*): 'The true poet dreams being awake. He is not possessed by his subject but has dominion over it.'

several directions: knowledge is the prerogative of the philosopher and is to be attained by the intellectual discipline of
dialectic; the poet lacks true knowledge and lacks even the
rational expertise of the craftsman; if he sometimes appears to
say what is true and useful his words are the chance outpourings of one possessed by frenzy.

Plato's picture of the inspired poet is so vivid and compelling
that it has been taken to represent Greek belief not only of his
own day but even as early as Homer. If this view is, as I
believe, untenable we have to decide whether Plato's picture is
entirely his own invention, and if so how it gained credence. In
the rest of this chapter I shall hope to show that Plato's message
is almost entirely new and that it is made acceptable by being
dressed in language and imagery familiar from tradition.

I return to the passage from the *Ion*. What first strikes the
reader is that this procession of images is untypical of Plato. In
his works symbol and myth are often hard to interpret and to
relate to the more austerely expressed philosophical argument
but they normally present a certain formal elegance and sym-
metry. By comparison our passage is almost rambling, the con-
nections made by a sort of free association. There are two
reasons for this: Socrates was talking to a rhapsode and gently
mocking his companion's style; Plato was hoping that his
reader would not notice that he was being led to an unexpected
destination.

The first two images need little comment: Plato likens poets
to Corybantic dancers and Maenads; the point of comparison
is obviously temporary lack of control, and Corybants and
Maenads are stock examples of the ecstatic state. The comparison of poetic composition and Dionysiac frenzy seems to be
new. What is interesting is the way Plato lets the apparently
fortuitous mention of the Maenads drawing milk and honey
from streams lead him on to the honeyed fountains in the
gardens of the Muses. Gardens had been associated more often
with the Nymphs (and we remember that Nymphs could send
men mad) or with the Graces than with the Muses.[1] Honey

---

[1] Gardens of Nymphs: e.g. *P.M.G.* 286.4.
 Gardens of Graces: e.g. P. *O.* 9.27–8.
 Meadow (of Muses): e.g. Choerilus fr. 1. Kinkel.

G

again and again symbolizes the sweetness of poetry,[1] but in this Platonic context we ought also to remember its connection with prophecy: in the Hymn to Hermes Apollo describes the three holy winged sisters, the Thriae, who fly hither and thither feeding on honey-combs. 'And when they are inflamed by eating yellow honey they are willing and ready to speak truth: but if they are deprived of the sweet food of the gods at once they utter lies.'[2]

When Plato speaks of the poet winging his way from flower to flower like a bee he is using a traditional comparison partly arising from the 'sweetness' of poetry, and in this passage leading to the general description of the poet as 'winged'. Bacchylides' allusion to the commissioning of one of his odes contains also the idea of the busy activity of the bee: the victor's sister's husband has roused to action the clear-voiced, island bee.[3] Pindar expresses his consciousness that an ode must not dwell too long on one topic by writing:

ἐγκωμίων γὰρ ἄωτος ὕμνων
ἐπ' ἄλλοτ' ἄλλον ὧτε μέλισσα θύνει λόγον.

'It is the glory of hymns to dart from one theme to another, like a bee.'[4] It seems likely that Plato had in mind a similar metaphor by the early tragic poet Phrynichus which we know from Aristophanes. The coryphaeus of the Bird chorus tells how he sings in the woodland dells and on the mountain peaks, 'whence Phrynichus, like a bee, feeding on divine songs, always brought home a sweet poem':

ἔνθεν ὡσπερεὶ μέλιττα
Φρύνιχος ἀμβροσίων μελέων ἀπεβόσκετο καρπὸν ἀεὶ
φέρων γλυκεῖαν ᾠδάν.[5]

In the *Frogs* Aeschylus wishes not to appear 'to cull the same sacred meadow of the Muses as Phrynichus.'[6]

'The poet is a light and winged and holy thing.' It seems probable that a whole complex of associations lies behind this

---

[1] e.g. Pindar fr. 223, *P.M.G.* 26.1, 954(b); speech is compared with honey at *Il.* 1.247–9 and *Theog.* 83–4. [2] 552–63.
[3] 10.9–10. The author of *P.M.G.* 947 speaks of the Muse as a bee. See p. 49.
[4] *P.* 10.53–4. [5] *Birds* 748–50. [6] 1299–1300.

statement: which, if any of them, was dominant in Plato's mind it is impossible to say. The association of words and flying goes back to the Homeric 'winged words',[1] and we shall see later how often fame is seen as lending wings.[2] More relevant here is the association of poets and flying. We think first of the shaman, whose soul, as Professor Dodds writes, 'is thought to leave its body and travel to distant parts, most often to the spirit world. A shaman may in fact be seen simultaneously in different places; he has the power of bilocation. From these experiences, narrated by him in extempore song, he derives the skill in divination, religious poetry and magical medicine which makes him socially important.'[3] The shamanistic tradition was certainly known to the Greeks: it may be represented by the legendary Thamyris who came from Thrace, and by Aristeas of Proconnesus who is said to have travelled north at the command of Apollo; Pythagoras, Parmenides and Empedocles have some shamanistic qualities.

One obvious use of this image is to symbolize a poet's supremacy. Both Pindar and Bacchylides are conscious that they can outsoar their rivals: in a famous passage Bacchylides writes: 'The eagle, cleaving the deep ether on high with his swift tawny wings, messenger of wide-ruling Zeus the lord of thunder, trusts boldly to his mighty strength; the shrill-voiced birds crouch in fear of him; the heights of the wide earth stay him not, nor the rough, steep waves of the unwearied sea; he plies his wing of delicate plumage in the illimitable void, sped by the breath of the west wind, conspicuous in the sight of men.'

>   βαθὺν
> δ᾽ αἰθέρα ξουθαῖσι τάμνων
> ὑψοῦ πτερύγεσσι ταχεί –
> αις αἰετὸς εὐρυάνακτος ἄγγελος
> Ζηνὸς ἐρισφαράγου
> θαρσεῖ κρατερᾶι πίσυνος
> ἰσχύϊ, πτάσσοντι δ᾽ ὄρνι –
> χες λιγύφθογγοι φόβωι
> οὔ νιν κορυφαὶ μεγάλας ἴσχουσι γαίας,
> οὐδ᾽ ἁλὸς ἀκαμάτας

[1] See p. 69.   [2] See p. 126.   [3] *The Greeks and the Irrational*, 140.

δυσπαίπαλα κύματα · νωμᾶ –
ται δ᾽ἐν ἀτρύτωι χάει
λεπτότριχα σὺν ζεφύρου πνοι –
αἷσιν ἔθειραν ἀρίγνω –
τος μετ᾽ ἀνθρώποις ἰδεῖν.[1]

Some passages of Aristophanes suggest that the image of flying conveys not only the poet's sense of superiority but also the kinship of poetry and air. In the *Acharnians*, Dicaeopolis has a word with Euripides' servant: 'Euripides in?' 'In and not-in, if you see what I mean. His mind's out picking sayings, but he's in, writing tragedies, with his feet up.'[2] No doubt Euripides' mind inhabits those same airy regions in which Trygaeus saw the souls of dithyrambic poets (whom the Clouds nourish) gathering preludes.[3] When the arch-dithyrambist, Cinesias, turns up in Cloud-cuckoo-city his effusion begins: 'I soar up, up to Olympus on weightless wings; I flit in my course from song to song.'[4]

In the *Phaedrus* Socrates spoke of the 'gates of poetry' and here too we know an earlier parallel in the remark of Bacchylides that it is difficult 'to discover the gates of verse before unspoken': ἀρρήτων ἐπέων πύλας ἐξευρεῖν.[5]

Socrates went on to compare the 'poetry of sanity' and that of the mad, and he has sometimes been taken to mean no more than that 'inspired' poetry is better than pedestrian verse. In the context of Plato's other writings about poetry this seems unlikely. The same problem of interpretation confronts us when we consider fragments of the fifth-century philosopher Democritus, who is a possible source for Plato's view of inspiration.[6] In fragment 21 Democritus describes and accounts for Homer's supremacy as a poet: Ὅμηρος φύσεως λαχὼν θεαζούσης ἐπέων κόσμον ἐτεκτήνατο παντοίων. ('Homer, by his possession of a

---

[1] 5.16–30, tr. Jebb. Pindar speaks of himself as an eagle at *O.* 2.95–7, *N.* 3.77–8.   [2] *Ach.* 395–400.

[3] *Peace* 827–31, *Clouds* 331–4. In the *Frogs* (889–94) Euripides prays to his personal divinities, among them 'Ether, on whom I feed'; cf. Eur. *Alc.* 963, fr. 911N[2].

[4] *Birds* 1373–4, and see the whole scene. Cinesias begins by quoting Anacreon, *P.M.G.* 378.

[5] fr. 5; cf. Timotheus' image of the Muses' treasure-chamber (*Pers.* 232–3).

[6] See Guthrie, *Philosophy* II, 459–51, 473–8.

86

divine nature, built an ordered structure of every sort of verse.')¹ This fragment comes from one of Democritus' literary works called 'About Homer, or Correct Diction and Rare Expressions', and it is reasonable to assume that he was praising Homer's wonderful ability in combining all types of diction in a poetic unity, an ability he owed to something god-like in his nature and not to temporary possession by a god. Fragment 18 is more difficult: Horace, stating his belief in the superiority of *technē* to inspiration, wrote 'excludit sanos Helicone poetas Democritus', ('Democritus denied sane poets a place in Helicon').² Horace is exaggerating: a milder account of the views of Plato and Democritus had been given by Cicero: 'I have often heard the view that no-one can be a good poet without a kindling of the spirit and a certain degree of inspired frenzy.'³ (Cicero is not directly translating any passage of either philosopher known to us.) The fragment which is supposed to lie behind the passage just quoted and which purports to be genuine Democritus runs as follows: ποιητὴς δὲ ἄσσα μὲν ἂν γράφηι μετ' ἐνθουσιασμοῦ καὶ ἱεροῦ πνεύματος, καλὰ κάρτα ἐστίν. ('Whatever a poet writes when possessed by god and with a holy breath (spirit ?) is particularly fine.')⁴ It is unlikely that these are Democritus' actual words, especially ἱερὸν πνεῦμα. If he did use some metaphor for breathing song into the poet he may have imitated the Homeric or Hesiodic use of the verb.⁵ This fragment is the more puzzling in that it seems out of keeping with Democritus' usual scientific, rational approach. Professor Guthrie points out that of attempts to bring it into line the most successful link it to his theory of sense-perception, in particular the fragment which reads: 'There are more senses (than the usual five ?) in animals, wise men and gods.'⁶ If 'wise men' here equals poets or seers or both, Democritus may be accounting for their supernatural knowledge.

We have seen that Plato's description of the poet in a trance-like state may be partly shamanistic in origin: a passage from

¹ θεαζούσης may, but need not, allude to a state of frenzied possession.
² *Ars Poetica* 295–6.   ³ *De oratore* II, 46, 194.   ⁴ D.-K. 18.
⁵ *Il.* 10.482, *Od.* 19.38, *Theog.* 32; cf. Eur. *I.A.* 760–1 (of prophecy); however Euripides makes Amphion (*Antiope* fr. 192N²) speak of 'time, the breath of the gods (θεῶν πνεῦμα) and love of song' presumably as causing his devotion to music.   ⁶ D.-K. A116.

87

the *Laws* refers to another manifestation of trance, that of the Pythia, the priestess of the Delphic oracle. 'There is an ancient tale that when the poet is seated on the tripod of the Muse he is not in possession of his mind; like a fountain he allows the stream of thought to flow freely, and since his art is mimesis he is often compelled to represent men in opposite circumstances and say contradictory things and he does not know which of the opposing views is the truth.'[1] It is interesting to see that here Plato is specifically applying an inspirational view of poetry to the mimetic branches of the art, epic and drama, not just to lyric. The two images used here again emphasize the poet's passivity: the first is familiar to us not from the Athenian source which Plato implies but from the works of Pindar and Bacchylides. It is not surprising that the Greeks should have seen a resemblance between the imparting of knowledge by the Muses and of oracles by their companion and leader, Apollo. But Pindar and Bacchylides see themselves not as the entranced Pythia but as the interpreter of the unintelligible oracular utterance. Both use the word *prophetes* of their role: Bacchylides (perhaps following Pindar) is 'the godlike interpreter of the violet-eyed Muses'[2] and Pindar 'the musical interpreter of the Pierians'.[3] Pindar made his meaning even plainer when he wrote:

μαντεύεο, Μοῖσα, προφατεύσω δ᾽ ἐγώ.

'Give me your oracle, Muse, and I shall interpret.'[4] In this use the poets convey their indebtedness to the Muse together with their sense that their own contribution is necessary.

We have seen that Plato in the *Ion* mentioned the Muses' streams from which poets could imbibe verse: this image of a source external to the poet was to become a cliché, but it is less important and less revealing than the picture of the fount of poetry within the artist. The comparison of flowing speech to a

[1] *Laws* 719C. In the *Phaedo* (60D-61C) Socrates says that he is writing poetry in the hope that he is obeying a command heard in a dream; according to Isocrates (*Helen* 65) Helen appeared to Homer in a dream; cf. the stories told of Ennius and Caedmon.　　　[2] 9.3.　　　[3] Paean 6.4.

[4] fr. 168; cf. *Birds* 725 μάντεσι Μούσαις, Aeschylus frs. 60 and 341N². In one sense this metaphor is an extension of the conventional 'messenger' or 'herald', another way of showing the poet as intermediary between gods and men.

river is as old as Homer[1] and is seen in a more developed form in, for example, Aristophanes' likening of Cratinus' eloquence to a torrent.[2] The image of the poet as a fountain in the passage just quoted from the *Laws* is unsophisticated: an earlier occurrence of the image in the *Phaedrus* is much more illuminating. In this dialogue Socrates found fault with Lysias' speech about love; with his usual self-depreciation he continues: ' I'm sure I have heard something better, from the fair Sappho maybe, or the wise Anacreon, or perhaps some prose writer. What ground, you may ask, have I for saying so? Good sir, there is something welling up within my breast, which makes me feel that I could find something different, and something better, to say. I am of course well aware it can't be anything originating in my own mind, for I know my own ignorance; so I suppose it can only be that it has been poured into me, through my ears, as into a vessel, from some external source; though in my stupid fashion I have actually forgotten how, and from whom, I heard it.' Socrates likens the onset of inspiration to something welling up inside him which cannot long be contained: we are reminded of Wordsworth's 'spontaneous overflow of powerful feelings'. Notice too that this welling-up is accompanied by feelings of confidence. This confidence, which is not the euphoria of manic states, is a conspicuous feature of Greek poetry from Homer onwards.

In the *Phaedrus* Socrates went on to say that the words he will speak cannot be his own: they have been poured into him from some external source. Moreover he has forgotten their precise origin.[3] It is worth considering the implications of this image in the context of Greek poetry. First, the absorption of what the poet has heard or read marks him out from the ordinary man, and the Greek practice of committing to memory great amounts of poetry gave the poet a large store to draw

[1] *Il.* 1.249.

[2] *Knights* 526–8. Pindar used a similar image when he wrote: 'Do not when in sight of the nectar from my spring go thirsty away to a salt stream' (fr. 106.41–42); cf. *P.* 4.295–9. See also Cratinus fr. 36.

[3] A similar irony about the source of Socrates' wisdom is expressed in the *Cratylus* (428C) where Cratylus says: 'You, Socrates, seem to me to be an oracle ... whether you are inspired by Euthyphro, or whether some Muse, without your knowing it, has long dwelt within your breast.' Socrates replies: 'I have long been wondering at my own wisdom, finding it beyond belief.'

upon. While the poet may be assumed to spend much time
consciously thinking about and shaping his verse the metaphor
of the well aptly describes the unconscious assimilation and
integration of what he has heard, until, in Housman's words,
'the spring bubbles up again'. The workings of this unconscious
stage in the genesis of a poem remain mysterious but often it
seems that the sound of words, not ideas or images, is most
important. As Socrates said in the *Ion*, it is when poets fall under
the power of music and metre that they are inspired. Eliot
amplifies this in *The Music of Poetry*: 'I know that a poem, or a
passage of a poem, may tend to realize itself first as a particular
rhythm before it reaches expression in words, and that this
rhythm may bring to birth the idea and the image.'

In the context of 'imbibing' poetry and of loss of control
while inspired it is natural to wonder whether the Greeks compared the excitement of composition with that engendered by
drinking wine. We shall see later that the sweetness of poetry
can be compared with that of wine,[1] but here I am concerned
only with the effect of wine on the creative faculties. The
amount of evidence is not very great, nor is it all to be taken
seriously. Archilochus wrote:

ὡς Διωνύσοι' ἄνακτος καλὸν ἐξάρξαι μέλος
οἶδα διθύραμβον οἴνωι συγκεραυνωθεὶς φρένας.

'I know how to lead the fair song of Dionysus, the dithyramb,
when my wits are fused with wine.'[2] Does Archilochus mean
that his skill deserts him when sober, or just that Dionysus is
to be honoured by drinking as well as singing? The comic poet
Cratinus wrote a play satirizing himself as a drunkard: his wife,
Comedy, complains that he has left her for his mistress, Drink,
and a surviving couplet (if both lines are genuine) puts the case
for the defence:

οἶνός τοι χαρίεντι πέλει ταχὺς ἵππος ἀοιδῷ,
ὕδωρ δὲ πίνων χρηστὸν οὐδὲν ἂν τέκοις.

'Wine is a swift horse for the poet; drink water and you'll pro-
duce nothing of value.'[3] This idea became a commonplace of

[1] See p. 125f.   [2] fr. 77D. See Pickard-Cambridge, *D.T.C.*[2], 9 f.
[3] Cratinus fr. 199; cf. 'Epicharmus' fr. 132 Kaibel.

90

Latin poetry,[1] partly as a justification for writing convivial verse, but it is not clear that it was seriously regarded by the Greeks during our period. The common observation that wine loosens the tongue and relaxes inhibitions is enough by itself to account for the passages cited.[2]

---

[1] See Horace *Ep.* 1.19.

[2] See the stories collected by Press, *op. cit.* 83, about the drinking habits of Jonson, Addison and Housman. Similarly e.g. Athenaeus (10.428F) and Plutarch (*Quaest. conv.* 7.10.715E) preserve stories about Aeschylus' fondness for drink.

5. Poetry as a Craft

We have seen the Homeric bard appealing to the Muses for knowledge: at least one passage in the *Odyssey* shows that it was also possible, even at this early period, to regard poetry as a craft. When Odysseus had defeated the suitors, the bard Phemius begged for his life, stating as part of his claim to mercy:

αὐτοδίδακτος δ'εἰμί, θεὸς δέ μοι ἐν φρεσὶν οἴμας
παντοίας ἐνέφυσεν.[1]

'I am self-taught and god has implanted in my mind songs of all kinds.' Phemius is putting forward two reasons why he should be spared: his songs, in all their variety, come from god; he himself does not repeat, by rote, verses learned from other poets. Phemius' exact meaning, which has been disputed, turns on the interpretation of 'self-taught'.[2] It would be unwise to take 'self-taught' too literally: the oral poet was no Grandma Moses, isolated from artistic influences, but a man accustomed to memorize and use the words of his predecessors. What Phemius claimed was originality in the context of oral poetry. We see here side by side an acknowledgment of divine inspiration and a consciousness that the poet *learns*.

The novice craftsman learns the rules of his trade, but most of his instruction comes through copying what his master does. We may imagine the 'Sons of Homer' as practising and handing on the epic in much the same way as our mediaeval guilds of craftsmen. *We* should probably think of training in a technique

---

[1] *Od.* 22.347-8; see also *Od.* 8.489 and the words of the Kirghiz minstrel quoted in F. M. Cornford's *Principium Sapientiae* (10): 'I can sing any song whatever; for God has implanted this gift of song in my heart. He gives me the word on my tongue, without my having to seek it.' The 'path of song' metaphor is discussed on pp. 64-9.

[2] Some scholars see the second clause as more important than, and contrasted with, the first. The lines are discussed by e.g. K. Latte, *A. und A.* 1946, 154, R. Sealey, *R.E.G.* 1957, 315, M. Bowra, *Heroic Poetry*, 427, W. K. C. Guthrie, *Philosophy* I, 414-15.

as developing inborn talent: for the writer of the Homeric Hymn
to Hermes this was not so. In a passage describing Apollo's
wonder at Hermes' invention of the lyre, Apollo asks the baby
god whether he was born with the ability to play it, or whether
some god or man gave him the gift and revealed to him the art
of song. A few lines later Apollo puts the question:

τίς τέχνη, τίς μοῦσα ἀμηχανέων μελεδώνων,
τίς τρίβος;

'What art is this? What the music that banishes harsh cares?
What is this path of song?'[1] *Technē* here is the skill required to
play on, and compose for, the new instrument. It is natural to
speak of skill in connection with poetry that normally had an
instrumental accompaniment: even if the poet thought of his
words as god-given he needed command of instrumental technique. The word *technē* does not occur in the early period as
describing actual poetic composition but the idea is present,
expressed by the verbs *epistamai* and *oida*.[2] In all three words
an element of knowledge is present, but this is not theoretical
knowledge divorced from practical ability: their meaning has
something of the modern 'know-how'; it is a combination of
knowing what to do and how to do it with the necessary physical
skill. When Homer said that the chorus depicted on Achilles'
shield 'danced with skilled feet'[3] he meant that they knew the
steps and performed them competently. Homer uses the verb
epistamai of bards: once specifically of a bard's narrative skill
when Alcinous congratulated Odysseus in this simile:

μῦθον δ' ὡς ὅτ' ἀοιδὸς ἐπισταμένως κατέλεξας.

'You told your story with a bard's skill.'[4]

When poetry is thought of primarily as a craft the poet is
called *poiētēs*, a 'maker', and his work is *poiēma* or *poiēsis*. It

[1] *h.Hom.* 4.440-2, 447-8. Technical skill may also be denoted by δεξιότης
(*Frogs* 1009; cf. 1114) while τέχνη may mean Art, as it does in Pherecrates fr.
94 and *Frogs* 939.
[2] J. Gould *Plato's Ethics* (Cambridge 1955) 6-15, discusses the development
of ἐπίσταμαι.
[3] *Il.* 18.599, ἐπισταμένοισι πόδεσσι; cf. *Od.* 21.406.
[4] *Od.* 11.368; cf. Hesiod, *Works* 106, Solon 10.52. Archilochus 1D,77D,
Theognis 769-72.

is significant that the words do not have this sense during the early period.[1] However terms borrowed from individual crafts are applied metaphorically to poetry before *poiētēs* comes into use. Such terms were needed because a language for talking about poetry did not yet exist; they are metaphorical because metaphor was the natural mode for expressing ideas at this stage of linguistic development.

Hesiod had used πλάσσειν, to 'mould', in describing how figures were made from clay.[2] When Xenophanes attacked Hesiod for his stories of warfare among the gods, he alluded to them as πλάσματα τῶν προτέρων, 'fabrications of former poets'.[3] If the fragment of Hesiod which talks of poets ῥάψαντες ἀοιδήν, 'stitching song', is genuine, we have another early example of a craft metaphor, one which became established in the name 'rhapsode', 'song-stitcher,' given to bards.[4] It is clear that some uses of the word 'rhapsode' were derogatory, laying stress on the reciter's patching together of other men's work as opposed to the original composition of the true poet. But even as late as Plato 'rhapsode' can be used of a genuine poet,[5] and the metaphor was probably colourless when first invented. 'Stitch', like 'weave' (also Homeric), can be a synonym for 'make': like 'weave', it can easily develop a pejorative tone. Pindar begins one of his odes by saying that he will follow the practice of the 'Sons of Homer' who begin most of their 'stitched songs' with a proem to Zeus.[6] The phrase is not emotionally loaded, and, as Sealey suggests, it may allude to those orally-composed poems in which formulae are joined together.

By the time of Pindar, craft metaphors are frequently found in lyric. Considering the richness and variety of Pindar's images it would be surprising if some of them were not drawn from the crafts, and indeed the range of crafts mentioned is wide. The stress however is not on the poet as maker, but on the poem as

---

[1] ποιητής first in Herod. 2.53, ποίημα Cratinus fr. 187, ποίησις Herod. 2.82. For the meanings of ποίησις and ποίημα see C. O. Brink, *Horace on Poetry* (Cambridge 1963) 62, 76–8. For ποιεῖν at Theognis 771 see p. 109.

[2] e.g. *Works* 70, *Theog.* 571–2; see further F. Solmsen, *J.H.I.* 1963, 473–96.

[3] Xenophanes 1D.22; cf. Pindar *N.* 5.29.

[4] Fr. 265 Rz. = *dub.* 357 M.-W. The etymology and meaning of ῥάπτειν are discussed by H. Fränkel, *Glotta* 1925, 3–6, H. Patzer, *Hermes* 1952, 314–25, R. Sealey, *R.E.G.* 1957, 312–15, G. Else, *Hermes* 1957, 17–46.

[5] *Rep.* 600D.   [6] *N.* 2.1–6.

comparable in beauty with other artefacts. Some of Pindar's metaphors are traditional: he adapts Homeric 'stitching' and 'weaving' of songs to his own purposes.[1] The conventional image of the epinician as a garland for the victor is exalted in Pindar's Seventh *Nemean*:[2] no longer is the wreath made of leaves which wither, but, like a jeweller 'the Muse binds gold upon white ivory with the lily growth, raised dripping from the sea'. These same qualities of brilliance and permanence are suggested when Pindar uses architectural metaphors, and this theme was to be developed by other poets, notably in Horace's 'exegi monumentum aere perennius', 'I have built a monument more lasting than bronze.' For Pindar, the visual effect of the building made it like a great poem: in the Sixth *Olympian* the poet is to build a palace which will be seen from afar; the treasure house of the Sixth *Pythian* is similarly radiant and will stand unharmed by rain and wind.[3]

When Pindar said that effort and training were of no avail to the man without inborn quality[4] he was thinking primarily of athletes, but his words are as apt for his own art. He would not wish to compare himself to a craft-practitioner and on one occasion he even rejects the comparison between poem and sculpture: his aim is to be widely-known and his songs must travel, unlike statues.

I am no maker of images, not one to fashion idols standing quiet on pedestals.[5]

The poem of Simonides written in answer to Cleobulus' epitaph for Midas casts doubt on the permanence of monuments: Cleobulus had claimed that a bronze statue set on a tomb would endure as long as trees, rivers and sun, and Simonides pointed out that everything is subject to the gods' will, and that, in fact, even men can shatter objects of stone. The message of this poem is chiefly that over-confidence is dangerous, but Simonides probably felt also that a poem 'alive on men's lips' has a better chance of survival than a statue.[6]

---

[1] ῥαπτός N. 2.1–6, ὑφαίνω fr. 207, cf. Bacch. 5.9, 19.8, πλέκω O. 6.86.
[2] N. 7.77–9.   [3] O. 6.1–4, P. 6.5–18; cf. P. 3.113, fr. 231.   [4] O. 9.107–10.
[5] N. 5.1–2. These lines raise the question of the currency of comparison of different arts at this period. See p. 142 f.
[6] P.M.G. 581; see D. A. Campbell, *Greek Lyric Poetry* (London, 1967), 393, for comment on the two poems.

POETRY AND CRITICISM BEFORE PLATO

The tragic poets do not seem to have written of poetry in terms of *technē* in their plays and fragments which survive,[1] but this class of metaphor is extremely common in Old Comedy. The context and tone of many of the passages suggest that the metaphors may be used to poke fun at contemporary literary criticism as well as in their own right. It is probable that some of these 'in-jokes' properly belong to the field of oratory and are thence transferred to literary criticism in general. Eupolis points out the importance of technique to the orator, saying that nature is the source of speech, technique of eloquence.[2] It was natural then that the practitioners of the new rhetoric who delighted in coining words should also be exuberant in applying fresh metaphors to their craft. These novelties were fit game for Comedy, and the joke became even better when the new-fangled phrases were applied to serious poetry.[3] A passage of the *Thesmophoriazusae* contains an amazing medley of craft-metaphors in which Agathon's servant describes how the tragedian works:

μέλλει γὰρ ὁ καλλιεπὴς Ἀγάθων . . .
δρυόχους τιθέναι δράματος ἀρχάς.
κάμπτει δὲ νέας ἁψῖδας ἐπῶν,
τὰ δὲ τορνεύει, τὰ δὲ κολλομελεῖ,
καὶ γνωμοτυπεῖ κἀντονομάζει
καὶ κηροχυτεῖ καὶ γογγύλλει
καὶ χοανεύει.[4]

'Agathon the fair of speech is about to lay the keel of a new drama, yea with mighty crossbeams shall it be constructed. For behold, he turneth the verses upon the lathe and sticketh them together; maxim and metaphor doth he hammer out, yea in melted wax doth he mould his creation: he rolleth it till it be round; he casteth it . . .'[5] The servant has just requested a holy

[1] Sophocles was the author of a treatise on the tragic chorus mentioned on p. 138 and wrote of the Muse as τεκτόναρχος or τεκτονουργός, fr. 162.
[2] Eupolis 116a.
[3] J. Taillardat (*op. cit.*, 468), suggests that it was the sophists in their capacity as critics who first applied the new images to serious literature. I should be willing to accept this for those metaphors which describe the style and content of a work, but the process of composition was, I believe, first expressed in craft-metaphor by the Comic poets.
[4] *Thesm.* 49–57.   [5] Translated by David Barrett.

96

silence and the co-operation of nature in providing fit working conditions for his master, and the noise and bustle suggested in the passage quoted make a mockery of his awe.

By the last years of the fifth century almost the whole range of Greek crafts is called into service for the description of literature. The metaphors from stitching and building continue and are expanded; ship-building, metal-work (including the minting of coins), carpentry and (perhaps) rope-making are all added, as are more general terms applicable to several crafts.[1]

The frequency of craft-metaphors in Aristophanes and his contemporaries reflects Comedy's tendency to express ideas and abstractions in visual, concrete terms: the mind that sees Peace as a beautiful, desirable woman also sees tragedies as solid objects with weight and dimension. But there is more to it than that: the cumulative effect of these craft-metaphors may be to devalue literature and authors, in one of two ways. The concentration on the processes of composition may reduce the poet to the level of the artisan, one who merely glues things together or hammers in nails. Again the attitude which regards poetry as a commodity like any other diminishes the mystique with which a Cinesias would like to surround it. Craft-metaphors of course are not intrinsically pejorative: one may compliment an author by drawing attention to his care, skill and industry in creating, and to the perfection of the finished work, as we do in terms like 'polished' and 'finely-wrought', and the Greeks with ποικίλος and στρογγύλος ('intricate', 'nicely-rounded'). Moreover craft-metaphors may exclude ideas of labour in making and concentrate on making the beauty of the object clear in visual terms, as when Pindar describes an ode as 'a grave-stone whiter than marble from Paros'.[2]

When a poem is regarded as 'made' we are aware that

---

[1] These metaphors will be found listed in additional notes at the end of this chapter.

[2] *N.* 4.81.

The Greek poets were sparing in referring to the labour of composition, or its pleasure. Cratinus (fr. 237) claims that his comedy has taken over two years of work, and Aristophanes says the *Clouds* caused him a lot of effort (523–4); the only explicit mention of the pleasure which the writer should feel occurs in Euripides (*Supp.* 180–3), but the Hymn to Hermes makes the young god's feeling of glee as he composes songs for his newly-invented lyre abundantly obvious (54–62; cf. 418–62).

something new has come into existence, to be valued because it is new. The stress on poetic originality comes to the fore at the end of the fifth century and is seen on the one side in metrical and musical innovations and on the other in the expression, by Euripides notoriously, of 'shocking' ideas and an iconoclastic attitude to tradition. The pleasure aroused by a new song had long been remarked,[1] but the poet had not previously felt the need for originality at whatever cost. We have seen that Bacchylides was conscious of the difficulties of discovering new material,[2] and a similar view was stated more elaborately by the fifth-century epic poet Choerilus in a proem begging his readers' indulgence:

ἆ μάκαρ, ὅστις ἔην κεῖνον χρόνον ἴδρις ἀοιδῆς,
Μουσάων θεράπων, ὅτ᾽ ἀκήρατος ἦν ἔτι λειμών·
νῦν δ᾽ ὅτε πάντα δέδασται, ἔχουσι δὲ πείρατα τέχναι,
ὕστατοι ὥστε δρόμου καταλειπόμεθ᾽, οὐδέ πῃ ἔστι
πάντῃ παπταίνοντα νεοζυγὲς ἅρμα πελάσσαι.

'Blessed the Muses' servant, skilled in song, who lived when their meadow was yet unreaped. Now when everything has been distributed and the arts have fixed limits we are left far behind in the race, nor can we, however far we look, reach a new chariot.'[3]

The poet who is confident of the novelty of his work may boast of it:

οὐδ᾽ ὑμᾶς ζητῶ ᾽ξαπατᾶν δὶς καὶ τρὶς ταῦτ᾽ εἰσάγων,
ἀλλ᾽ ἀεὶ καινὰς ἰδέας ἐσφέρων σοφίζομαι,
οὐδὲν ἀλλήλαισιν ὁμοίας καὶ πάσας δεξιάς.

'I don't try to deceive you, bringing out the same play two or three times over. I'm a clever playwright, my ideas are always new, never alike, invariably clever.'[4] Aristophanes is implicitly running down his rival comic dramatists, not dismissing all

---

[1] e.g. *Od.* 1.351–2; cf. Pindar *O.* 9.52.
[2] fr. 5; see p. 56.
[3] Choerilus fr. 1 Kinkel, discussed in Arist. *Rhet.* 1415a.
[4] Aristophanes, *Clouds* 546–8; cf. *Wasps* 1044 (καινοτάταις διανοίαις) and Cratinus fr. 135. Professional rivalry is mentioned as early as Hesiod, *Works* 25–6; Pindar's 'Praise old wine but the blossoms of hymns that are new' (*O.* 9.52–3) may allude to Simonides' old-fashioned poetry.

previous poetry; but even this extreme is found in a fragment
of Timotheus: what is new is good, what is old is bad.

οὐκ ἀείδω τὰ παλαιά,
καινὰ γὰρ ἀμὰ κρείσσω ·
νέος ὁ Ζεὺς βασιλεύει,
τὸ πάλαι δ᾿ ἦν Κρόνος ἄρχων ·
ἀπίτω Μοῦσα παλαιά.

'I don't sing the old songs, the new ones I write are better.
Zeus is the new king; once upon a time Cronos reigned. Away
with the ancient Muse.'[1]

It seems likely that it is musical innovations that were
Timotheus' chief boast, although his language is also marked
by extravagant coinages and compounds and his nome, the
Persians, of which considerable portions survive, breaks with
tradition too in abandoning strophic organization. This poem
ends with a statement of his poetic creed: 'Now come, exalter
of the new-wrought Music of the golden lyre, come to aid my
hymns, Apollo, healer. For the great leader of Sparta, her
people, noble and long-lasting, teeming with the flower of youth,
is blazing; they shake and chase me with burning rebuke
because in my new hymns I dishonour old-fashioned music. But
I keep none from these hymns, old, young or my own age. Those
I reject are the defilers of ancient music, who mutilate song and
prolong their howling like a herald with his shrill, penetrating
cry.

'Orpheus, Calliope's son, was first begetter of the lyre (? in
Pieria). Next came famous Terpander of Antissa in Aeolian
Lesbos and yoked Music to the ten melodies of the Nome. But
now it is Timotheus who brings to life a cithara of eleven strings
with its measures and rhythms; he has opened a private
treasure-house of the Muses rich in hymns. Miletus was the city
that reared him, her people in their twelve towns first among
Achaeans.'[2]

The new music did not at once sweep out the old, and Aristophanes, who prided himself on his own originality, mocked some

---

[1] *P.M.G.* 796.
[2] *P.M.G.* 791.202–36. P. Maas (*R.E.* VI A2, 1232) dates the poem between
420 and 415.

H

of the modern excesses while borrowing others. Nor did old poetry lose its currency although the younger, sophisticated men might despise it.[1] Pheidippides in the *Clouds* would recite neither Simonides nor Aeschylus, and a fragment of Eupolis which accuses Stesichorus, Alcman and Simonides of being out of date, though probably ironical in tone, at least shows that 'old-fashioned' is a term of abuse.[2]

Along with the poet's pride in his originality goes a new poetic possessiveness[3] and a sensitivity to charges of plagiarism. The best-known example of this tendency is the much-discussed 'Seal' poem of Theognis, who seems to have been afraid not only that his lines might be pirated but also that they might be changed for the worse. He asks that a seal should be placed on them: 'as a result everyone will say "These are the verses of Theognis of Megara: his name is known among all peoples." '

ὧδε δὲ πᾶς τις ἐρεῖ · 'Θεύγνιδός ἐστιν ἔπη
τοῦ Μεγαρέως · πάντας δὲ κατ᾽ ἀνθρώπους ὀνομαστός.'[4]

In this connection one should remember that as early as Hesiod the poet had taken steps to ensure the survival of his name. In the *Theogony* he refers to himself in the third person; Alcman names himself in a passage quoted later in this chapter, and the author of the Hymn to Apollo writes of himself as the blind man who lives in rocky Chios.[5]

Traditionally the Greek poet had borrowed not only themes but whole phrases from Homer, and this practice continues, but now in the fifth century we find also attacks on contemporaries for their thefts. Aristophanes accused another dramatist not only of stealing a play but of using its material for three of his own: 'From my large cloak he makes three small ones.'[6]

[1] Old Comedy demonstrates the currency of some earlier poetry; e.g. Stesichorus (Eupolis fr. 361), Alcaeus and Anacreon (Ar. fr. 223), Aeschylus (Ar. fr. 153). [2] *Clouds* 1353–78; Eupolis fr. 139.

[3] Poetic possessiveness is discernible in Pindar if Bacchylides is the 'ape' of the Second *Pythian* (72–3; 'in the judgment of children the ape is fair'). Bowra (*Problems*, 74 ff.) argues that there is an allusion to Bacchylides, and that the ape here symbolizes mimicry, not trickery. This view is disputed by Burton, 126–7, and re-stated in Bowra's *Pindar*, 136.

[4] Theognis 19–26; see D. A. Campbell, *Greek Lyric Poetry*, 347–50, and references there cited.

[5] *Theog.* 22, *P.M.G.* 39, *h. Hom.* 3. 166–73. [6] fr. 54.

Eupolis' *Autolycus* presents two poets in conflict: A. 'Chasing after newer ideas you led a shocking life.' B. 'You're not one to talk: you've licked the rims of plenty of dishes.'[1] Eupolis' first speaker may be Aristophanes; at any rate the rivalry between the two is well attested, since Eupolis' claim that he helped to write the *Knights* is counterbalanced by Aristophanes' charge that he had plagiarized that play.[2] It is poverty that leads to theft: Euripides' powers of invention were so poor, his attackers thought, that he could write nothing by himself, his effrontery so great that he could outface all accusations of dependence on collaborators. Socrates' help is mentioned in a comedy by Telecleides: 'This play's a new one by Euripides, the *Phrygians*: kindling by Socrates.'[3] Nor could Euripides manage without borrowing from Sophocles or without aid from members of his own household.[4]

While poetry and music were regarded as a gift from the gods there was no need to theorize about their origins, but during the fifth century a man-centred and sceptical enquiry into the beginnings and development of civilization included the arts in its scope. The older view had not ruled out the human contribution altogether by accepting the divine: Alcman, for example, as long ago as the seventh century had said πῆρά τοι μαθήσιος ἀρχά ('the basis of learning is trial and experiment'), and Xenophanes in the next century maintained that 'the gods have not revealed all things from the beginning, but by seeking men find out better in time.'[5] Moreover from early times not only gods but men had been credited with musical discoveries, Hermes inventing the lyre, Athena the Many-headed Tune for the flute, Arion the dithyramb, Terpander the Orthios Nomos. This search for a πρῶτος εὑρετής, or 'First founder', of an art was accompanied by the construction of a system of descent by which poets were said to be 'children' of some divinity or semi-mythical individual.[6] Thus Orpheus was son of Calliope, and

---

[1] fr. 52.
[2] See *Knights* 531, 1291, *Clouds* 554, Eupolis fr. 78, Cratinus fr. 200; similar attacks are alluded to in Hermippus fr. 64, Cratinus fr. 335, Plato fr. 70.
[3] Telecleides fr. 39; cf. fr. 40, Callias fr. 12, Aristophanes fr. 376.
[4] Aristophanes fr. 580, 581, *Frogs* 943–4, 1046–8, 1452–3, *Ach.* 395.
[5] *P.M.G.* 125 (Alcman); D.-K. 18.
[6] There is a full treatment of the πρῶτος εὑρετής by A. Kleingünther, *Phil.*

father or teacher of Musaeus, whose son was Eumolpus; Stesichorus was called son of Hesiod.[1] Such a system is seen in more prosaic form in the history of the 'Sons of Homer', in some ways an equivalent of our craft-guilds. This alliance of the human and divine in the development of art is typical of the Greek outlook which survived into the fifth century.

The philosopher Democritus produced a rationalizing theory of the origin of music; its details are now hard to reconstruct, but we can recover two essential points. The early arts, according to Democritus, evolved by necessity; music, more recent, did not evolve by necessity but out of an already existing abundance.[2] Music accordingly is seen as a luxury, an adornment of civilization. The technique of the arts was learned by imitating animals: from the singing-birds, swan and nightingale, men learned music.[3] This latter belief may long have been current among the people: there is only late authority for the tale that Stesichorus learned lyre-playing from Apollo while still in his mother's womb and song from a nightingale which perched on his infant lips,[4] but two fragments of Alcman point to a similar account: in the first the poet claims to know the tunes of all birds; in the second he says:

Ϝέπη τάδε καὶ μέλος Ἀλκμὰν
εὗρε γεγλωσσαμέναν
κακκαβίδων ὄπα συνθέμενος.

Text and interpretation are uncertain but Alcman may mean that he invented the present poem by paying heed to the song of partridges.[5]

In conclusion it will be helpful to put side by side two

Supplementband 26 (1934), 1–155. εὕρημα is the usual Greek word for invention; so Pindar prays to be εὑρησιεπής (O. 9.86; cf. O. 3.4), Tynnichus' poem is εὕρημά τι Μοισᾶν (P.M.G. 707), Pherecrates draws attention to a metrical innovation as ἐξευρήματι καινῷ (fr. 79); cf. the pun ἐξυρημένον | ἐξηυρημένον (Aristophanes fr. 327), Eccles. 882–3.

[1] cf. the names Terpiades (Od. 22.330) and Ligyastades (Suda, s.v. Mimnermus).

[2] D.-K. 144; see G. Vlastos, A.J.P. 1946, 51–9. Democritus wrote eight works on literary subjects.

[3] D.-K. 154.   [4] Pliny, N.H. 10.82, Anth. Pal. 2.125 (P.M.G. 281e).

[5] P.M.G. 40.39, with references ad loc.

fifth-century views about *technē*, one scientific and the other combining traditional and modern ways of thinking. The author of *On Ancient Medicine*, writing towards the end of the century, and very likely aware of Democritus' work, said that the *technē* of medicine originates in dissatisfaction with the existing circumstances and proceeds by observation and trial to ameliorate them. It is man's need and his nature which call forth the art.[1] Aeschylus in the *Prometheus* is similarly aware that mankind is wretched before the discovery of the civilized skills, but, unlike the 'scientific' writers, he keeps the old beliefs, only developing and modifying them in a way that reflects the period at which the play was written (surely not long before his death in 456). The Titan Prometheus claims: 'all men's skills and arts come from Prometheus'.

πᾶσαι τέχναι βροτοῖσιν ἐκ Προμηθέως.[2]

If we examine Prometheus' list of blessings from a modern standpoint it seems curiously unsystematic and inconsistent. His traditional role of fire-bringer is enlarged by making him also an educator. Prometheus promises that once men have fire they will learn many skills: that is, their own intelligence will come into play; similarly, Prometheus needed only to show them veins of metallic ore.[3] Another aspect of his work was to teach men to observe natural phenomena and to systematize their observations.[4] Thirdly, he revealed new possibilities to man, those of living in houses, using animals and sailing the sea, for example. Finally, he taught them practical skills like carpentry and the theoretical basis of number, writing, divination and medicine. Throughout the passage we find an awareness that man's progress depends on his use of Prometheus' gifts; Prometheus gives practical help and instruction and enlarges

[1] See H. Miller, *T.A.P.A.* 1949, 187–202. The technical works of artists and writers are discussed in Chapter Seven.
[2] The speech of which this line is the climax occurs at *P.V.* 442–506; cf. the sophist Protagoras' account of Prometheus and civilization (Plato, *Prot.* 320D–328D) and another version of the myth by the Eleatic Stranger (*Politicus* 274C–D). Aristophanes parodies stories of this sort, which hover between science and myth, at *Birds* 685–736. The subject of Palamedes, the 'Muses' nightingale' and inventor of writing, treated by Aeschylus, Sophocles and Euripides, is a further indication of interest in the πρῶτος εὑρετής theme.
[3] *P.V.* 254, 500–4. [4] 447–8, 454–8.

103

man's horizons: men respond by developing both skill and knowledge.

The message of Prometheus' speech of self-justification is, in essentials, the same as that of Phemius quoted at the beginning of this chapter: 'I am self-taught, and god has implanted in my mind every kind of song.' There need be no conflict between the belief that poetry is a gift and the observation that the poet needs skill and knowledge: the opinion of William Morris that 'poetry is a craft, and only a craft' is as hard to support as Plato's denial of the poet's claim to be considered a craftsman.

Additional Notes

The categories given below cannot be rigidly defined: for more detailed information see Taillardat, *op. cit.*

1. Terms applicable to more than one craft: *Frogs* 799–802, 956, Crates fr. 19 (measurement), *Thesm.* 56, 67–69, fr. 699 (wax moulds).
2. Carpenter: Cratinus fr. 70, *Frogs* 820 (τέκτων), *Thesm.* 53 (glueing).
3. Builder: Pherecrates fr. 94, *Peace* 749, *Frogs* 1004, *Clouds* 1024 (πυργόω and οἰκοδομέω), Plato fr. 67 (γωναῖος, 'corner-stone'), *Frogs* 854 (κεφαλαῖον ῥῆμα).
4. Stonemason: Plato fr. 67, *Clouds* 1367, 1397.
5. Shipwright: *Thesm.* 52, Teclecleides fr. 40, *Frogs* 824 (γόμφος, 'bolt').
6. ? Ropemaker: *Frogs* 1297.
7. Wheelwright: *Thesm.* 53–56, *Ach.* 686, *Peace* 28, fr. 471.
8. Smith: fr. 699 (ἀκροφύσιον), *Knights* 782, 1379, *Thesm.* 55, *Clouds* 950, *Frogs* 877 (τυπόω).
9. Tailor: ? Pherecrates fr. 79, Aristophanes fr. 54.
10. Shoemaker: Anon. com. fr. 46.
11. Domestic: *a*) ? Ar. fr. 638 (preparation of wool)
    b) cooking: Teclecleides fr. 39, 40, Metagenes fr. 14, Com. adesp. 12 Demianczuk, Ar. fr. 130, 151, *Knights* 538–9.

6. The Poet and his Audience

In this chapter I shall survey the material, mainly poetic, which deals with the effect of poetry on the community as a whole and on the mind and emotions of the individual hearer. This is a subject which can be studied broadly or narrowly. The broad approach, demonstrated most notably in Werner Jaeger's *Paideia* and Bruno Snell's *Poetry and Society*, seeks to illuminate the connection between the life and *mores* of the Greeks in successive periods and their literature, whether poetry, philosophy or history. (All poetry, even personal lyric, can be made to reveal some degree of information about the poet's conception of his role.) I shall limit myself to explicit statements about the purpose and value of Greek poetry and its power to persuade or delight. Material of this sort is important for the history of literary criticism, apart from its intrinsic interest. Firstly it provides a background to the philosophical argument about poetry and society in Plato's *Republic*, which has exerted its great influence on subsequent critics from Aristotle to the present day. In addition, the practical critic, as opposed to the theorist, shapes his judgement of a particular work by criteria of worth and pleasure, even if he does not mean to do so, and early amateur critics can hardly have thought this process dangerous.

In the *Frogs* of Aristophanes, produced in 405, we find expressed, in the mouths of Aeschylus and Euripides, the traditional views of the poet's function *vis-à-vis* the community. Euripides is given the basic principle to proclaim: 'Poets make men better citizens.'

βελτίους τε ποιοῦμεν τοὺς ἀνθρώπους ἐν ταῖς πόλεσιν.

A little later Aeschylus says that children are taught by schoolmasters, grown men by poets.[1] Aeschylus also describes how the earliest poets benefited the state, Orpheus by teaching religious rites and the duty of refraining from killing, Musaeus by giving

---

[1] 1009–10, 1054–6.

oracles and cures for diseases, Hesiod by advice to farmers, Homer by exemplifying skill and valour in war.[1]

We are today out of sympathy with the idea of the poet as teacher. For modern readers, didactic poetry is a small and unimportant genre, at best tedious, at worst condescending. While we should readily admit that great poetry is in some sense educative (Johnson's 'enlargement of sensibility'), the term didactic poetry has come to be used to denote the sort of bloodless verse which conveys unexceptionable moral precepts, or merely the addition of metre and rhyme to ease the learning of lists of facts. Even the great didactic poems of Lucretius and Virgil are sometimes regarded as containing 'an intolerable deal of chaff', as though their authors lived only for the hour when they could compose a simile or describe a cavern. It must be said at once that the Greeks did not use verse to make palatable what would more naturally be written in prose, and we should remember also that poetry is the normal medium in early stages of civilized communities for the expression of anything important and worthy of preservation. If we are to recover the Greek view we need to free ourselves as far as we can from the modern view by which poetry is the preserve of a cultural élite, by whom it is seen chiefly as a form of recreation and is valued for its effect on the mind and emotions of the individual, not the group. The Greeks would have thought Yeats irresponsible for writing:

I think it better that in times like these
A poet's mouth be silent, for in truth
We have no gift to set a statesman right.

The first thing that strikes us as we look at Aeschylus' list of early teachers is its strange mixture. Aeschylus apparently lumped together what we should see as moral, practical or theoretical training, nor did he distinguish as we should between, for instance, the teaching of Homer which is indirect and conveyed through example, and that of Hesiod in a fairly systematic treatise. If we add later poets to the list the diversity becomes even more apparent: in the medium of elegiacs, Tyrtaeus exhorts soldiers, Solon advises citizens, Theognis imparts ethical

[1] 1029–36.

principles to his friend; Pindar's choral lyric teaches indirectly through praise as well as directly through precept, and the iambic writers teach through blame of an individual or type. Where we see differences in aims, method, medium and material the Greeks saw one process: education through poetry.

Before we dismiss all this mixture as unsophisticated confusion and rush to join fifth-century critics of traditional education we need to pause and consider two circumstances (among several others) which help to justify the conservatives. The first needs only a brief mention. The Greeks were in fact educated through poetry (with music) at school and learnt large portions of the major poets by heart.[1] Secondly, the Greek concept of *aretē* (the quality by whose possession you do well all that you have to do) was so wide that it embraced not only the skill and valour of the soldier or athlete but the more tranquil virtues of the private citizen as well. It would be hard to find Greek poetry which did not tend to inculcate *aretē* or at least to reveal its lack as odious.

It is undisputed fact that Homer was for several centuries the source of moral, and probably of much practical, education and that a large part of his work was known by heart. What remains doubtful is how far his aim was consciously didactic. Homer is a reticent poet whose own voice we hear rarely and with difficulty in his invocations of the Muse and echoed in the words of his bards. We have already seen some of the difficulties involved in trying to make a clear picture of the relationship between the Muse and the poet, and we shall have to return to one aspect of it, the problem of poetic truth, later in this chapter. For the present it need only be said that a didactic poet is of necessity a believer in the truth of what he says. The question of Homer's didacticism has been raised again recently by Professor Havelock in his *Preface to Plato*. Havelock maintains that Homer's purpose was to write a poem 'not as a piece of creative fiction, but as a compilation of inherited lore'. In his illustration from what he calls the 'Homeric Encyclopaedia' he finds examples of preserved usage in fields as various as the setting up of cults, family life and seamanship. This is an

---

[1] For the role of poetry in school education see e.g. F. A. G. Beck, *Greek Education 450–350 B.C.* (London, 1964) 117–22.

extreme view, and one which finds no support in the words of Homer's bards, who plainly did not think of themselves as teachers. It is hard to know what sort of audience Havelock visualizes for Homer: were his hearers supposed to be more interested in social usage (most of which was already familiar to them) than in the wrath of Achilles? No, Havelock's Homer must surely have been writing for posterity, and this is a large assumption to make. Havelock's thesis gains even less support from the *Odyssey* in which the proportion devoted to inherited lore is much smaller and there is greater emphasis on romance, magic and adventure. What practical advantage is there in learning how to deal with the Cyclops? If Homer was consciously didactic, his aim can only have been the broad one shared by the greatest writers, to teach by illuminating the ways of gods and men with his own particular insight. However it is likely that later Greeks would have said that Homer intended to teach since their criticism was largely concerned with his factual accuracy and his provision of moral examples.

The literary contest in the *Frogs* shows the weaknesses of the conservatives and the strength of their critics: its first section is concerned with teaching through example. Dionysus ridicules Aeschylus' declaration that Homer taught skill and valour in war by pointing to one Pantacles who did not even know how to fix his helmet. A feeble enough joke, but symptomatic of one sort of attack. Aeschylus' defence was only to point to those who still exemplified the Homeric ideal.[1] Although we do not look to poetry for technical instruction, we do still discuss whether literature should present edifying examples of conduct. When a play like *Saved* (Edward Bond, London, 1966) is put on or in any censorship debate we hear again the words of Aeschylus proclaiming that ordinary people are corrupted by seeing evil characters and wicked actions on the stage. The argument continues on familiar lines with the defence that immorality was not invented by the dramatist and a counter-objection that the writer should nevertheless hide what is shameful.[2] It is perhaps

[1] 1034–44; cf. Aeschylus' argument that the *Seven against Thebes* and the *Persians* inspired men with warlike spirit, 1012–30.

[2] 1043–66. A similar remark in Euripides (*Tro.* 384–5) is more concerned with the pain of recounting what is shameful.

worth while to mention two lines of defence which were *not* used in the debate: one, that no one was ever corrupted by a book, would have invited the riposte that no one was ever improved by one; the other, that works of art have an aesthetic value independent of their moral content, would not have satisfied any Greek of this period.[1]

The acceptance of moral responsibility by both poets in this contest was not exceptional. Because their attitude was both normal and obvious we rarely find it stated although it is implicit in fields as widely disparate as Old Comedy and the Pindaric ode. The poet did not inhabit a private world but moved in the community, often accepting public office. His sense of his relationship with his hearers is exemplified when he speaks of himself as a messenger or herald of the Muses, and his responsibility is explicitly stated by Theognis:

χρὴ Μουσῶν θεράποντα καὶ ἄγγελον, εἴ τι περισσὸν
εἰδείη, σοφίης μὴ φθονερὸν τελέθειν,
ἀλλὰ τὰ μὲν μῶσθαι, τὰ δὲ δεικνύναι, ἄλλα δὲ ποιεῖν ·
τί σφιν χρήσηται μοῦνος ἐπιστάμενος;[2]

Theognis, as van Groningen sees, is comparing the poet to a rich man: as the possessor of exceptional skills he must not be miserly but must use his wealth in various ways; what can he gain by hoarding his knowledge?[3]

On the few occasions on which the poet's social status is mentioned he is classed not with rulers (unless, like Solon, he is

---

[1] I ought to add that I do not see the contest in the *Frogs* as one between conservatives (Aeschylus) and modernists (Euripides) with all the right, and the support of author and audience, on Aeschylus' side. At times both poets are united, *qua* poet, against all outsiders and their shared beliefs should interest us as much as their differences.

[2] 769-72.

[3] I follow the general line of interpretation proposed by B. van Groningen (*Mnem.* 1957, 103-9). He faults, with justice, earlier explanations of the difficult third line. His own theory that three categories of poetry are here denominated, hortatory (μῶσθαι), didactic (δεικνύναι), the creation of μῦθος (ποιεῖν), is not entirely convincing, for two reasons. First, there are no parallels to show the existence of such a system of categorizing poetry at this time; nor is Theognis likely to have thought that poets *created* myths. I suspect that the verbs all allude to different aspects of the same poetic process, not to different types of poetry. I wonder if Theognis is saying that the poet ought to have an enquiring mind, that he ought to teach, that he ought to work at his technique.

one) but with others whose profession benefited the people; for example, in Homer, with seers and physicians.[1] Xenophanes wrote a poem claiming that poets should be held in greater honour than athletes since they were more likely to benefit their city.[2] But although there is an element of self-advertisement in the poet's remarks about his esteem there is no doubt that *qua* poet he was held in honour even by leaders and that he could address them with considerable freedom, witness Pindar's advice to Hiero. Odysseus remarks that bards are honoured and respected by all men,[3] and they are often distinguished in epic with the epithet *theios*, 'divine'.[4] The poet's chief reward was fame: not only the spread of his reputation through Greece but the prospect of undying honour in years to come. In this way he could escape the common fate of extinction at death. Hesiod tells with pride how he competed in the games of Amphidamas in Chalcis: 'And there I proclaim that I won a victory with a hymn and bore off a handled tripod. I dedicated it to the Muses of Helicon in the place where first they set me in the path of clear song.'[5] The author of the Hymn to Apollo was the first to voice the yearning for fame: he asked the chorus of Delian maidens to make mention of his name in the future whenever a visitor from abroad wanted to know who was the best poet at Delos. They were to answer

τυφλὸς ἀνήρ, οἰκεῖ δὲ Χίῳ ἔνι παιπαλοέσσῃ,
τοῦ πᾶσαι μετόπισθεν ἀριστεύουσιν ἀοιδαί.

'A blind man, his home rocky Chios, and all his songs are famous henceforward.' The chorus are to share the fame of the 'blind man from Chios' for he will carry it to all cities and be believed since their fame is genuine.[6] We shall see later how closely the poet's fame is related to the immortality he confers on his subject. The harshest censure that Sappho can direct at a rival is to deny her the prospect of immortality through fame:

κατθάνοισα δὲ κείσηι, οὐδέ ποτα μναμοσύνα σέθεν
ἔσσετ᾽ οὐδὲ πόθα εἰς ὕστερον · οὐ γὰρ πεδέχηις βρόδων

---

[1] *Od.* 17.382. See also Empedocles 146 D.-K.   [2] fr. 2.
[3] *Od.* 8.479-80.   [4] e.g. *Od.* 8.43, 87; cf. *Margites* 1 and *Il.* 2.600, 8.498.
[5] *Works* 656-9.   [6] *h.Hom.* 3.165-76.

THE POET AND HIS AUDIENCE

τὼν ἐκ Πιερίας, ἀλλ᾿ ἀφάνης κἀν ᾿Αίδα δόμωι
φοιτάσηις πεδ᾿ ἀμαύρων νεκύων ἐκπεποταμένα.

'When you have died, you shall lie there, and there will never
be memory of you or longing hereafter; for you have no share
in the roses from Pieria; but in the House of Death also you
shall walk unseen with the unsubstantial dead, when you have
flown from here.'[1]
About the poet's financial rewards we know little.[2] We have
a 'Homeric' epigram of unknown date which says 'I will sing for
you, Potters, if you pay me', and a joke in Aristophanes' *Peace*
about Simonides and money,[3] but only in Pindar do we find a
fuller treatment of the poet's attitude. On one occasion he
expresses regret that he should need to charge a fee for his
professional services: the poets of old freely sang love-songs for
their friends;

> The Muse in those days was not mercenary nor worked for
> hire,
> nor was the sweetness of Terpsichore's honeyed singing for sale
> nor her songs with faces silvered over for their soft utterance.
> Nowadays she drives us to hold with that Argive's word, that
> mounts close to the truth itself.

> *Money is man*, he said, forlorn alike of possessions and friends.

6 ἁ Μοῖσα γὰρ οὐ φιλοκερδής πω τότ᾿ ἦν οὐδ᾿ ἐργάτις ·
7 οὐδ᾿ ἐπέρναντο γλυκεῖαι μελιφθόγγου ποτὶ Τερψιχόρας
8 ἀργυρωθεῖσαι πρόσωπα μαλθακόφωνοι ἀοιδαί.
9 νῦν δ᾿ ἐφίητι τὸ τὠργείου φυλάξαι
10 ῥῆμ᾿ ἀλαθείας ὁδῶν ἄγχιστα βαῖνον,
11 'χρήματα χρήματ᾿ ἀνήρ᾿ ὃς φᾶ κτεάνων θ᾿ ἅμα λειφθεὶς καὶ
φίλων.[4]

[1] Text and translation as in Bowra, *G.L.P.* 206–7. The 'roses of Pieria' stand
for the gift of poetry, in a metaphor without parallels.
[2] J. A. Davison, *Phoenix* 1962, 141–56; see especially 141.
[3] Epigram 14 (Baumeister). The joke at *Peace* 697–9 is obscure: when Hermes
is asked how Sophocles is getting on he replies: 'Very well, but he's had an odd
experience; he's turned into Simonides and now he's so old and mellow that
he'd even put to sea on a hurdle if you payed him.' (Simonides is supposed
to have been the first poet to charge a fee and so was open to charges of greed.)
[4] *I.* 2.1–11. The general meaning is clear: charging fees, an unpleasant
necessity, is doubly repugnant when the poem's recipient is a personal friend.

111

Elsewhere Pindar speaks of the binding force of his contract with a patron: 'Muse, if you contracted for payment to provide your voice in return for silver, it is your duty to set it in motion at different times on different themes, *now* for Thrasydaeus or his father'.[1]

The most dangerous attack on the poet's position was to charge him not with being mercenary but with telling lies. The Greek words for 'lie' are wider in range of meaning than 'lie' in English and need not imply an intention to deceive, but the authority of the teacher-poet depended upon his reliability. 'Fiction', 'imagination', 'literal (poetic, psychological) truth' are among the terms which the Greeks lacked in discussing litera-ture: 'lie' had to cover everything from factual error through literary invention to deliberate deceit.[2] The question of truth in literature is crucial from Hesiod to Plato, and even Aristotle has not fully resolved it. I take first our earliest, and perhaps most difficult, passage on lies in literature. When the Muses appeared to Hesiod they said:

ἴδμεν ψεύδεα πολλὰ λέγειν ἐτύμοισιν ὁμοῖα,
ἴδμεν δ᾿, εὖτ᾿ ἐθέλωμεν, ἀληθέα γηρύσασθαι.

'We know how to tell many lies like the truth but also how to tell the truth when we wish.'[3] The many interpretations of this

---

The imagery is difficult, particularly in the Pindaric compression of line 8, and has been much discussed (see the summary in Bowra, *Pindar* 355–6). Are we to see the Muse and her songs as prostitutes or merely as hired servants? The first line quoted above denies only that the Muse (the art of music) of former times worked for pay; in the next two lines poetry itself is personified: 'sweet songs' are sold (πέρνημι is chiefly used of exporting slaves), Terpsichore's songs, not those of the semi-abstract Muse, since her name means 'pleasure in choral song'. The prostitute interpretation then rests entirely on ἀργυρωθεῖσαι πρόσωπα and may be supposed to refer to the practice of whitening the face as an aid to beauty – if this is so, the implication must surely be that songs are not saleable without some extra adornment. While I doubt that Pindar would have wished to say this (or indeed that he would have likened his art to prosti-tution even in a light-hearted poem), no other interpretation can be proved to be correct. I should like line 8 to mean that 'songs are rewarded with silver for their beauty because of their gentle utterance'.

[1] *P.* 11.41–4, Burton 68–70: Μοῖσα, τὸ δὲ τεόν, εἰ μισθοῖο συνέθεν παρέχειν | φωνὰν ὑπάργυρον, ἄλλοτ᾿ ἀλλᾷ ταρασσέμεν | ἢ πατρὶ Πυθονίκῳ | τό γέ νυν ἢ Θρασυδάῳ.

[2] In translating Plato, for example, we are justified in writing variously 'fiction' or 'lie' or even 'error' for ψεῦδος. [3] *Theog.* 27–8.

puzzling remark fall into two categories: either Hesiod had a genuine religious experience which he reported faithfully, or (for reasons of prestige?) he invented the whole thing, attributing to the Muses whatever suited him. I believe that Hesiod was recounting a genuine experience, what he saw and heard on Helicon, and I think that the Muses were warning him: although he was to be the recipient of their gifts he was to remember that the Muses, like other deities, were capricious and would not guarantee their favours unconditionally as an outright gift. If Hesiod were to offend, he would be punished, and punished in the most harmful way: he would believe himself to be publishing a revelation from the Muses, but in fact he would be misled into recording a lying vision.[1]

The late sixth-century philosopher Heraclitus of Ephesus believed that true knowledge resulted from insight denied to the majority and attacked the doctrine that poets are reliable teachers: 'What sense or mind have they? They believe popular bards and take the crowd as their teacher, not realizing that "the majority are worthless, the good are few".'[2] Heraclitus contrasted true knowledge with polymathy: 'Polymathy doesn't teach sense; if it did, it would have taught Hesiod, Pythagoras, Xenophanes and Hecataeus.'[3] Apart from generalized criticism ('Homer and Archilochus ought to be expelled from the contests and whipped')[4] we have one fragment directed against a specific passage in Hesiod: 'Most men's teacher is Hesiod; they believe he knew most things – a man who couldn't tell day and night. For they are one.'[5] This is an allusion to *Theogony* 124, where Hesiod made Day the daughter of Night. The aristocratic feeling that truth can be discerned only by the chosen few is echoed by Pindar and influences the respective attitudes of Aeschylus and Euripides in the *Frogs*. Pindar wrote: 'There are many swift

---

[1] Hesiod's vision has been much discussed: a recent summary of conflicting views may be found in Hesiod: *Theogony* ed. M. L. West, *ad loc.* The most favoured interpretation of the Muses' remarks about lies has been to see in them a slighting allusion to Homer (e.g. A. Lesky, *A History of Greek Literature*, 92, T. A. Sinclair, *J.H.S.* 1935, 267), or if such an allusion seems improbable at this early date (J. A. Davison, *Eranos* 1955, 125–40), to epic fictional narrative in general. To the discussions cited by Dr West add P. Walcot *R.E.G.* 1960, 36–9, H. Wade-Gery, *Phoenix* 1949, 86.

[2] D.-K. 104.   [3] D.-K. 40.   [4] D.-K. 42.

[5] D.-K. 57; cf. 106 and the attack on Homer in 105.

arrows in the quiver beneath my arm which have a voice for
the intelligent: the majority need interpreters. The wise man is
he who knows many things by nature.'[1]
We have noticed already, in the *Frogs*, the view that what is
shameful should be passed over in silence. A related attitude,
that what is shameful cannot possibly be true, was first expressed by the poet-philosopher Xenophanes in the sixth century. Xenophanes posited a new divine being and criticized the
gods of Homer ('from whom all have learned', fr. 9) as immoral
and anthropomorphic.[2] In a poem giving instructions for the
right conduct of a symposium he advises the participants not to
relate the battles of Titans, Giants and Centaurs which were
fabrications of former poets:

οὔ τι μάχας διέπειν Τιτήνων οὐδὲ Γιγάντων
οὐδέ ⟨κε⟩ Κενταύρων, πλάσματα τῶν προτέρων.[3]

Xenophanes need not be accusing Hesiod of deliberate lying,
although *plasso* etc. is used pejoratively.[4]
Xenophanes' words find an echo in Pindar when he says 'let
be war and all discord apart from the immortals'.[5] Again we
discover in Pindar a reluctance to disclose what horrifies him:
he breaks off the story of Bellerophon with the words 'On his
fate at the last I will keep silence'.[6] Bacchylides is equally concerned with truth, but in a different way. For him, truth is
intimately connected with fame, as we shall see later in the
chapter.
The existence of incompatible versions of a myth complicated
the question of truth in poetry, and it may be this that Solon
meant when he wrote πολλὰ ψεύδονται ἀοιδοί, 'bards tell many
lies'.[7] The most famous instance of the problem is found in
Stesichorus' Palinode addressed to Helen:

οὐκ ἔστ᾽ ἔτυμος λόγος οὗτος,
οὐδ᾽ ἔβας ἐν νηυσὶν εὐσέλμοις
οὐδ᾽ ἵκεο πέργαμα Τροίας.

---

[1] *O.* 2.91–5; these lines no doubt compliment Theron, the ode's recipient, on
his intelligence.   [2] frs. 10–41.   [3] fr. 1.21–2.
[4] e.g. Aeschylus, *P.V.* 1030, Gorgias, *Helen* 11, Plato, *Tim.* 26E.
[5] *O.* 9.43–4.   [6] *O.* 13.87b; cf. *N.* 1.18, fr. 244.
[7] fr. 21; cf. Eur., *H.F.* 1346.

'This is not the true story; you made no journey in well-benched ships, nor did you come to Troy's citadel.'[1] It is likely that elsewhere in the poem Stesichorus said that he had been blinded for repeating the version of the tale of Helen in which she deserted her husband for Paris and so caused the Trojan war: Stesichorus should have said that the real Helen was faithful; only her phantom went to Troy. An ancient commentary, recently published, tells us that there were two Palinodes, both opening with an appeal to the Muse, one of them containing our Palinode and the other recanting a false version of the tale of Helen first told by Hesiod.[2] Perhaps we shall never know the answers to all the questions raised by the poem and the commentary: what is important here is that the Palinode itself rapidly became legendary. In the *Phaedrus* Socrates says that the perils of speaking ill of a god are well known. 'Yet there is an ancient method of atonement if myths are wrongly told; Stesichorus knew it, but not Homer. Because of his slander of Helen he was blinded; unlike Homer, because he was a true poet, he recognized his fault and at once wrote' – and here Plato quotes the Palinode – 'and when he had finished the poem called the Palinode his sight was immediately restored'.[3] The legend that 'lying' poets were blinded by the gods demonstrates the importance attached to truth in poetry. One may rationalize the source of the legend by saying that the bardic calling was one of the few open to a blind man in Homeric society, and that his lack of sight was compensated by the gifts of memory for which the blind are well known and which were essential to an oral poet.[4] But it is easy to see how blindness came to be regarded as a punishment, particularly if its onset was sudden, as the result of a stroke. When Teiresias saw what he should not have seen he was deprived of sight: the punishment fitted the offence.[5] Teiresias' physical sight was replaced by the inner vision of the

[1] *P.M.G.* 192.
[2] *P.M.G.* 193 (P. Oxy. xxix); Bowra suggests (*C.R.* 1963, 245–52) that the other Palinode referred to a story of an earlier intrigue of Helen. See now L. Woodbury, *Phoenix* 1967, 157–76.   [3] *Phaedrus* 243A.
[4] Hesiod may have been represented as blind on a relief in the sanctuary of the Muses (P. Jamot, *B.C.H.* 1890, 546–51); Xenocritus, an early lyric poet, is said to have been blind from birth; the story of Homer's blindness may be as old as the Hymn to Apollo.   [5] Callimachus, Hymn 5.

seer; when the Muses blinded Demodocus they gave him the gift of song, a gift, that is, of knowledge hidden to ordinary people.[1] When Thamyris was blinded it may be that he was deprived of both physical and poetic sight; this would explain the attraction of his legend for Sophocles, who is much concerned with blindness as a symbol of lack of insight.[2] And so from the observed fact that blind men become poets arose the poetic truth that the poet has his own sort of sight; the legend is exemplified in different ways: in the case of Stesichorus, physical blindness sharpened his moral awareness and he wrote his recantation, dedicated to the goddess who loves song. Metaphorical blindness is mentioned in an incomplete poem of Pindar; the line of thought seems to be that the poet who tries to write without the Muses is blind.[3]

In the fifth century the discussion of truth in poetry takes two new directions. In the first place there seems to have been a groping towards a general aesthetic theory by means of explaining the principles of one art in terms of another. At the time painting was much admired for being lifelike: witness the story told of Zeuxis' grapes. It is in this context that we should place the statement of the anonymous sophist who wrote the *Dissoi Logoi* perhaps near the end of the fifth century. The best tragedian or painter, he says, is the one who produces the greatest illusion by making his works lifelike.[4] This paradoxical judgement, which seeks common ground between tragedy and painting, is an early example of the confusion which has so often been caused by generalizing about Art. The fifth century too saw an increased concern with the power of language; to speak well was more than ever the key to success, and 'speaking well' too often meant a quick-witted, cynical juggling with points to confuse the hearer. Moreover one of the orator's resources was to quote from established authors or even to adapt a scene borrowed from epic or drama to lend pathos or conviction to his argument: the authority of the original must be damaged by

[1] *Od.* 8.64.
[2] *Il.* 2.594–600; for symbolic blindness in Sophocles see e.g. John Jones *On Aristotle and Greek Tragedy*, 167–70, 212.
[3] Paean 7b.13–15, quoted and discussed on p. 60.
[4] D.-K. 90.3.10; cf. Gorgias D.-K. 23: on both these passages see T. Rosenmeyer, *A.J.P.* 1955, 231–60 ('Gorgias, Aeschylus and Apate').

this practice. And as rhetorical skill came to be seen as a matter of following certain rules and using certain devices people became able to spot the techniques of persuasion used in literature also.

The persuasive power of language was not, of course, a new discovery: Homer shows Odysseus' ability to tell convincing lies,[1] and Hesiod accounts for the eloquence of princes in the proem to the *Theogony*: 'whomsoever of heaven-nourished princes the daughters of great Zeus honour, and behold him at his birth, they pour sweet dew upon his tongue, and from his lips flow gracious words. All the people look towards him while he settles causes with true judgements: and he, speaking surely, would soon make wise end even of a great quarrel; for therefore are there princes wise in heart, because when the people are being misguided in their assembly, they set right the matter again with ease, persuading them with gentle words. And when he passes through a gathering, they greet him as a god with gentle reverence, and he is conspicuous amongst the assembled: for such is the holy gift of the Muses to men. For it is through the Muses and far-shooting Apollo that there are singers and harpers upon the earth; but princes are of Zeus, and happy is he whom the Muses love: sweet flows speech from his mouth.'[2]

If a writer as early as Hesiod had found it necessary to comment on the power of language to influence people we may wonder whether belief in the truth of epic, for example, was really prevalent. Since our evidence shows that scepticism was exceptional, we ask the further question, 'How could the Greeks believe that epic was literally true?' Thucydides understandably saw the *Iliad* as history: how did the unsophisticated regard the *Odyssey*? Before we accuse the Greeks, at least down to the fifth century, of credulity, we should remember that some modern myths enjoy a wide currency and that impossibility does not preclude belief. When myths were told in epic they were made persuasive by the musical and histrionic skill of the bard. When they were told in choral lyric they were enacted in dance, gesture and song and engaged more than the critical faculty of the spectator. Pindar was probably the first to try to describe

---

[1] *Od.* 19.203: 'in his pretence he spoke many lies like true words', ἴσκε ψεύδεα πολλὰ λέγων ἐτύμοισιν ὁμοῖα.

[2] *Theog.* 81–97, H. Evelyn-White's translation in the Loeb edition.

this strange power of literature which is more than just persuasiveness. Although he believed that in time truth would prevail,[1] he had a clear understanding of the glamour of poetry. He wrote of myths which deceive because they are 'subtly worked with intricate falsehoods' and says that Charis (the spirit of grace and beauty) adds fame by making the incredible credible.[2] His insight is even more remarkable in the passage about Odysseus:

ἐγὼ δὲ πλέον᾽ ἔλπομαι
λόγον ᾽Οδυσσέος ἢ πάθαν διὰ τὸν ἁδυεπῆ γενέσθ᾽ ῞Ομηρον.
ἐπεὶ ψεύδεσί οἱ ποτανᾷ τε μαχανᾷ
σεμνὸν ἔπεστί τι · σοφία δὲ κλέπτει παράγοισα μύθοις · τυφλὸν
δ᾽ἔχει
ἦτορ ὅμιλος ἀνδρῶν ὁ πλεῖστος.

I think the tale
of Odysseus is greater than his deeds, all through the grace
of Homer.
Upon his lies and the winged intelligence
there is a kind of majesty; genius persuasive in speech
deceives us; blind
is the heart in the multitude of men.[3]

When Aristotle discussed lies in literature he was careful to keep the subject outside the sphere of morality: his concern is with making the incredible credible and how this can best be done, not with whether it should be done. The discussion is part of his comparison of the merits and demands of epic and tragedy.[4] 'The astonishing has a place in tragedy, while epic will go farther and admit the irrational or absurd (a common ingredient in the astonishing) since in epic one does not actually see the subject of the narrative in action.' There follows an example of an epic scene which would look ridiculous on the stage. Aristotle continues: 'the astonishing gives pleasure, as can be seen from the fact that no one tells a story without embroidery: the additions are meant to please. It is from Homer above all that every other poet has learned how to lie.'[5] So far Aristotle has given lies a place in an author's technique

[1] e.g. *O.* 4.20.   [2] *O.* 1.28–34.   [3] *N.* 7.20–4.
[4] *Poetics* 1460 a11–b5.   [5] cf. Thuc. 1.10.3, 1.22.4, 2.41.4.

of holding his hearer's amazed attention: he goes on to show
how lies obtain credence, by explaining how false reasoning
works. It is a false assumption that, if B is true, then A, which
precedes it, is also true. Here Aristotle's argument is shifting
from the broader question of exaggerating and embellishing a
story to the narrower issue of the logical fallacy. This latter
however leads to the dictum that 'probable impossibilities are
preferable to implausible possibilities' and then to a discussion
about the avoidance of absurdities in the plot-structure of
tragedies. It is clear throughout this passage that Aristotle is
not only avoiding the position 'lying is morally wrong' but also
seeking to demonstrate that the audience's acceptance of a work
of literature is complex and varies with the genre: in any
case the successful writer is one who can evoke wonder and
amazement.

We have seen evidence of an awareness that eloquence could
be misused and that literature has a special magic, hard to
define. The sophist Gorgias attempts a definition. It was probably towards the end of the fifth century that he produced his
display-speech, the encomium of Helen, which is as much concerned with the power of *Logos* as with Helen's fall from grace,
and contains a passage about the effects of language which
deserves to be quoted at length. 'Language is a powerful tyrant:
although it is invisible and insubstantial its works equal a god's.
Language has power to stop terror, remove suffering, promote
joy and increase compassion. . . . As one listens to poetry one is
invaded by a tremor of panic, by tears of pity or by wistful
longing: it is through language that we experience in our own
soul the happiness and misfortunes which affect the actions and
persons of others. . . . This inspired magic of language induces
delight and banishes sorrow. For when the influence of the spell
meets the opinion-forming (receptive) part of the soul it soothes
and persuades it and finally changes it through its wizardry.
But two arts of enchantment and magic are known, namely
errors of soul and deceptions of opinion. There are many who
have persuaded, and still do persuade, a great mass of people
when all they have done is to manufacture lies on all topics.'[1]

[1] D.-K. 11.8–11. Gorgias' theories of art are discussed by C. P. Segal,*H.S.C.P.*
1962, 99–155 and T. S. Duncan, *C.J.* 1938, 404–5.

This is almost certainly the earliest psychological explanation of the persuasiveness of language: Gorgias picks up the Hesiodic belief that the Muses inspire both poets and princes and develops the theory that *Logos* is a single, self-existent power which by rousing emotion makes individuals and crowds act. He sees something in language itself, apart from the matter it conveys, which works like a drug, actually having an effect on the soul. His remarks about panic, pity and longing are plainly a source of the Aristotelian 'pity and fear' but they also expand and systematize earlier, isolated remarks about the emotional response to literature. Gorgias' reputation as a thinker has suffered partly because the search for unity of thought in his scanty fragments has been unsuccessful, but still more because his ornate style has made him seem a mere rhetorician: 'starting with the initial advantage of having nothing particular to say, he was able to concentrate all his energies upon saying it'.[1] Nevertheless his importance in that branch of criticism concerned with the effect of literature should not be underestimated.

The unknown sophist who wrote the *Dissoi Logoi* remarks that poetry aims at pleasure, not truth.[2] We may infer from his words the existence of a rudimentary hedonistic theory of art by the end of the fifth century, but when earlier writers mention the capacity of song to give pleasure we should regard them as recording what they had observed and not as promulgating a theory which limited the function of poetry to that of giving pleasure. Homer and Hesiod make it clear that the Muses sang to give pleasure on Olympus: not only the content of their song but their grace of movement and beautiful voices delighted the gods.[3] Pleasing the gods with song was one way in which men could obtain prosperity. The association of music with all public and private occasions of rejoicing in Greece is too well known to need detailed comment; the evidence of art reinforces that of literature.[4] What does need to be stressed however is that often the enjoyment was in participation; one thinks first of the guests at symposia singing in turn as the wine circulated, but

[1] J. D. Denniston, *Greek Prose Style* (Oxford, 1952) 12. In his edition of Plato's *Gorgias* (Oxford, 1959, 6–10) Professor Dodds, who denies that Gorgias should be called philosopher or sophist, speaks of his 'dazzling insincerity'.
[2] D.-K. 90.3.17.   [3] *Theog.* 10, 39–45, 60–1, 65–70; *Il.* 1.604–5.
[4] See e.g. Solon 20.

even the more professional performances in drama or victory-song must have involved comparatively large numbers in active music-making, and this must have affected the emotional response of performers and audience.

The emotional power of music as revealed in Homer and Hesiod is not simply that of giving pleasure. Poetry heightens feeling, sometimes unbearably: Homer shows both Penelope and Odysseus moved to tears when they hear a bard singing. When Penelope heard Phemius reciting the Return of the Achaeans she asked him to sing a different tale since he knew 'many other ways of soothing men'.[1] During Alcinous' entertainment arranged in his honour Odysseus was twice overcome by his feelings when Demodocus sang, first when he heard the story of his own quarrel with Achilles and again at the tale of the Wooden Horse.[2] The latter occasion is described more fully: Odysseus himself had chosen the subject, yet as he heard it 'he was melted and a tear moistened his cheeks'. Homer likens Odysseus' piti-ful weeping to that of a woman who bewails her husband as he dies in his defeated city and is herself wounded and led into captivity. The content of the stories by marking the contrast between Odysseus' past and present fortunes contributed to his breakdown but was less important than their immediacy and vividness, as Odysseus himself knew when he praised the bard for his singing:

λίην γὰρ κατὰ κόσμον Ἀχαιῶν οἶτον ἀείδεις,
ὅσσ᾽ ἔρξαν τ᾽ ἔπαθόν τε καὶ ὅσσ᾽ ἐμόγησαν Ἀχαιοί,
ὥς τέ που ἢ αὐτὸς παρεὼν ἢ ἄλλου ἀκούσας.

'You sing with astonishing exactness of the fate of the Achaeans, of all their deeds, suffering and exertion, just as if you had been there yourself or heard the tale from an eye-witness.'[3] The very quality which gives pleasure to the uninvolved causes unbear-able pain to one personally concerned. In Plato's *Ion* Socrates asks the rhapsode whether he loses awareness of himself and his surroundings and believes he is actually present in Ithaca or Troy as a witness of the deeds he is recounting. Ion replies: 'When I recite something pitiable my eyes fill with tears and when my subject is frightening or awe-inspiring my hair stands

[1] *Od.* 1.325–64.　　　　[2] *Od.* 8.83–92, 487–531.　　　　[3] 489–91.

on end in fear and my heart thumps.' A little later he describes his effect on his hearers: 'Every time I recite I look down on them from the platform and see them weeping and looking tense at my story, and sharing in a common awe.'[1]

As early as Hesiod we learn that music can relieve suffering. This anodyne power is manifested in two ways as Greek literature develops: music may either distract the anxious mind or soothe it and even hold it spellbound. (We shall see that the word *thelgo* and its cognates range in meaning from 'soothe' to 'enchant'.) In the proem to the *Theogony* Hesiod wrote: 'If a man with the grief of a recent sorrow in his mind feels his heart dried out with suffering, and then a bard, the Muses' servant, hymns the deeds of men of old and the blessed gods of Olympus, at once he forgets his distress and no longer remembers his cares: the goddesses' gifts swiftly divert him.'[2]

In the praise of the lyre which opens the First *Pythian* Pindar shows how its music soothes and enchants:

> 'Zeus' eagle sleeps on his staff, folding
>   his quick wings both ways to quiet,
> Lord of birds; you shed a mist on his hooked head,
> dark and gentle closure of eyes; dreaming, he ripples
> his lithe back, bound in spell
> of your waves. Violent Ares even, leaving aside
>   the stern pride
> of spears, makes gentle his heart in sleep.
> Your shafts enchant the divinities by grace of the
> wisdom of Lato's son and the deep-girdled Muses.'[3]

These twin powers were also manifested by the Sirens, who, like the Muses, knew past, present and future.[4] Circe's warning and Odysseus' own experience make it clear that they could draw men to them by their singing and keep them in entire forgetfulness of their homes and children; a fragment of Pindar speaks

[1] *Ion* 535C–E.
[2] *Theog.* 98–103; there is no need to see in 98 an allusion to a specific recent bereavement (M. L. West, *Theog.*, 45). Hesiod is saying that music can relieve any suffering, even the sharpness of recent grief; cf. Sophocles, fr. 238N².
[3] *P.* 1.6–12; for the Muses as givers of sleep see p. 13.
[4] *Od.* 12.39–54, 156–200. Alcman (*P.M.G.* 30) equated Muse and Siren: see M. L. West, *C.Q.* 1965, 200.

of the Siren's voice which quells the gale, while Aristophanes'
complimentary reference to Euripides' poetry as a 'blend
of honey and Sirens' must again emphasize their power of
attraction.[1]

The idea of enchantment is uppermost in a fragment of
Archilochus: 'all men are enchanted by songs' (κηλεῖται δ᾽ ὅτις
ἐστὶν ἀοιδαῖς).[2] Enchantment may not only hold the listener
spell-bound but impel him to action against his wishes. So
Pindar, convinced of his song's power to sway even the centaur
Chiron, if he were still alive, writes of his wish that his 'honey-
voiced hymns might set a philtre in his heart'.[3] Here song is
likened to a drug, and the same metaphor is used by Gorgias in
the *Helen* when writing of the power of language. For Gorgias
a drug (*pharmakon*) may heal or destroy: 'the power of language
has the same effect on the disposition (*taxis*) of the soul as the
prescribing (*taxis*) of drugs has on the nature of the body. Just
as some drugs draw specific infections from the body while
others put a stop to an illness or to life itself, so with language.
Words sometimes cause pain, sometimes joy, panic or courage in
the hearers; some words however are evil propaganda, drugging
and bewitching the soul.'[4] This quasi-physical effect of poetry
may be seen as entirely beneficent, soothing disordered or
savage emotions[5] and, in the Fourth *Nemean*, relieving fatigue:

Ἄριστος εὐφροσύνα πόνων κεκριμένων
ἰατρός · αἱ δὲ σοφαί
Μοισᾶν θύγατρες ἀοιδαὶ θέλξαν νιν ἁπτόμεναι.
οὐδὲ θερμὸν ὕδωρ τόσον γε μαλθακὰ τεύχει
γυῖα, τόσσον εὐλογία φόρμιγγι συνάορος.[6]

The train of thought here is that the celebration which follows
a victory helps the athlete recover from the pain of exertion, and
that it is the hymns of praise during the festivity which con-
tribute most to his recovery. Pindar regards the celebration as

[1] Pindar fr. 106.7–11; Aristophanes fr. 676b. Hesiod is said to have named
the Sirens as Thelxiope or Thelxinoe, Molpe and Aglaophonus (Σ Apollonius
Rhodius iv. 892).
[2] fr. 106; cf. *Od.* 11.334, Pindar fr. 86.18; Pindar also speaks of the Keledones,
who were like the Sirens, but kindly (fr. 49.24).
[3] *P.* 3.63–7; cf. 1–7.   [4] D.-K. 11.14.
[5] e.g. *O.* 2.14/15, *P.* 1.6–14.   [6] *N.* 4.1–5.

123

a doctor and song as the doctor's assistant with soothing touch; the healing image is continued in the simile which follows: praise is more relaxing even than warm water. 'When the contest is decided, the joy of celebration is the best doctor for labours endured, and skilled songs, the Muses' daughters, soothe the victor by their touch. Not even warm water makes his limbs as relaxed as praise accompanied by the lyre.'[1]

The metaphor of poetry as a drug or philtre is a specialized development of the traditional image of words 'streaming' from the mouth. In the proem to the *Theogony* Hesiod uses this metaphor of the Muses ('their untiring voice flows sweetly from their mouths'), of any prince whom they honour ('on his tongue they pour sweet dew and from his mouth stream soothing words') and of any bard whom they love ('sweet flows the voice from his mouth').[2] These passages, with their later imitations, draw attention to the remarkable unbroken flow of eloquence. 'On his tongue they pour sweet dew and from his mouth stream soothing words.' Here 'soothing words' are the result of the Muses' gift of 'sweet dew', and this idea may lie behind descriptions of song as 'honey-voiced' and the like.[3] Such descriptions, which often praise content as well as delivery, are richer than the conventional 'lovely' applied to song.[4] The same word for 'dew' is found in a Pindaric ode in a slightly different connection: 'Hail, friend: I send you a late gift, honey mixed with pale milk, a draught of song; the commingled dew crowns the draught among the breathing of Aeolian flutes.'[5] These lines complete the metaphor of the ode's commencement: 'Each exploit has its

---

[1] I take νιν in v. 3 to refer to the victor, not to εὐφροσύνα; θέλξαν and ἁπτόμεναι probably convey a secondary meaning 'hold and enchant'. For θέλγω cf. *Od.* 1.337, 12.40, Aeschylus *P.V.* 173–4, Plato *Symp.* 197E.

[2] *Theog.* 39–40, 83–4, 97; cf. *Od.* 8.170–3. *Il.* 1.249.

[3] 'Honey-voiced': e.g. *I.* 6.8, *P.* 3.64; 'honey-tongued': e.g. Bacch. 3.97, fr. 4.63; cf. Pindar fr. 223. For the connection between honey and dew, see e.g. Virgil, *Georgics* 4.1, Pausanias 9.23.2. The famous description of Pericles' oratory, Eupolis 98.5–8 owes something to this idea: 'A sort of persuasiveness sat on his lips (such was his power of enchantment) and he was the only orator to leave his sting in the listeners.' Cf. Ar. fr. 580a, 581 of the honey on Sophocles' lips.

[4] e.g. in Archilochus fr. 1, Solon 1.52, Anacreon fr. 32D., Simonides fr. 79D.

[5] *N.* 3.73–7; the image is difficult (see editors *ad loc.*, Norwood, *Pindar* 170 and 267) because the meaning of ἔερσα is uncertain. I am inclined to think that the honey is imagined as a distillation of dew which, when the liquids have been blended, causes a translucence on the surface of the draught.

own thirst: athletic victory welcomes song above all, the skilled servant of valour crowned.'[1] The thirst for song that Pindar mentions is specific: he is not making a generalization about humanity's need for poetry, even in the Ninth *Pythian* where he writes: 'I then, quenching the thirst for song, am driven by his compulsion to waken again the reputation of his forebears.'[2] The thirst here is likely to be that of the ode's commissioner, not Pindar's desire for self-expression.

The comparison of poetry with wine normally continues the idea of sweetness and adds ceremonial and festive associations but does not say that poetry intoxicates.

> As one who takes a cup from a lavish hand,
> bubbling within the foam of the grape,
> presenting it
> to a young bridegroom, pledging hearth
>   to hearth, the pride, sheer gold, of possession,
> the joy of the feast, to honour his new son, render him
> among friends present admired for the bride's consent:
> so I, bringing poured nectar of victory,
> gift of the Muses, the mind's sweet yield,
> offer it up
> to the conquerors at Olympia and Pytho.[3]

This is the most elaborate presentation of a theme familiar elsewhere: in a fragment of Aristophanes the taste of wine is the point (a harsh poet is like Pramnian wine but what people really prefer is a sweet, fragrant vintage), whereas in an *Isthmian* ode 'the cup of the Muses' songs' is associated both with symposia and the celebration of three prizes.[4] Just as the power of speech is personified in the deity Peitho who is both Persuasion and Attractiveness, so the pleasure-giving capacity of song is symbolized by Charis (Grace) and the Charites. In a chorus of the *Helen* Euripides associates the Graces with the Muses in the task

---

[1] 6–8.

[2] 107–9. It is possible to translate ἀοιδᾶν δίψαν as 'thirst of songs', meaning that songs already exist somewhere and long to be expressed.

[3] *O*. 7.1–10; Bowra, *Pindar* 24–6.

[4] Ar. fr. 579, *I*. 6.1–8; cf. *O*. 6.91, *I*. 5.21–2, *Ach*. 484. For the inflammatory effects of wine on the poet see p. 90f. For Homer's poetry compared to a banquet, see Athenaeus 8.347E.

of relieving grief.[1] The Graces make a song pleasing and convincing to the hearer and so help in establishing its fame or that of its subject. 'What is said lives longer than what is done if the tongue, aided by the Graces' goodwill, thrusts it forth from a profound mind.'[2] For the individual the best hope of escaping death was to be sung by a poet or represented by a sculptor. The theme of the Homeric hero as of the Homeric bard was the deeds of men (κλέα ἀνδρῶν).[3] Whereas the statue is fixed in one place, the poem can carry fame everywhere.[4] It has wings.

> I've given thee wings shall waft thee forth with ease
> High o'er the land, high o'er the boundless seas;
> No feast shall ever be but thou'lt be there
> Couch'd on men's lips, for oft the young and fair
> With ordered sweetness clear shall sing thy praise
> To the clear flute; and when in after-days
> To the dark and dolorous land thou com'st below,
> Ne'er even in death shalt thou thy fame forgo,
> But men will keep in memory unchanging
> The name of Cyrnus, who shalt, all Greece ranging,
> Mainland and island, pass the unharvested
> Home of the fish, not Pegasus-wise, but sped
> By the grand gifts of Them of the Violet Crown,
> To all that ope their doors, and up and down
> While earth and sun endure, world without end,
> Shalt live a song to men: – yet I, sweet friend,
> I have no honour small or great with thee,
> But like a child, with words thou cheatest me.[5]

We have seen already that Pindar and Bacchylides thought of themselves as soaring like eagles;[6] Pindar prays that the athlete too 'may be raised on the bright wings of the tuneful

---

[1] 1341–5.

[2] N. 4.6–8. At N. 1.11–12 Pindar says that the Muse loves to remember great contests, and at N. 3.79 the victor's fame depends on Clio's willingness. There is a full treatment of the Charites in Duchemin, 55–94. See also E. Schwarzenberg, *Die Grazien*, Bonn, 1966.

[3] *Il.* 9.189, 524–5, *Od.* 8.73; at *Il.* 6.357–8 Helen remarks that she and Paris will be made famous in song; cf. Eur. *Tro.* 1242–5.

[4] N. 5.1–5, cf. *P.M.G.* 954.

[5] Theognis 237–54, J. M. Edmonds' translation.   [6] See p. 85f.

Muses' and gain victories at Delphi and Olympia. This almost suggests that the prospect of immortality through song is an incitement as well as a reward.[1]

The interdependence of the fame of the poet (or his song) and the dedicatee is a frequent theme in Bacchylides, but it appears earlier as well, in Ibycus' address to Polycrates, ruler of Samos:

καὶ σύ, Πολύκρατες, κλέος ἄφθιτον ἑξεῖς
ὡς κατ' ἀοιδὰν καὶ ἐμὸν κλέος.

'You shall have undying fame too, Polycrates, because of my poem and my fame.'[2] Bacchylides' lines about fame normally lay an emphasis on truth: the achievement celebrated must be genuine. 'It is the Lydian stone which tests gold, but men's valour is tried by wisdom and all-conquering truth.'[3] He is less concerned with the ubiquity of fame than with its survival after death: 'a noble deed, provided it receives genuine hymns, is treasured on high by the gods; if it is true, it remains among men, even after the victor's death, the noblest of the Muses' playthings.'[4] Bacchylides makes the same points more explicitly in an ode for Hiero: 'the brightness of valour does not fade with the body: the Muse nurtures it. . . . Silence brings no adornment for the man who has succeeded; among deeds truly fine, someone will praise the charm of the honey-tongued nightingale of Ceos.'[5] If it is a high compliment to suggest that a man's name will live for ever, then the harsh critic can foretell oblivion: Sappho's words are echoed by Aeschylus in the *Frogs*: *his* poetry still lives, Euripides' died with him (and so he can refer to it).[6] Pindar gives new wealth to the theme of immortality when he says, in praise of Arcesilas and the rulers of Cyrene who preceded him, that dead kings listen attentively beneath the earth to 'great valour showered with gentle dew in the outpourings of revel-songs.'[7] Here valour is a flower watered by streams of praise, but more commonly praise itself is seen as a

---

[1] *I.* 1.64–7.

[2] *P.M.G.* 282.47–8. See Bowra, *G.L.P.*, 252–7, D. L. Page, *Aegyptus* 1951, 158–72, J. P. Barron, *C.R.* 1961, 187.   [3] fr. 14.   [4] 9.82–7.

[5] 3.90–8; cf. Euripides fr. 1028, *P.M.G.* 842.17–21 (Aristotle), *Protag.* 339A, *Symp.* 209D.

[6] *Frogs* 868–9; cf. Socrates' criticism of Tynnichus (*Ion* 534D). Sappho's poem is quoted on p. 110f.   [7] *P.* 5.96–103.

flower or a garland, as is appropriate in view of the fact that the victorious athlete was crowned with a wreath. There are two other Pindaric passages using the stream-motif in connection with fame. In the simpler of the two Pindar makes a promise to the athlete and his family: 'I will give them the pure water of Dirce to drink, the spring which the deep-girdled daughters of Mnemosyne of the golden robe caused to appear by the fortified gates of Cadmus.'[1] These lines imply not only that Pindar's poetry is a draught (sent from Thebes) for which the victor thirsts, but that coming from the daughters of Memory it will slake the thirst for fame. A similar passage in a *Nemean* ode has more complex imagery, but its concern with fame is obvious. 'If a man prospers he casts the pleasing cause of his success in the Muses' stream, since great feats of strength, left without song, lie in deep darkness. We know of only one mirror for noble deeds; if by grace of Mnemosyne with her gleaming crown is found requital of toils in famed verses.'

εἰ δὲ τύχῃ τις ἔρδων, μελίφρον᾽ αἰτίαν
ῥοαῖσι Μοισᾶν ἐνέβαλε · ταὶ μεγάλαι γὰρ ἀλκαὶ
σκότον πολὺν ὕμνων ἔχοντι δεόμεναι ·
ἔργοις δὲ καλοῖς ἔσοπτρον ἴσαμεν ἑνὶ σὺν τρόπῳ,
εἰ Μναμοσύνας ἕκατι λιπαράμπυκος
εὕρηται ἄποινα μόχθων κλυταῖς ἐπέων ἀοιδαῖς.

In prosaic language this means that a successful man commissions a poem of celebration. The imagery turns on the conventional contrast between the darkness of obscurity and the light of fame. Poetry here is a mirror reflecting success; the mirror belongs to Mnemosyne, the Recorder (the light image is reiterated in 'gleaming crown'). But poetry is also a stream which carries fame wherever it goes. (The images may be united by the picture of a sparkling stream reflecting light.)[2]

The garland metaphor owes its rich possibilities to the variety of associations it can use or suggest.[3] When an epinician ode is said to be a garland it means that the athletic triumph is

[1] *I.* 6.71–2; cf. 19 (ῥαινέμεν εὐλογίας), *P.* 8.60 and *I.* 5.60.

[2] *N.* 7.11–16. For the light of fame see also e.g. *I.* 7.23, *N.* 10.2–3, and p. 75.

[3] For φυλλοβολία (throwing flowers at athletes) see G. Giglioli, *Arch. Class.* 1950, 31–45.

crowned with song, and may suggest in addition the garlands worn by participants at symposia and banquets. As the poet weaves the garland we are reminded of the processes of composition, the joining together of words and melody, of myth, precept and praise, as when Pindar writes of 'weaving an intricate hymn'.[1] Since garlands might be made of flowers (although the garlands for victorious athletes were of bay, olive or wild celery) this image may focus attention simply on the beauty of flowers or on the flower as a symbol of abundance and fulfilment. The majority of occurrences of this metaphor in Pindar and Bacchylides are simple and lack elaboration:[2] the richest is found in a *Nemean* ode where Pindar, writing for an Aeginetan, assures him that the Muse is making him a garland of gold, ivory and coral. This garland will not fade or lose its value, a compliment appropriate to both victor and poet.[3]

[1] *O.* 6.86–7; cf. *O.* 6.105.
[2] ἄνθος, *O.* 6.105, *O.* 9.52; Bacch. 16.9, Paean 4.63–4; cf. *I.* 3 and 4.62, fr. 91.7–8, *O.* 1.14, *O.* 7.8.
[3] *N.* 7.77–9.

7. The Beginnings of Criticism

'The words of Mercury are harsh after the songs of Apollo.' When we study the fragmentary, scattered evidence of the earliest criticism proper we cannot help being conscious of a sense of anti-climax: in place of the glorification of the Muses' gifts apparent earlier we are apt to find a destructive attitude, niggling criticism of details, gossip, or, at best, summary praise. Almost for the first time we become aware that the 'critic' is being clever at poetry's expense. Yet it would be wrong to condemn the early theorists or the sophists out of hand: they are not the only critics to have adopted a negative attitude; their work has formed the basis for various aspects of literary studies.

In this chapter I shall be mainly concerned with the critical parts of Plato's *Protagoras* and Aristophanes' *Frogs*, but first I shall look briefly at some less familiar material. Our chief interest in studying the criticism of the fifth century probably lies in discovering what the critics said and in comparing it with the views propounded by Plato and Aristotle and their successors, but we shall also want to know who the critics were and how and where they published their work. Again, it should be possible to find out something about their methods.

First, who were the critics? We have seen that as early as the sixth century the philosophers Xenophanes and Heraclitus made known their opinions on literary topics; in the fifth century philosophers were joined by lyric poets, dramatists, sophists, historians and theorists in several branches of learning;[1] accordingly, we find relevant material in authors both famous and obscure, presented in allegory, in lyric poems or in

---

[1] G. Lanata, *Poetica Pre-Platonica* (Florence, 1963) collects a number of literary fragments, other than those occurring in Old Comedy, relevant to criticism. For convenience, I list here the names of less well-known writers of the sixth and fifth centuries whose critical fragments are not discussed in detail in the chapter: Pherecydes of Samos, Theagenes of Rhegium, Hellanicus of Lesbos, Damastes, Stesimbrotus of Thasos, Metrodorus of Lampsacus, Glaucus of Rhegium.

jokes. Unless the passages are very brief we shall know how specialized the critic's vocabulary is and whether he analyses, parodies or makes direct statements about his subject. Moreover, when we find an author recasting a myth we may suspect that he is implicitly finding fault with a predecessor who had told it differently. Finally, we need to try to read between the lines in the hope of learning about the critical principles and awareness of the writer and his age. Does the critic disclose beliefs about the essential nature and purpose of literature? Does he see literature as a manifestation of art or hold any general aesthetic theory? Is the critic accustomed to compare different authors' works in the same genre and to trace influences?

It is likely to be clear already not only that critical remarks occur piecemeal but that they are found in rather surprising surroundings. The works of the allegorists are a case in point. Where the ethical approach to literature had earlier resulted in attacks on Homer or Hesiod, in the hands of these writers it took the form of positive, allegorical interpretation.[1] It is possible that Pherecydes of Syros, a sixth-century cosmologist, had already found a hidden meaning in Homer, but the practice of allegory may best be illustrated from fifth-century writers and from Plato: Anaxagoras, for example, said that the true subjects of Homer's poetry were virtue and justice, and Metrodorus made Homer's gods, his Greeks and his Trojans all forces of nature.[2] Near the beginning of the *Phaedrus* Socrates puts forward a rationalizing interpretation of the myth of Boreas and Orithyia, but noticeably refrains from praising the allegorical method.[3] Allegory is a tool which the critic may use simply for exegesis of a difficult passage or for defence of one that is apparently 'immoral' or nonsensical (and in either case he may be drawing attention to the superiority if his own insight); there is also the possibility that allegorical interpretation of a respected author may be devised only to reinforce or illustrate some theory of one's own.

The ethical approach is evinced also by the musical theorist,

---

[1] J. Tate, *C.R.* 1927, 214–15, *C.Q.* 1929, 142–54, 1930, 1–10, 1934, 105–14.
[2] Pherecydes, D.-K. 5; Anaxagoras, D.-K. A1.11; Metrodorus, D.-K. 3; cf. 2, 4, 5.   [3] 229B–230A.

Damon, the associate of Prodicus and teacher of Pericles. Instruction in music had previously been committed to writing by Lasus of Hermione, Pindar's music teacher, probably fairly late in the sixth century, but it need not have conveyed ethical precepts.[1] The modern moralist may deplore the verbal content of songs and sometimes the orgiastic effect of their rhythmic reiteration, but Damon, and Plato after him, saw all music as inevitably affecting the soul of the hearer. Damon is a controversial figure, about whom we should like to know more: did he, for example, justify the assertions made in the following remark? 'Song and dance necessarily arise when the soul is in some way moved; liberal and beautiful songs and dances create a similar soul, and the reverse kind create a reverse kind of soul.'[2]

Damon's book, which we should perhaps rather describe as a pamphlet, illustrates the tendency for fifth-century theorists to publish handbooks containing their teaching. The surviving information about the titles and contents of these handbooks is not extensive, but we know that their subjects included art, literature and rhetoric: in the field of art we know of Parrhasius on painting, Polyclitus on sculpture, Agatharchus on scene-painting, Democritus and Anaxagoras on perspective; some of Plato's dialogues preserve reflections of early rhetorical teaching and its specialized vocabulary, and Sophocles' *On the Chorus* demonstrates the existence of a purely literary work.[3] One may make guesses about the needs and motives which led to the production of handbooks: rivalries among teachers might have caused a possessive attitude to doctrine, some of the material may have been too bulky for easy memorization or unsuitably formulated, or a book may have been produced to correct or amplify theories so far disseminated by word of mouth. Whatever the economics of the book trade in the last part of the fifth century, it is certain that the possession of a book could be

[1] *Suda s.v.* Lasus; cf. *P.M.G.* 702, about the Aeolian mode. See also Philolaus, D.-K. 11.
[2] D.-K. 6; see W. D. Anderson, *Ethos and Education in Greek Music* (Harvard/O.U.P. 1966) 38–42, 74–80, and *T.A.P.A.* 1955, 88–102; R. P. Winnington-Ingram, *Lustrum* 1958, 51–5.
[3] In general, see T. B. L. Webster, *C.Q.* 1939, 166–79, L. Radermacher, *Artium Scriptores* (S.B.Ö.A. 1951), G. A. Kennedy, *The Art of Persuasion in Greece* (Princeton 1963) 52–79 and *A.J.P.* 1959, 169–78. For Plato, see e.g. *Phaedrus* 266–7.

matter for a joke when the *Frogs* was written: unfortunately the joke is obscure.[1] The chorus conclude the *agon* proper by urging Aeschylus and Euripides to further intellectual bouts: 'if you're afraid that the spectators' ignorance may hinder their understanding of your subtleties, don't be anxious: it's not like that at all now. They're seasoned campaigners; each has a book and understands technical points; by nature they are powerful; now they're sharp as well.'[2] This military metaphor follows the picture of the contestants as epic warriors which has been established from the beginning of the contest and extends it to the audience, although not in epic language. The metaphor seems to say that the audience are good warriors by nature, that they are experienced in fighting and have been given an understanding of the practice of war by a military manual. If the metaphor is all of a piece, we are being told that the audience had already heard literary disputes and had read a book about literature (not a book about the art of war, nor any unspecified book): in the circumstances, the book might be about Homer or tragedy; that such a book had recently been published and quite widely circulated need not be doubted, but Aristophanes was flattering his audience, I suppose, in saying that they *all* had a copy.

The training of orators is likely to have included material we should classify as literary or linguistic, the study of grammar, figures of speech, vocabulary and metre; since illustrative material must often have been drawn from Homer and the poets, the boundary between rhetoric and criticism must have been crossed and re-crossed. Among the sophists, Protagoras, Prodicus, Gorgias and Hippias were known for work of this sort which must have seemed to the outsider otiose or pedantic.[3] At the same time, the foundations for another type of study were

[1] See E. G. Turner, *Athenian Books in the 5th. and 4th. centuries B.C.* (Inaugural lecture, 1952).

[2] *Frogs* 1109–16, discussed by L. Radermacher *ad loc.*, V. Ehrenberg, *The People of Aristophanes* (Oxford, 1951) 287.

[3] For mockery of Protagoras' work on gender see *Clouds* 658–79; for Gorgias' classification of figures of speech D.-K. A2; his teaching methods D.-K. 14 (Arist. *Soph. el.* 183b 36) and Plato *Phaedrus* 261B. For Prodicus see Plato *Cratyl.* 384B; for his work on synonyms etc. *Protag.* 337A, *Meno* 75E. For Hippias' work on Music and Rhythm see D.-K. A2, for his Homeric criticism *Hipp. Mi.* 364C, for his linguistic studies *Hipp. Ma.* 285B, *Hipp. Mi.* 368B.

being laid: literary history. One example will serve to show the writers' approach: 'However Anaximenes and Damastes and Pindar the lyric-poet say that Homer is Chian. Damastes says he belongs to the tenth generation after Musaeus.'[1] Interest is focused on the relative and absolute chronology of poets and on their birthplace or on anecdotes about their lives and characters. This sort of material was conveyed in works with titles like 'About the Poets' and also in general histories: witness Herodotus' opinion about the dates of Homer and Hesiod.[2]

The major source of surviving criticism is the work of poets and dramatists in the fifth century: some of their criticism is implied; in other cases they refer to their predecessors or contemporaries in such a way as to demonstrate their own artistic values as well as the existence of rivalries. Some of this material will be quoted and discussed later in the chapter, but first something needs to be said about Old Comedy as a vehicle for criticism: first, a writer, like any well-known contemporary figure, may be the victim of a joke; next, in the parabasis the comic dramatist often defends himself by attacking his rivals; finally, and most important, a writer may be the subject of one or more scenes in a play. The interpretation of critical material found in lyric poetry and in comedy is often difficult, whether because we lack the knowledge to grasp what was clear to the author's contemporaries or because he was deliberately allusive.

In Plato's *Ion* the rhapsode boasts that he can talk about Homer better than Metrodorus, Stesimbrotus, or Glaucon 'because of his more numerous and excellent insights'.[3] The writers Ion named are known to us as allegorists and historians; Homer was subjected to every possible variety of criticism from the anecdote to the encomium.[4] For the derivative poet of the *Birds* Homer is the poet *par excellence* and he ends each verse with the phrase κατὰ τὸν "Ομηρον, 'according to Homer'.[5] It may have

---

References to figures of speech include the intrusive *antonomasia* at *Thesm.* 58, *antitheton* (Ar. fr. 327), *eikon* (*Clouds* 559, *Frogs* 905).

[1] Damastes 5F 11a *F.G.H.*; cf. Democritus 16 D.-K., Glaucus 2 *F.G.H.*

[2] Herodotus 2.53; cf. 2.116–17; Glaucus wrote 'About Poets and Musicians', and similar titles are given for Antiphon and Damastes, among others.

[3] *Ion* 530C.

[4] Anecdote: e.g. Heraclitus, D.-K. 56; Democritus' reasoned praise is quoted on p. 86 f. [5] Aristophanes, *Birds* 910.

been during the fifth century that some of the *Certamen*, an account of a contest between Homer and Hesiod, was written.[1] The very fact that Homer was an authority and regularly quoted was enough to irritate fifth-century iconoclasts, who seem to have criticized factual and verbal inaccuracies in epic.[2] In the *Poetics* Aristotle provides several examples of detailed, sometimes rather petty, criticism of Homer: one he attributes to Protagoras, but no doubt many originated with the sophists: when Homer wrote 'Goddess, sing the wrath' he was uttering a command where he should have been praying.[3] Much more penetrating is Pindar's assessment of Homer's 'seductive narrative' already quoted: in the space of a few lines Pindar conveys his insight into Homer's poetry and the way it affects the hearer and also makes clear why he both admires and disapproves of him.[4]

The poems of Pindar show something of his attitude to other forerunners and contemporaries as well as to his own poetic task. I have already referred to the possible allusion to Simonides and Bacchylides in the Second *Olympian*; Pindar also wrote about Archilochus, comparing the iambographer's venom with his own idea of what was fitting: Archilochus, he says, 'fattens himself on the heavy phrases of his hatred'; this perhaps implies that the poet's character is affected by what he writes, the converse of the usual belief.[5]

Before I turn to the aims and methods of fifth-century criticism I must discuss briefly the problem of implicit criticism. Ibycus' address to Polycrates, as we have seen, hardly flatters the manner of epic,[6] but criticism of Homer is not the main

[1] See G. S. Kirk, *C.Q.* 1950, 149–50.

[2] *Il.* 6.146 is quoted in an elegiac poem (29D.1–2) attributed to the iambographer, Semonides of Amorgos; this may be the earliest Homeric quotation, but for this and other possible instances see J. A. Davison, *Eranos* 1955, 125–40.

[3] *Poetics* 1456b 15, cf. 1461a. See also Protagoras A 30 D.-K. and H. Apfel, *T.A.P.A.* 1938, 245–58.

[4] *N.* 7.20–4; see p. 118.

[5] *O.* 2.94–5; *P.* 2.54–5. The stories suggesting rivalry between Pindar and Myrtis or Pindar and Corinna are discussed by D. L. Page, *Corinna* (London, 1953) 31, 72. Myrtis was Pindar's contemporary, but Professor Page dates Corinna in the third century; the earlier dating is supported by A. E. Harvey, *C.Q.* 1955, 180, T.B.L. Webster, *Lustrum* 1956, 102.

[6] *P.M.G.* 282a; see p. 127, and cf. *P.M.G.* 298.

point of this poem. When we set the recognition scene of Euripides' *Electra* beside that of Aeschylus' *Choephori* it is hard to resist the belief that Aeschylus' version was unacceptable to Euripides, but was he criticizing the older dramatist?[1] Scholarly argument has considered the credibility of Aeschylus' account and his debt to tradition and also the motives which might have induced Euripides to create a sceptical Electra. An audience familiar with Aeschylus' play is likely to have been reminded of his treatment when they heard Electra discussing the lock, footprints and embroidery, but they need not have felt that the reminder was an indecorous interruption of the play they were watching: an awareness of novelities in treatment of myth or character is likely to have added to their enjoyment.

Although no fifth-century writer gives an account of structure in the systematic detail of the *Poetics* it is clear that it was recognized as a topic: the Aristotelian terms *synthesis* and *systasis* do not occur, but comments on several aspects of structure are not infrequent. Cratinus said that the tragic poet Acestor would deserve a beating if he failed to achieve unity and economy of incident, ἐὰν μὴ συστρέφῃ τὰ πράγματα, and a similar dislike of unwieldy length is noticeable in the *Frogs*.[2] Another comic poet, Metagenes, most likely in a parabasis, praises the variety of his invention: 'I vary my story with "episodes" so as to give the spectators a feast with plenty of novel side-dishes' (κατ᾽ ἐπεισόδιον μεταβάλλω τὸν λόγον, ὡς ἂν πολλαῖσι παροψίσι καὶ καιναῖς εὐωχήσω τὸ θέατρον).[3]

We have seen that Homer's use of the 'path of song' metaphor has structural implications and have noted in Odysseus' praise

[1] *Electra* 520–44, *Choephori* 167–232; see the brief discussion and references in J. D. Denniston's edition of *Electra*. See also *Phoenissae* 749 ff. and *Septem* 375 ff.

[2] Cratinus fr. 85, *Frogs* 911–15. For στοιβή, 'padding', see *Frogs* 1178.

[3] Metagenes fr. 14; see G. Norwood, *C.P.* 1930, 217–29. I suspect that 'episode' here means neither what is irrelevant to the plot nor whatever occurs between choral odes: Metagenes may introduce new characters, or attractive song and dance, to enliven the progress of his story. His boast is not quite like that of Aristophanes in the *Clouds*: ἀλλ᾽ ἀεὶ καινὰς ἰδέας ἐσφέρων σοφίζομαι, οὐδὲν ἀλλήλαισιν ὁμοίας καὶ πάσας δεξιάς (547–8). 'I show my mastery by the continual novelty of my dramatic ideas, all different, all skilful.' ἰδέας probably refers to scenes like that of Socrates in a basket communing with the air, where the stage picture presents immediately and vividly what would take several sentences to explain; cf. Protagoras A30 D.-K.

of Demodocus' narrative skill the expression *kata kosmon* which
seems to allude to the precise and vivid ordering of the story so
that the listener feels he is participating in the events described:
subsequent uses of *kosmos* in a literary context also tell us about
the shaping of material.[1] An early elegiac poem by the Athenian
statesman Solon began

αὐτὸς κῆρυξ ἦλθον ἀφ' ἱμερτῆς Σαλαμῖνος
κόσμον ἐπέων ᾠδὴν ἀντ' ἀγορῆς θεμένος

'I myself have come as a herald from fair Salamis, having composed, instead of a speech, a poem, an ordered structure of
verse.'[2] With *kosmos* Democritus used the verb τεκταίνομαι,
'build', not 'compose'.[3]

Readers of the later critics in antiquity are familiar with their
practice of distinguishing an author by one adjective, often
metaphorical, which usually describes his manner or style.
The poets of Old Comedy, too, often attached one-word labels,
but the effect of these tended to be as much humorous as
critical. The most obvious example is calling the poet Agathon
agathos, 'good', but there is also play with the critical vogue-
word ψυχρός which is used where we might say of a joke or a
story 'it leaves me cold'. In the *Thesmophoriazusae* Aristophanes
connects character, or personality, and the work produced: the
writer Theognis, frigid by nature, makes frigid plays (ψυχρὸς ὢν
ψυχρῶς ποιεῖ).[4] It is probably popular belief, hardly to be called
a critical doctrine, that an artist's work reflects his nature, and
the cliché is exploited for comic purposes, as when Euripides in
the *Frogs* accounted for Aeschylus' failure to portray women in
love by saying that he lacked Aphrodite.[5] The view that the
poet should keep silence about what is shameful is turned
against Archilochus by Critias when he says that we should have
remained ignorant of all that was disreputable in the parentage,

---

[1] *Od.* 8.489, quoted above, p. 121. Another possible Homeric allusion to structure has been seen in *Od.* 8.170: θεὸς μορφὴν ἔπεσι στέφει ('God puts a crown
of beauty/shapeliness on his words'); cf. 11.367, which may well be an inter-
polation; μορφή is not found elsewhere in Homer. See D. L. Page, *The Homeric
Odyssey* (Oxford, 1955), 35, 49, n.17.

[2] Solon 2D; cf. Eupolis fr. 303 διάθεσιν ᾠδῆς.

[3] Democritus 21 D.-K., quoted above p. 86 f.; cf. Parmenides 8.50-2 D.-K.
and Pindar fr. 231.

[4] *Thesm.* 170; cf. 848, *Ach.* 140 and Eupolis fr. 244.   [5] 1043-8.

career and character of Archilochus if he had not told us himself. This literal, humourless approach to what an author says is an extreme manifestation of the identification of poetry and poet; perhaps Critias writes ironically.[1] A passage of Euripides reinforces the idea expressed in comedy that a writer has, as it were, to get into the skin of the character he is creating, an idea which recurs in some form in the pages of Aristotle, Horace and Quintilian. Euripides says only that a poet who desires to evoke joyful emotions must experience them himself as he writes, but Aristophanes shows Agathon in the guise of a woman when he is creating a tragic heroine, and he suggests that Euripides writes more effectively about cripples when he is lying down.[2] A fragment of Aristophanes interestingly contrasts the nature and work of Euripides: the same Euripides who is awkward and humourless even after wine is the one whose verse has the taste of Sirens and honey.[3] A saying attributed to Simonides uses the simple metaphorical description to introduce a fuller comparison of Homer and Hesiod: 'Simonides called Hesiod a gardener, Homer a maker of garlands. Hesiod created stories about gods and heroes: Homer wove them into garlands – the *Iliad* and the *Odyssey*.'[4] The sophist Gorgias, who seems to have had a special interest in tragedy, provides an early instance of the characterization of a literary work in one telling phrase, 'a play full of Ares' applied to the *Seven against Thebes*.[5] Forceful or revealing as these passages may be, as criticism they are primitive in comparison with Sophocles' remarks reported by Plutarch and others.

We are told that Sophocles 'formed a thiasos in honour of the Muses', and it is possible that this was a literary circle whose discussions influenced the production of Sophocles' handbook *On the Chorus*.[6] According to Plutarch Sophocles was conscious of three stages in the evolution of his style, first the heavy pomposity of Aeschylus, next a style of his own, but one with

---

[1] Critias 44 D.-K.

[2] *Supplices* 180–3; *Thesm.* 148–52; *Ach.* 410–11.　　　[3] fr. 676b.

[4] Gnomol. Paris, p. 59, n. 217.

[5] Gorgias 24 D.-K., *Frogs* 1021; see Arist., *Rhet.* 1406b 14.

[6] *Life* 6: ταῖς Μούσαις θίασον ἐκ τῶν πεπαιδευμένων συναγαγεῖν. The members may have been actors, but cf. the use of παιδεύω 'educated', 'cultivated' e.g. at *Laws* 685D.

forced and unpleasing characteristics, finally a style that was
adaptable and so better than the earlier two.[1] Sophocles seems
to have believed not only that he was influenced by Aeschylus
at the beginning of his own career, but that the evolution of
style is under the control of the writer and that he is conscious
of his aims: it is in this connection that his reproach to Aeschylus
should be read: 'If you do write as you should, it's not by
design'.[2] The comparison of Euripides' character-drawing with
his own is too well known to need discussion here, but it is
perhaps worth speculating on the arrangement of a work which
may have included comparisons of tragedians with regard to
style and character.[3] We should very much like to know
whether Sophocles considered tragic writers one by one or
whether he dealt with topics like construction, lyric and character. As we shall see later, the criticism in the *Frogs* shows
familiarity with a method of proceeding by topics whereas in the
Protagoras exegesis of a single poem is the rule; titles like *On the
Poets* suggest that writers were treated separately.[4]

It is unfortunate that Sophocles' account of the development
of his style does not appear verbatim in Plutarch, since our
information about stylistic and other critical vocabulary in the
fifth century has many gaps. We know that, in addition to the
ordinary adjectives 'good', 'fine' and the like, certain critical
adjectives became fashionable in the fifth century; ψυχρός I have
mentioned already; ὀρθός ('correct'), ἀστεῖος ('witty'), κομψός
('elegant'), στρογγύλος ('round') and γλαφυρός ('hollow') belong
in the same class: these words are either metaphorical, or they
are specialized uses of common terms, and in these characteristics they resemble other critical vocabulary.[5]

The adjectives listed in the previous paragraph were no doubt

[1] *de profect. in virt.* 7, p. 79B. It is possible that this and the two passages
next quoted originated in Sophocles' book. See T. B. L. Webster, *An Introduction to Sophocles* (Oxford, 1936, paperback edition, London, 1969) 7, 57,
Bowra, *Problems*, 108–25, H. Lloyd-Jones, *J.H.S.* 1955, 158–9.
[2] Athen. 428F.   [3] *Poetics* 1460b 33.
[4] See *Protag.* 347B for Hippias' readiness to expound Simonides' *aretē* poem.
[5] ὀρθός and cognate words were important in the terminology of Protagoras
and Prodicus; see e.g. Plato *Phaedrus* 267C, *Euthyd.* 277E, Ar. *Ach.* 397,
Birds 692; for ἀστεῖος see Arist. *Rhet.* 1410b 20, *Clouds* 204, *Frogs* 901, κομψός
Birds 195, *Rhesus* 625, Isocrates 12.1, στρογγύλος *Ach.* 685, Ar. frs. 199, 471,
Phaedrus 234E, γλαφυρός *Birds* 1272.

first used critically by men professionally engaged in rhetoric, and there are a few other terms we can safely attribute to sophists and their fellows, but many uncertainties remain; as a result, we cannot always distinguish between terms used by ordinary people in talking about poetry and those coined or modified to meet the needs of a literary coterie.[1] What adds to our difficulties is that it sometimes happens that a word retains its everyday meaning while also developing one or more limited or colloquial significances, rather like 'book' or 'lyric' in English. Even if we did not know from reading Homer that there were terms denoting particular types of poetry at this early period we should probably have guessed that songs for weddings or funerals would acquire their own names. Some quasi-technical terms must have been needed for arranging a performance or commissioning a particular type of song; some musical terms must have been indispensable, and after the birth of drama author and chorus-leader at least could do with quick ways of referring to parts of plays.

In view of the importance of criticism by genres from antiquity down to recent times it is unfortunate that we often cannot securely interpret words like dithyramb or iambic: in some cases difficulties arise from insufficiency of examples, in others the name changes its application. Again, the categories of lyric poetry established by Alexandrian scholars can mislead us if we assume them to be those of the fifth century.[2]

There is, however, fifth-century evidence for critical theories about genres which does not depend on disputed terminology. Aeschylus in the *Frogs* maintains that diction and costume should match the tragic dignity of heroic characters: that a less

[1] The verb διαιρεῖν is used of the sort of close analysis established by the sophists: see *Protag.* 338E, *Hipp. Mai.* 285C, *Clouds* 740–2. For 5th century noun-formations in -σις and -μα see E. Handley, *Eranos* 1953, 129–42 and C. Peppler, *A.J.P.* 1916, 459–65.

[2] For categories of lyric poetry see *Ion* 534C, *Laws* 700A–B, 764D–E, H. Weir Smyth, *Greek Melic Poets* (London, 1900), intro. xxiii–cxxxiv, M. Bowra, *G.L.P.* 5–9, H. Färber, *Die Lyrik in der Kunsttheorie der Antike* (Munich, 1936), A. E. Harvey, *C.Q.* 1955, 157–75; see also K. J. Dover, *Archilochus* (Fondation Hardt *Entretiens* Tome X), 181–212 (elegy and iambus), D. L. Page in *Greek Poetry and Life*, 206–30 (elegy), A. W. Pickard-Cambridge, *D.T.C.*[2] 1–59 (dithyramb), A. M. Dale, *Eranos* 1950, 14–20 (stasimon and hyporcheme), A. Delatte, *Ant. Class.* 1938, 23–9 (δαμώματα in Stesichorus *P.M.G.* 212), W. B. Stanford, *Hermath.* 1957, 65–72 (ἔπη).

grand function was considered appropriate for comedy is perhaps shown by comic poets' claims to be taken seriously; in the *Frogs* the chorus pray that they may say 'much that is funny, much that is serious', and in the *Acharnians* the line τὸ γὰρ δίκαιον οἶδε καὶ τρυγῳδία ('Comedy, too, knows what is right') has a similar implication.[1] Some of the effectiveness of parody, as we shall see, depends on a clear demarcation between genres: to take an early example and one unconcerned with literary criticism, Hipponax' attack on a glutton shows what is gained when content and treatment collide:

Μοῦσά μοι Εὐρυμεδοντιάδεα τὴν ποντοχάρυβδιν,
τὴν ἐγγαστριμάχαιραν, ὃς ἐσθίει οὐ κατὰ κόσμον,
ἔννεφ᾽ ὅπως ψηφῖδι κακὸς κακὸν οἶτον ὄληται
βουλῇ δημοσίῃ παρὰ θῖν᾽ ἁλὸς ἀτρυγέτοιο.

'Tell, Muse, of Eurymedon's son, sea-swallower, knife-belly, who eats without order or decency; tell how he will meet the evil fate he deserves, by stoning, by decree of the people, at the edge of the unwearied sea.'[2] The use of epic phrases and of devices like the Muse-invocation emphasizes the difference between the glutton's repulsive ways and the conduct admired in epic heroes, but at the same time gives the abuse a scale and amplitude it would otherwise lack.[3] The hexameters which the poet and politician Critias wrote about Anacreon about the end of the fifth century show that he had a very clear idea of the characteristics of one genre at least: he seems to be in the course of describing writers of love-poetry and associates Anacreon's poems with symposia, seductions, the music of auloi and barbiton; like wine, his poetry is sweet and grief-assuaging.[4]

We have now seen what tools were available to the fifth-century critic and some of the ways he used them. It remains to consider a major problem, the origin and development of theorizing in general and of specific individual theories.[5] It is

---

[1] *Frogs* 1058-61, 389-90; *Ach.* 500. See also Arist. *Rhet.* 1419b 3.

[2] Hipponax 77D; see the commentary in D. A. Campbell, *Greek Lyric Poetry*, 376.

[3] There is a similar difference between conventional and actual material in (?) Simonides' 'epitaph' for Timocreon (99D) and in Timocreon's encomium attacking Themistocles (*P.M.G.* 727).

[4] Critias 8D.   [5] See T. B. L. Webster, *C.Q.* 1939, 166-79.

necessary at the outset to make a distinction between the expression of an opinion and the formulation of a theory: for example, someone may say, perhaps giving utterance to a widely-held, tacit assumption, 'Poetry gives pleasure.' He is not a theorist, but his remark may lead a successor to proclaim that it is poetry's function to give pleasure, not to educate, and now we have, in embryo, the hedonistic theory. It is difficult to read Aristotle's account of Catharsis or Plato's of Mimesis without being affected by subsequent interpretations and distortions, still less without curiosity as to the origins of the theory. It would be possible to look for signs of a catharsis-theory in Gorgias or Antiphon, but it seems better to concentrate here on the problem of Mimesis since it must involve consideration of the relationship between different arts. The chief question must be: did Plato invent the theory of Mimesis, saying for the first time that Art was only a copy of reality? We shall not detract from Plato's originality as a thinker if we suppose that the word Mimesis, together with some idea that, for example, a painting imitates a real object, was already known to him. We need to examine earlier occurrences of words cognate with *mimesis*, noticing them particularly when they are used in a literary or artistic context, but it is just as important to discover, if possible, early evidence that the excellence of an artist was thought to depend on his skill as an imitator, or that poet and painter, *qua* imitators, were thought to serve one mistress, Art.[1] It is possible to find introductions to aesthetic theory which assume that the Greeks had discovered an essential kinship between the arts, in the processes of creation and in their effect on the spectator or listener, and that they had discerned that works of art, together with experiences and emotions peculiar to them, belonged together, with the label 'aesthetic' attached to them. This assumption seems to be made partly because analogies between arts are undeniably old, but also because stylistic and other resemblances between different arts at any one period have so often been observed. When Xenophanes called impious

---

[1] The history of the word *mimesis* has been studied by G. Else, *C.P.* 1958, 73–90 and G. Sörbom, *Mimesis and Art* (Stockholm, 1966). I use 'imitate' rather than 'represent' or 'enact' to make the discussion easier to follow in English.

legends *plasmata* he demonstrated his realization that legends, like clay figures, can be made; that poet and modeller are to this extent alike.[1] I doubt, however, that we should go on to infer that men are misled by clay figures, as they may be by impious myths. Xenophanes has used a metaphor in which the disparate objects compared are like in one respect. Similarly with Pindar when he finds resemblances between what he writes and a building or statue.[2] In the Fifth *Nemean* Pindar points out that his poems travel; they are not fixed in one place like a statue.[3] We can see that near the beginning of the fifth century it was possible, and perhaps customary, to compare products of the different arts with regard to their beauty, their share in honouring gods or men, the fact that they were 'made'. There is no evidence that a building or painting was considered to be 'inspired' in the way that a poem was inspired, or to influence men for good or ill.

We do not know when to date either of Simonides' fragments about poetry, but his death in 468 antedated the introduction of the illusionistic style of painting, so the grounds on which he compared the two arts are different from those of the author of the *Dissoi Logoi*, who believed that the creation of illusion was the artist's greatest achievement.[4] When Simonides remarked 'Painting is silent poetry, poetry is painting which speaks' the epigrammatic, almost paradoxical tone of his words makes his observation sound new.[5] The second fragment is plain in expression but new, as far as we know, in content: ὁ λόγος τῶν πραγμάτων εἰκών ἐστι.[6] The plain style does not accompany transparently-clear meaning: is Simonides' emphasis like that of Plato – 'a story (only) imitates reality'? Or is he saying that it is real events which are represented in literature? Or would this paraphrase convey his thought – 'when you hear a story you picture the events taking place'? If the third version is right Simonides is drawing attention to the same qualities which Odysseus commended in Demodocus. I am inclined to think that either the second or third version fits better than the first with the observation preserved by Plutarch. Simonides must be comparing painting and poetry on the ground that both imitate: an

[1] Xenophanes 1D.22, quoted on p. 114. [2] See p. 95. [3] *N*. 5.1–2.
[4] See p. 116. [5] Plutarch, *de gloria Ath.* 3.346F. [6] Simonides fr. 190D.

143

incident in the Trojan War could be described by a poet or painted on a vase and conveyed equally vividly in either medium. It is possible to go one step further, remembering Aristotle's distinction between narrative and *mimesis* in epic, and suggest that Simonides is comparing the silent scene on the vase with the one in which the characters speak. It may be that this interpretation limits Simonides' meaning too strictly, but a reading of the Danae poem shows the value Simonides placed on pictorial narrative.[1]

A writer like Pindar uses analogies with the visual arts in order to fill the minds of his hearers with splendid pictures: his interest in the relationship between a poem and a statue has different motives from those of the prose writers. It is unfortunate that we know little about the attitude of writers towards music: we have seen evidence that music was held to affect the moral character of the listener, and in this respect it could obviously have been compared with poetry, but, on the other hand, it seems unlikely that music was felt to have the permanence of song or a building. During the course of the fifth century it is probable that making comparisons between the arts became fashionable and led to the belief that they were allied in a more essential way than had previously been thought.[2] It is not impossible that some critic thought that the most important characteristic linking the arts was the fact that they imitated reality: a doctrine of this sort is unlikely to have been put forward by a sophist concerned to demonstrate the power of Logos or to have been widely accepted.

There survive two examples of 'practical criticism' in the fifth century; in each, criticism is an object of laughter. Plato's dialogue, the *Protagoras*, is set in the house of the wealthy Callias, a comfortable gathering-place for intellectuals. The 'dramatic' date of the dialogue is the late 430s when Protagoras was about sixty and Socrates in his thirties. Two other well-known sophists, Hippias of Elis and Prodicus of Ceos, were among the company. Protagoras claims that his pupils acquire *aretē*, which can therefore be taught: he attempts to overcome Socrates' scepticism by describing how men learned to live in communities and to acquire political wisdom and morality.

---

[1] *P.M.G.* 543.   [2] See *Phaedrus* 275E and Xenophon, *Mem.* 3.10.

Socrates, as in the *Meno*, proposes that *aretē* must be defined before one can decide if it can be taught. Among the attempts at definition is the long passage in which Simonides' poem about *aretē* is criticized.[1] This section does not advance the philosophical argument, but it does show some of the participants in a ridiculous light.

The criticism is framed by two general statements, one enunciated by Protagoras and the other by Socrates. 'In my opinion, Socrates, the most important part of a man's education is to be expert in poetry (περὶ ἐπῶν δεινὸν εἶναι), that is, to be able to recognize, understand and distinguish the correct and the incorrect in poetry and give reasons for one's opinions.' There is no cause to doubt that the beliefs of the historical Protagoras are here expressed, and it is interesting to see that he requires criticism to be more than *ex cathedra* pronouncement; it is just possible that he saw the need for literary perceptiveness, something more than pure intelligence. He judges poetry by the standard of ὀρθότης, 'correctness'.

Socrates' concluding remarks constitute a crushing and clever attack on poetry: talking about poetry is like having paid entertainers at a party, a thing only vulgar people do. Educated people entertain one another out of their own intellectual and musical resources, needing no outsiders, not even poets. So discussions like the present should be concerned to test truth and the participants themselves. It is impossible to ask a poet what he means and impossible to reach agreement about his meaning.[2] Socrates does not actually say that poets tell lies or liken them to dancing-girls, but the smear is implicit.

Formally the Simonides section balances Protagoras' account of evolution, allowing Socrates a parallel opportunity of displaying one aspect of *his* sophistic technique, and, incidentally, of ridiculing Prodicus as well as Protagoras. As in a dramatic *agon*, the loser speaks first. Simonides' poem on *aretē* does present real difficulties of interpretation,[3] but the solution proposed by Socrates is dishonest and quibbling.

---

[1] *Prot.* 339–348B. The Simonides poem, which is incomplete, is *P.M.G.* 542.

[2] 347C–348A; cf. *Phaedrus* 275E.

[3] See A. W. H. Adkins, *Merit and Responsibility* (Oxford, 1960) 165–8, 196–7, 355–9, and L. Woodbury, *T.A.P.A.* 1953, 135–163.

Protagoras begins by setting the inconsistent passages side by side:

> Hard is it on the one hand to become
> A good man truly, hands and feet and mind
> Foursquare, wrought without blame

and

> Nor do I count as sure the oft-quoted word
> Of Pittacus, though wise indeed he was
> Who spoke it. To be noble, said the sage,
> Is hard.[1]

Protagoras requires that the poem should be both καλός and ὀρθός 'beautiful', and 'correct', and suggests that an inconsistent poem cannot be καλός. Socrates denies inconsistency and introduces the first of his hair-splitting verbal definitions, calling for Prodicus' support. 'Be' and 'become', he says, mean different things. He adduces a quotation from Hesiod in support of his argument. Protagoras makes a common-sense reply, but Socrates continues with a misinterpretation of the word 'hard', which he is forced to recant, thereby leaving his ally Prodicus out on a limb.

The second stage in the discussion is Socrates' explanation of the poem: the motive of his lengthy preamble is no doubt mockery of the 'long speeches' of the sophists and rhetoricians, and his subject-matter too is unexpected. Socrates says that the Spartans purport to be superior in courage and warfare, but disguise their superior wisdom for fear it may be imitated. However, their wisdom can be seen in their brilliant, pithy sayings. This gnomic style has been copied by the sages, among them Pittacus, and Simonides, ambitious for philosophical repute, realized that he must be seen to excel Pittacus. His poem therefore was so constructed as to refute Pittacus' saying.

If this introduction is typical of sophistic criticism, it gives us two interesting facts: first that criticism could already include discussion of a writer's personal motives, and, second, that there was some attempt at setting a poem in a wider historical or national context: that the present attempt is futile is beside the point.

Now the exegesis proper. Its technique is the close scrutiny

[1] Professor Guthrie's translation.

146

of a passage, its syntax, word-order and thought. The tools are reputable enough, and, if rightly used, could help to elucidate this difficult poem. What is surprising is to find linguistic and philosophical criticism closely allied: had the sophists' critical methods reached this point? The argument is long, unnecessarily so, and tedious, as mockery of pedantry is likely to be, and I choose two passages to illustrate it, again from Professor Guthrie's translation. The first (343D–4A) demonstrates verbal, the second (344C–D) philosophical, analysis. 'At the very beginning of the poem, it seems crazy, if he wished to say that it is hard to become a good man, that he should then insert "on the one hand". The insertion seems to make no sense, except on the supposition that Simonides is speaking polemically against the saying of Pittacus. Pittacus said, "Hard is it to be noble", and Simonides replied, disputing the point, "No; to *become* a good man is hard truly" – not, by the way, "to become truly good": he does not refer the "truly" to that, as if some men were truly good and others good but not truly so. That would strike people as silly and unlike Simonides. We must transpose the word "truly" in the poem, thus as it were implying the saying of Pittacus before it, as if he spoke first and Simonides were answering his words. Thus "O men, hard it is to be noble"; and Simonides replies, "That is not true, Pittacus; not to *be* but to *become* a good man, foursquare in hands and feet and mind, wrought without blame, that is hard truly." ' 'A little further on Simonides says, as if he were developing an argument, that although to become a good man is truly difficult, yet it is possible, for a while at least; but having become good, to remain in this state and *be* a good man – which is what you were speaking of, Pittacus – is impossible and super-human. This is the privilege of a god alone, whereas

> he cannot but be bad, whom once
> Misfortune irredeemable casts down.

Now who is cast down by irredeemable misfortune in the management of a ship? Clearly not the passenger, for he has *been* down all the time. You cannot knock down a man who is lying on the ground, you can only knock him down if he is standing, and put him on the ground. In the same way irredeemable misfortune may cast down the resourceful, but not the man who is helpless all the time. The steersman may be reduced to helplessness by the onset of a great storm, the farmer by a bad season, and the doctor from some analogous misfortune; for the good may become bad, as another poet has testified in the line

"The good are sometimes bad and sometimes noble;"

but the bad man cannot become bad, but *is* so of necessity. So it is that the resourceful and wise and good, when irredeemable disaster brings him to nought, cannot but be bad.'

The tone of this criticism is didactic; its author is not trying to spread appreciation of the poem but to win others to his interpretation. He praises it in passing ('an elegant and well-thought-out production') but sees himself as superior to, and uniquely able to understand, the poet; he cannot resist the temptation of adding otiose, 'learned' footnotes ('note that he uses the Lesbian dialect here because he is addressing Pittacus').[1]

Aristophanes' *Frogs* had its first performance in 405, about fifteen years before the *Protagoras* was written; its literary criticism is at least as difficult to assess, since it forms only one part of a rich and complex whole. Dionysus succeeds in reaching Hades in his quest for Euripides, and finds him on the point of competing with Aeschylus for the throne of tragedy; the second half of the play is concerned with the contest. Formally the core of the literary competition is the *agon* (894–1088), but this is preceded by an introductory scene between two slaves (756–811) and a preliminary bout when the rivals first appear. After the *agon* proper four scenes are devoted to individual aspects of the poets' work, prologues, lyric, monody and 'weight'. The play ends with Aeschylus' triumphant return to Athens.

Aeschylus, Euripides, Dionysus and the chorus practise literary criticism: their author, through them, criticizes criticism. These two functions are not accomplished by straightforward exegesis, but dramatically and humorously. I should like to illustrate this richness of material and texture by examining the dialogue between Dionysus' slave and Pluto's, and the choral songs at the beginning of the contest. The two slaves (755) have just become sworn allies when Xanthias hears

[1] 344B, 346E.

148

a shouting-match. The tragic poets, shorn of tragic pomp, have
quarrelled about the free meals and place of honour given to the
best artists. The criminal classes, we learn, went mad about
Euripides' crooked double-talk, and demanded a contest.
Aeschylus' supporters were few: the better type of citizen is as
scarce in Hades as in Athens. So Aristophanes implies a connection between Aeschylus, aristocracy, goodness, while giving
the audience the pleasure of hearing themselves abused; he picks
up the theme of the parabasis (718–37) which will recur in the
political questions at the play's end (1420–65). The latter part
of the scene establishes that literature is for Euripides a commodity whose shape and dimension can be measured and tested
(it will be weighed later): here Euripides is shown as devotee of
the new criticism, working in craft-metaphors. So this preliminary scene has essentially a debunking purpose, the slaves'
eye view of brawling poets and of poetry put to the test.

There is one hint of the different picture to follow: Aeschylus,
according to Pluto's slave, responding to Euripides' challenge,
lowered his head and glared like a bull. And it is as animals that
the chorus see the tragedians. Their four stanzas, whose immediate dramatic purpose is to whet our appetite for the
emergence of Aeschylus and Euripides, describe the coming
struggle in epic terms. Warriors are like wild animals, words like
weapons, as in Homer. The battle-imagery is to be continued in
two succeeding odes: this is not just a quarrel but a heroic conflict, and it would not be impossible to find points of resemblance
between, say, Aeschylus and Achilles or Euripides and Odysseus.
The song has Aeschylean features too, not only in its fondness
for compound adjectives and its 'difficulty', but metrically (and
so, one would suppose, in melody and movement as well).[1]
Euripides gets a smaller share of the chorus' attention, although
there is probably a hint of his fondness for s's as well as his
dependence on talk and his finicky intellectualism:

> Soon the tester of verse, the smooth tongue, solely sound,
> Issues forth, putting spurs to the horse of its envy . . .

> ἔνθεν δὴ στοματουργός, ἐπῶν βασανίστρια, λίσπη
> γλῶσσ᾽, ἀνελισσομένη φθονερούς κινοῦσα χαλινούς[2] . . .

---

[1] I discuss the metrical parody with that of 1264 ff.   [2] 826–7.

The inborn valour of the true warrior will be matched against the acquired skill of the craftsman: *physis* against *technē*.

Major and minor themes have been prepared, and the contestants' portraits sketched: the moment they appear, blows strike home. Aeschylus is silent, with the boring, customary silence of a character from one of his plays, until Euripides goes too far: 'I know him, I've had my eye on him, writes about savages, says what he likes, him with his unbridled, uncontrolled, unbarrèd tongue, his one-track mind, his bags of boasts.' Aeschylus: 'Say you so, you offspring of the green goddess? You say this to me, you picker-up of mini-maxims, you patchwork poet with your mendicants; you won't get away with this.'[1] Name-calling and bad temper, but the material has been used before (at least as far back as the *Acharnians* of 425) and will be used again.

What features of the tragedians' work are directly attacked in this contest? The prime targets are Euripides' characters and Aeschylus' style. Aeschylus is hard for ordinary people to understand because of his unbroken flow, his long words, his exotic subject-matter, his tautology and irrelevance.[2] Euripides' characters are either downright wicked ('all these erring Cretan ladies' as Miss Dale calls them in the introduction to the *Alcestis*), unsuitably talkative or lacking in tragic stature.[3] Direct criticism, which is mainly contained in the preliminary bout, the agon proper and the first of the subsequent scenes, also reveals Euripides' desire to communicate with rich and poor alike, and Aeschylus' determination to inspire men to heroism. Aeschylus also enunciates one more purely literary principle, the belief that lofty subjects demand a similar style of utterance and stage-production, while Euripides provides a glimpse of less elevated motives when he sees the Aeschylean silent character as a device for producing what Dryden called 'a yawning kind of expectation'. We deduce from reading these passages that fifth-century critical discussion dealt not only with the moral effects of literature, but with the concept of the 'appropriate' and with the practical aspects of tragic structure. It seems likely, too, that Euripides has some experience of systematic criticism;

[1] 836-43.   [2] See especially 923-42, 1126-79.
[3] See especially 1042 ff. and 1078-827.

at least, he specifies component parts of a play – dialogue, lyric and plot (if νεῦρα, 'sinews', in 862 does mean 'plot'), and he attacks Aeschylus' prologues before his lyrics.

Not surprisingly, both poets are aware of their poetic inheritance, Aeschylus seeing himself as the follower of Phrynichus, Euripides of Aeschylus.[1] Again, Euripides personifies the dramatic art, perhaps adopting a newly-fashionable way of talking. When Aeschylus wishes to perform one of his rival's lyrics and calls on Euripides' Muse to perform the accompaniment, the comic extension of the traditional function of the Muses is not difficult: grotesque lyrics, therefore grotesque Muse. The passage in which tragedy is a fat woman is a little bolder: Euripides says: 'But the minute I inherited the Art from you, swollen with bombast and overweight phrases, I put her on a diet and reduced her weight with pithy sayings and exercise and pale beetroot, and gave her essence of verbosity distilled from books. Next I built her up again with monodies.'[2] This passage is typical of Aristophanes' exuberance in mixing medical and literary terminology, but its view of literature as a human being is not unparalleled. Near the beginning of the play Dionysus condemned the dramatists who trifled with tragedy: 'You could look and look and not find a seminal poet, one to voice a highborn speech'. Heracles: 'What do you mean, "seminal" (γόνιμος)?' 'I mean one who will utter something a bit daring, like "atmosphere, Zeus' apartment", or "Time's foot".'[3] Simonides' likening of Hesiod to a gardener who can make new plants grow finds a parallel later in the century in the use of τίκτω, 'give birth to' in the writings of comic poets and Euripides.[4] Aeschylus' swollen Tragedy has a sister in Music as depicted by the comic poet Pherecrates: she has been ill-used by a succession of progressive composers, Melanippides, Phrynis, Cinesias, Timotheus.[5]

It is noteworthy that Euripides more often defends himself

---

[1] 1298 ff., 940.   [2] 939–44.
[3] 92–102. The metaphor from procreation, now 'faded', was also newly-borrowed from medicine.
[4] *Clouds* 530, *Frogs* 1059, Cratinus fr. 199, Eur. *Supplices* 180–3, *H.F.* 767; cf. Plato, *Symposium* 196E.
[5] fr. 157K (144B, 145E); see I. Henderson, *The New Oxford History of Music*, vol. i. (London, 1957), p. 394 (with n. 2).

with reasoned argument while Aeschylus counter-attacks with abuse. The reason for this may be partly to show Euripides the know-all intellectual, partly to accompany Aeschylus' characteristic epic wrath with something more at home in comedy. The picture of the craftsman Euripides fussing over the polishing of his phrases is set against that of Aeschylus, the poet whose genius (*physis*) drives him irresistibly on. It is Aeschylus, for instance, who is deliberately rude about Euripides' mother and his marriage and implies that he spends his time drinking with harlots.[1] Of course, the old jokes about Euripides must be heard, but the Aeschylus of this play delivers them with relish. Aeschylus, too, makes the more broadly comic attacks, destroying Euripides' prologues with a 'little oil-flask' and demonstrating his lack of weight for all to see. The strongest contrast between the two methods is presented in the lengthy prologue-scene (1119–1248). Euripides gives an example of word-by-word criticism (κατ᾽ ἔπος 1198) of the type practised in the *Protagoras* and no doubt made fashionable by the sophists: his targets are inaccuracy and tautology, and his pedantry is made harder to stomach by his excitement, shown in exaggerating the number of his rival's faults, conceit and petulance. Dionysus' reaction is bewilderment and a feeling that he'd better keep count with pebbles to prevent any further exaggeration (1263). Aeschylus' response is apparently to use the same technique (1180–1), but it is interestingly different: 'Once was Oedipus a happy man.' 'Nonsense,' replies Aeschylus, 'born unhappy,' and he goes on to recount the story of Oedipus in the least pedantic way imaginable: he didn't *become* the most wretched of men; why, as soon as he was born (it was winter too) they exposed him so that he shouldn't grow up and kill his father; when he was still a lad he married an old woman; worse, she was his mother. Next Aeschylus threatens to destroy all Euripides' prologues with one little oil-flask. Whatever the exact object of Aeschylus' ridicule, whether it is Euripides' fondness for commonplace words and diminutives, his monotony of sentence-structure or metre, there is no doubt of the comic effect of the scene: as the recitation of each prologue is interrupted by the ludicrous 'lost his little oil-flask', nonsense overcomes reasoned fault-finding.

[1] 840 and 946–7, 1046–7, 1301.

The treatment of tragic lyric which follows appeals on both levels: it is funny in a simple, almost farcical way and it also contains indirect criticism. Euripides, threatening that he will 'cut all his rival's lyrics into one', sings a pastiche of warlike, solemn lines drawn from a variety of plays, linked by a refrain whose meaning becomes increasingly irrelevant.[1] This song ends: 'I am empowered to voice the fateful command, expediting the warriors (Ah, the beating, comest thou not to the rescue?)', and is followed by another even less intelligible collocation of lines with a meaningless refrain. The choral song which precedes this scene is written in a style typical of comedy, and the music and delivery, no doubt exaggerated, of the Aeschylean lyrics must have made an amusing contrast. There are problems for us in deciding exactly what Euripides is ridiculing, but they arise chiefly through our ignorance of Greek music. We are not sure, for example, why Euripides attributes the second stanza to the 'citharodic nomes' or what is the point of the refrain *tophlattothrat*, although some features of metrical parody are clear (and have been prepared by the choral songs of 814–29 and 875–82).

The choral lyric of 814–29, which had portrayed the warriors making ready for battle, had used long runs of dactyls, starting off from a spondee, each stanza ending with a short trochaic line. A similarly Aeschylean metrical pattern is discernible in the prayer to the Muses of 875–84.[2] In the lyric Euripides chooses to parody a slightly less common Aeschylean opening for dactyls: instead of, for example,

— — — ∪∪ — ∪∪ — ∪∪ — ∪∪ — — (814 etc.)

we have Φθιῶτ᾽ Ἀχιλλεῦ, τί ποτ᾽ ἀνδροδάικτον ἀκούων

— — ∪ — — ∪∪ — ∪∪ — ∪∪ — — (1264; cf. 1270, 1285).[3]

What sort of response did Aristophanes expect to mockery like this? First, the content of the lines is recognizably Aeschylean

[1] Euripides' threat εἰς ἓν γὰρ αὐτοῦ πάντα τὰ μέλη ξυντεμῶ probably contains a culinary metaphor since pastiche is like a hash, but ξυντέμνω may also have its meaning 'abridge', in view of the notorious length of Aeschylean lyrics (1262).

[2] Cf. *Pers.* 886, *Eum.* 347, 526 ff., and see A. M. Dale, *The Lyric Metres of Greek Drama*, 44–5.

[3] The lekythion scene has accustomed us to an interruption after — — ∪ — — e.g. (1240) Οἰνεύς ποτ᾽ ἐκ γῆς ᾽ ληκύθιον ἀπώλεσεν.
This rhythm may be deliberately echoed in Φθιῶτ᾽ Ἀχιλλεῦ.

– war, religion and 'air-roaming hounds' – and individual lines may have been familiar as 'quotations'. It is a reasonable assumption that the music was recognizably Aeschylean: just as there are now many people who could say that a piece of music is by Chopin, and that it is a mazurka, so Athenians are likely to have been able to discern the characteristics of the different styles, even if they could not say *why* a piece sounded Aeschylean. Demonstrating, and remembering, the difference between a polonaise and a mazurka is one thing, explaining it in words alone, quite another. The response to this type of scene is pleased recognition – 'Yes, that's just like Aeschylus' – and enjoyment of the incongruity of the intrusion of the operatic manner into scenes of buffoonery.

Aeschylus' parody of Euripidean lyric, both choral and solo, may be rather broader comedy, but it seems to work in much the same way as the passages just described. The choral lyric (1309–22) is provided with a female accompanist, Euripides' Muse, playing the castanets as Hypsipyle had done in the tragedy; no doubt she is as hideous as her author's poetry. In fact the song begins rather charmingly with halcyons twittering over the sea and continues, in increasing incoherence, with dolphins and vines, to an intelligible close: 'Embrace me, my child.' Much of this farrago, perhaps all, is quotation. At one point Aeschylus imitates Euripides' fashionable prolongation of a syllable: the word is εἱλίσσετε ('twine' or 'wind') and its first syllable, presumably in an attempt at word-painting, was sung to more than one note, perhaps to two notes in genuine Euripides but to several in the exaggerated parody. The other target of the song is Euripides' freedom in using short syllables in this particular class of metre, aeolo-choriambic, so that the conventional pattern — — —◡◡— —might give way to ◡◡— ◡◡ ◡◡ — —.

The monody which follows (1331–64) draws attention to Euripides' liking for this sort of intensely emotional expression. In it a tragic heroine tells a story by episodes: she has had a terrifying dream, and calls on her handmaids to help in the rites of purification. Next she notices that one of her domestics has stolen a fowl and vanished. This must have happened while she was preparing the spun thread for market. Her laments give way to a plea to Cretan guards and divinities to help her catch the thief. At this point Dionysus and Aeschylus decide they have had enough. Undoubtedly the monody contains some close parody of style and characteristic subject-matter, like the dream.[1] Euripides' catch-word φροῦδος appears, as it does as early as the *Clouds* (718-22); the quasi-hysterical repetition of 1352-5 with its successive short syllables is also typical: 'And left me suffering, suffering, and I dripped, dripped rivulets, rivulets, from my eyes, ah me.' But the parody is not all close, since the desire for accuracy comes second to the desire to amuse. It is true that Euripides can place tragic events in an almost homely setting and true that his characters' speech in suitable scenes is more colloquial than that of other tragedians. It is not true that his monodies mingled elevated and ordinary language or commonplace and mysterious subject-matter, but if Aristophanes can make them do so the song will be all the funnier.

Finally we come to the weighing-scene, proposed by Aeschylus, of course. The scene is absurd. Aeschylus' style, by common consent, is more 'weighty' than that of Euripides, but he wins by reciting lines which mention heavy objects. Once again, Aristophanes is making us think about critical terminology, particularly when it uses metaphor. By the logic of comedy, once talk about weight and you are in danger of seeing poetry as a commodity to be judged by the ounce or the yard.

We have seen that the contest is given shape by the contrast between the personalities of the two tragedians, and, true to his nature, the victorious Aeschylus returns to the upper world flinging a last insult at Euripides: 'Mind that lying clown, that stop-at-nothing Euripides never seats himself on MY throne, even by accident.' In the actual *agon* the chorus fulfil their customary task of spurring on the competitors, but afterwards they rarely intervene, perhaps because there is plenty of other singing. Their last song before the *exodos* helps to bind together the literary and moral questions raised in the play: 'Blessed are the sharp in mind, abundant evidence of that: look at Aeschylus on his way back up home again – he proved he'd got sense – he'll do the city some good, and his family, and his friends, just because he's bright. No blessing then to sit around with Socrates and chat, slighting all that matters in Tragedy and throwing out

[1] 1331-41; cf. *Hec.* 68-72, *I.T.* 42 ff., 150 ff.

Music. Highbrow discussions, silly pedantry, unproductive time-wasting – sure signs of insanity.' Intellect, good sense, wisdom, sanity: in its own way the *Frogs* is as much concerned as the *Bacchae* in revealing the blessings and limitations of these qualities, in particular as they affect one's judgment of men and books. In the end, the clever critics are seen to be on the losing side, with Socrates, Euripides, orators; clever, but not right-minded.

But one cannot conclude that Aristophanes was against all criticism, or even against all the 'new criticism', any more than that he was against Euripides and for Aeschylus. Let us finally look at the part Dionysus plays in all this. In his scene with Heracles Dionysus tells of his love for Euripides: 'And then, while I was reading the *Andromeda* to myself my heart was smitten with desire' (52–4), a desire that he can hardly describe, save by comparing it with Heracles' lust for soup. In quest of Euripides he is resolved to go to Hades. In the ensuing dialogue it emerges that Dionysus values Euripides for his cleverness and, for various reasons, disapproves of all contemporary dramatists. For the most part Dionysus uses the language of the amateur enthusiast, simply praising Sophocles as 'equable', for example, but presently his language becomes more extravagant (89–102), and he sets up as an expert. After a ludicrous mis-quotation of the notorious line from the *Hippolytus* Heracles asks, 'You like *that*?' 'I'm more than crazy about it.' 'It's rubbish, of course – you think so too.' 'I won't have you living in my mind: you've got a home of your own.' 'What's more, it's obviously completely pernicious.' 'You're the expert – at food.' The Dionysus of the contest has several tasks: when there is a third party in contest-scenes he may conciliate or provoke either of the opponents, and also make flippant interventions to relieve the seriousness of debate. So Dionysus from time to time quells Aeschylus and makes silly remarks, which on occasion reveal him as a foil to the literary experts. This Dionysus finds Aeschylean tragedy difficult, although he likes it (916–17, 932–3, 1028–9). He is positive that drama ought to improve citizens, while unconvinced by Aeschylus' claim that his plays make better warriors (1012–38). He does his best to understand the bewildering new criticism, compliments the contestants and

156

admits 'I haven't an idea what you're talking about' (1168). Let Aeschylus and Euripides discuss myth, Dionysus cares about the practical application of their remarks as it might affect contemporary Athenians. This quality in Dionysus, although evidence of his limited intellectual range, is a pointer to the conclusion of the contest when Dionysus says that he made the descent to Hades in search of a poet who would rescue the city that she might celebrate the festivals. In the event, unable to decide between the political advice of the tragic poets, in accordance with the dictates of his soul he chooses Aeschylus.

I have tried to show that in the *Frogs* Aristophanes treats as one issues that we should divide into religious, political and artistic, if no more, and, further, that as a comic poet he is perpetually shifting the ground of his humour. If this is true, we cannot expect him to sketch fifth-century criticism for us or state his view of it. Nevertheless some sort of summary must be attempted. First, literature is an integral part of the life of the city, giving pleasure and instruction (which are not mutually exclusive here). Moreover, there is no opposition between 'life' and 'literature', no idea that literature provides an escape from life nor that it is an adornment to the city nor that it supplies objects for aesthetic contemplation. The methods by which criticism proceeds are in part those of normal argument, plus a good deal of abuse and absurdity. Thus no special expertise or knowledge is needed in the discussion of character and morality in the *agon*. At the other extreme, the passages of analysis, and to some extent those of parody, presuppose the existence of a professional criticism, strange to the layman, dealing with matters of semantics, metre and syntax. At the mid-point we suspect a certain, non-technical familiarity with formal nomenclature and the like. In my belief Aristophanes did not see criticism in its entirety as inimical to literature, nor new criticism as inimical to old. It is possible that he combined a conviction that the fashionable in literature and criticism was unworthy with delight in exploiting the new developments.

There is no doubt that the parodist enjoys the exercise of his skill, the realization that he can exactly hit off the manner of X. So parody may be only a *jeu d'esprit*, and the parodist may have

157

no employment except that intermittently offered by *New Statesman* competitions. This is perhaps one reason for our dismissive attitude to the genre. But parody is a mode of criticism as well as a mode of humour (sometimes wit). Here is part of the prospectus of W. H. Auden's daydream College for Bards: the curriculum includes learning by heart of thousands of lines of poetry in three or four languages. 'The library would contain no books of literary criticism, and the only critical exercise required would be the writing of parodies.'[1] Note the alliance of learning by heart and the writing of parody.

Let us first consider parody as a mode of humour. In parody, especially parody performed on the stage, there is an element of mimicry. Children delight in catching the mannerisms of those well known to them and exaggerate until what in truth is mildly odd becomes hilariously funny: their motive may not be malicious. In the end, the oddity ridiculed is inseparable from their image of the man. The cartoonist by a similar technique fixes the image of a politician in the public mind and makes him less of an ogre (in the case of a Hitler), or less worthy of respect. (The satirist, by contrast, exaggerates what is repulsive or alarming in order to increase fear, scorn and loathing.) The Greek comic poet who ridiculed the public figure of his day by mimicry used a specialized form of mimicry in literary parody. Some of the appeal of parody arises through incongruity, which may be produced in more than one way. In paratragedy, for example, the tone and feeling appropriate to tragedy may embody material apt for comedy; similarly, trivial subject-matter may be set to a tune more fit for tragedy, and within a scene of parody a quotation may be distorted by the insertion of a colloquial or obscene word. Stage parody, then, amuses as mimicry and burlesque amuse, pleasing the eye as well as the ear and the mind, and to some in the audience it gives the additional joy of knowing themselves well-informed: such men not only follow the broad outlines but pride themselves on their awareness of all the details of the parody.

As a literary genre parody today lacks the setting which gave Greek parody its special character. Although parody is not restricted to the intellectual parlour-game its appearance in, say,

[1] *The Dyer's Hand*, 77.

Ulysses or the poems of T. S. Eliot does not guarantee it wide-spread enjoyment. There were two prerequisites for the success of parody, one the distinctness of genres, the other the ordinary man's familiarity with a sufficient bulk of poetry. 'Poet is heir of poet': one poet could use Homeric phrases as part of his own poem, without in any sense 'quoting', while another could amplify or correct a predecessor's words.[1]

As a mode of criticism parody achieved much the same results as critical analysis has achieved in recent times, and I do not think it extravagant to claim that it was a more subtle and accomplished form of criticism than any other then practised.[2] In the *Acharnians*, produced in 425, Aristophanes began the caricature of Euripides he was to perfect in the *Frogs* twenty years later.[3] The hero, Dicaeopolis, has to defend his private peace-treaty against the violent attack of the chorus; thinking that pitiful accoutrements will stir their compassion he sets off to borrow from Euripides. There is no need to comment on the humour of the hundred lines which follow, nor on their dramatic effectiveness, save to point out that the scene *is* a suppliant-scene, as well as being a parody of one. By a mixture of cheek, cajolery and persistence Dicaeopolis gets all he came for. By the time he departs, we have absorbed, almost without noticing, the following 'facts' about Euripides: the chief character of each play is likely to be blind, crippled or impoverished, and to be represented realistically upon the stage; his pitiful costume may make him seem other than he is, and when he speaks antithesis and mystification will be the rule. The rags and the beggar's kit which accompanies them constitute the Euripidean drama: remove them, and there is nothing left. The style of Euripides is a strange amalgam of diminutives, which sound colloquial, and self-apostrophe in the Homeric manner: 'My soul, there is a journey, Far away from chives' (480); his vocabulary is partly

---

[1] For Semonides' quotation of Homer see p. 135; Bacchylides (5.191) refers to, and Simonides (*P.M.G.* 579) amplifies, Hesiod. Solon (22) amended Mimnermus, according to Diogenes Laertius 1.60. The incidence of Homeric phraseology in e.g. early elegiac is amply attested by Diehl.

[2] For parody in general see G. Kitchin, *Burlesque and Parody in English* (London, 1931), D. Macdonald, *Parodies* (London, 1961); for Aristophanic parody and paratragedy E. W. Handley and J. Rea, *The Telephus of Euripides*, *B.I.C.S.* Supplement 5, 1957, P. Rau, *Paratragodia* (Munich, 1967), A. C. Schlesinger, *T.A.P.A.* 1936, 296–314, *A.J.P.* 1937, 294–305.   [3] 393–489.

that of his associates, the sophists, and is full of neologisms. Euripides himself is taciturn, given to displays of hauteur, the worshipper of a strange Zeus. This personality differs from the characterization in the *Frogs*: here it is Dicaeopolis who is excitable, as he shows by verbal repetition and a much greater loquacity than Euripides. The personality indicated in the *Acharnians* accords better with the moroseness mentioned by other sources, but Aristophanes may have been more concerned to make a contrast with Dicaeopolis and Aeschylus respectively than to portray accurately. Nevertheless, personality cannot be ignored since it was held to colour a writer's work.

Since the fabric of this scene is woven of quotation, misquotation, paratragedy, ordinary colloquialisms and those favoured by Euripides, it is hard to be sure whether Aristophanes intends us to think that Euripides was wrong to introduce homely objects into tragedy, or wrong to combine realism and high-flown diction ('The fellow waxes insolent: bar up the palace gates' 479), or whether he is ensuring the maximum tension between the manners of tragedy and comedy in order to increase the effectiveness of Dicaeopolis' remarks about Euripides' mother (457 and 478) and of the obscenity which ends Dicaeopolis' long speech (435–44). It is certain, I think, that the scene as a whole implies that Euripides' plays were primarily a source for the orator, it may be for the unscrupulous orator. The modern reader might think this a damning indictment, a denial that Euripides' tragedies had any literary or dramatic worth, but it must be remembered that one theme of this play, as of the *Clouds*, is oratory: should the ordinary citizen have a voice in public affairs? will he be heard if he is not an accomplished orator? The old men of the chorus, after appealing to the Muse who is associated with their country occupation of charcoalburning to give them forceful utterance, point out that the old and uneducated are at a disadvantage when faced with clever young orators (665–718). Dicaeopolis, after 'swallowing Euripides' (484), succeeds in persuading the chorus that they and the military are wrong to oppose peace with Sparta. The message is clear: oratory does some harm, but without oratory, here embodied in Euripides, not in Protagoras, Socrates or a demagogue, peace would be impossible.

160

All this may seem a far cry from literary criticism, but the fact that the Euripides-scene cannot be discussed without mention of oratory, nor the contest between Euripides and Aeschylus without mention of war and politics, illustrates the fact that still at the end of the fifth century literary criticism as an independent branch of study was the exception, literary criticism as an expression of political and social morality the rule. Moreover, the parodist, by the very nature of his art, picks out and exaggerates what is new or outré in his subject. Fifth-century criticism contained in comedy is therefore likely to be biased in that its context is not literature divorced from life, and in that it is expressed in a style which distorts. It is as we see the strains which developed in the fifth century whenever the simple belief that poetry was given by gods to men for the enjoyment of gods and men came into collision with scepticism and with the growth of specialization in arts and sciences, and as we see the loss of political confidence, that we begin to understand how Plato's literary sensitivity and perceptiveness came to issue in the repressive attitudes of the *Republic* and begin to estimate Aristotle's stature as the first critic to concentrate all his powers on literature. By his work, the quarrel between poetry and philosophy was put on one side and criticism allowed to begin its slow growth to maturity. The modern reader has gained much from just and reasoned estimates of writers and their works, from systematic analysis and the dissemination of understanding and enjoyment, but our gratitude for these benefits should not cause us to undervalue the fifth-century achievement; in particular, the insight, vitality and skill with which Pindar, Euripides and Aristophanes wrote about the Muses' art.

Select Bibliography

CRITICS AND CRITICISM

J. W. H. Atkins, *Literary Criticism in Antiquity*, 2 vols., Cambridge, 1934, and London, 1952.

G. W. Baker, 'De comicis Graecis litterarum iudiciis', *H.S.C.P.* 1904, 121–240.

S. H. Butcher, *Aristotle's theory of Poetry and Fine Art*, London, 1894, and New York, 1957.

I. Bywater, *Aristotle on the Art of Poetry*, Oxford, 1909.

D. Daiches, *Critical Approaches to Literature*, London, 1956.

J. F. D'Alton, *Roman Literary Theory and Criticism*, London, 1931, and New York, 1962.

J. D. Denniston, *Greek Literary Criticism*, London, 1924.

G. F. Else, *Aristotle's Poetics, the Argument*, Harvard, 1957.

G. M. A. Grube, *The Greek and Roman Critics*, London, 1965.

L. Radermacher, *Artium scriptores*, Vienna, 1951.

G. Saintsbury, *A History of Criticism*, London, 1908.

E. E. Sikes, *The Greek View of Poetry*, London, 1931.

F. Solmsen, 'The origins and methods of Aristotle's *Poetics*', *C.Q.* 1935, 192–201.

P. Vicaire, *Platon: critique littéraire*, Paris, 1960.

G. Watson, *The Literary Critics*, London, 1962.

T. B. L. Webster, 'Greek theories of art and literature down to 400 B.C.', *C.Q.* 1939, 166–79.

RELIGION AND THOUGHT

A. W. H. Adkins, *Merit and Responsibility*, Oxford, 1960.

P. Boyancé, *Le culte des Muses chez les philosophes grecs*, Paris, 1937.

F. M. Cornford, *Principium sapientiae*, Cambridge, 1952.

A. Delatte, *Les conceptions de l'enthousiasme chez les philosophes présocratiques*, Paris, 1934.

E. R. Dodds, *The Greeks and the Irrational*, Berkeley, 1951.

O. Falter, *Der Dichter und sein Gott*, Würzburg, 1934.

H. Fränkel, *Dichtung und Philosophie des frühen Griechentums*, New York, 1951.

W. Jaeger, *Paideia*, tr. G. Highet, 3 vols. Oxford, 1939–44.

H. I. Marrou, *Histoire de l'éducation dans l'antiquité*, Paris, 1950.

W. Otto, *Die Musen*, Darmstadt, 1956.

J. Press, *The Fire and the Fountain*, Oxford, 1955.

E. Schwarzenburg, *Die Grazien*, Bonn, 1966.

B. Snell, *Poetry and Society*, Indiana, 1961.

A. Sperduti, 'The divine nature of poetry in antiquity', *T.A.P.A.* 1950.

F. De Waele, *The magic staff or rod in Graeco-Italian antiquity*, Ghent, 1927.

AUTHORS AND WORKS

T. W. Allen, *Homer: the origins and the transmission*, Oxford, 1924.

C. M. Bowra, *Early Greek Elegists*, Cambridge, Mass., 1938.

Heroic Poetry, Oxford, 1952.

Pindar, Oxford, 1964.

C. O. Brink, *Horace on Poetry*, Cambridge, 1963.

C. Brooke-Rose, *A Grammar of Metaphor*, London, 1958.

A. R. Burn, *The Lyric Age of Greece*, London, 1960.

R. W. B. Burton, *Pindar's Pythian odes*, Oxford, 1962.

J. Carrière, *Theognis, poèmes élégiaques*, Paris, 1948.

P. Chantraine, *Grammaire Homérique*, 2 vols., Paris, 1948, 1953.

A. M. Dale, *Euripides: Helen*, Oxford, 1967.

The Lyric Metres of Greek Drama, Cambridge, 1948.

J. D. Denniston, 'Technical terms in Aristophanes', *C.Q.* 1927, 113–21.

E. R. Dodds, *Plato: Gorgias*, Oxford, 1959.

J. Duchemin, *Pindare, Poète et Prophète*, Paris, 1955.

J. M. Edmonds, *The Fragments of Attic Comedy*, 3 vols., Leiden, 1957–61.

A. W. Gomme, *The Greek Attitude to Poetry and History*, Berkeley, 1954.

R. Hackforth, *Plato's Phaedrus*, Cambridge, 1952.

Fondation Hardt, *Entretiens sur l'antiquité classique*, Vandœuvres – Génève:

Tome 1 *La notion du divin depuis Homère jusqu'à Platon*, 1952.

Tome 7 *Hésiode et son influence*, 1962.

Tome 10 *Archiloque*, 1964.

E. A. Havelock, *Preface to Plato*, Oxford, 1963.

J. Jones, *On Aristotle and Greek Tragedy*, London, 1962.

G. A. Kennedy, *The Art of Persuasion in Greece*, Princeton, 1963.

A. Koller, 'Die Parodie', *Glotta* 1956, 17–32.

G. Lanata, *Poetica pre-Platonica: testimonianze e frammenti*, Florence, 1963.

A. Lesky, *A History of Greek Literature*, London, 1966.

O. Masson, *Hipponax*, Paris, 1962.

G. Norwood, *Pindar*, Berkeley, 1945.

D. Page, *Alcman: the Partheneion*, Oxford, 1951.

Sappho and Alcaeus, Oxford, 1955.

L. Radermacher, *Aristophanes: Frösche*, Vienna, 1954.

P. Rau, *Paratragodia*, Munich, 1967.

W. Ritchie, *The Authenticity of the Rhesus of Euripides*, Cambridge, 1964.

H. Weir Smyth, *Greek Melic Poets*, London, 1900.

F. Solmsen, *Hesiod and Aeschylus*, Ithaca, 1949.

POETRY AND CRITICISM BEFORE PLATO

W. B. Stanford, *Aristophanes: Frogs*, London, 1958.

Greek Metaphor, Oxford, 1936.

M. Treu, *Archilochus*, Munich, 1959.

T. B. L. Webster, *Greek Art and Literature 700–530 B.C.*, London, 1959.

Greek Art and Literature 530–400 B.C., Oxford, 1930.

M. L. West, *Hesiod: Theogony*, Oxford, 1966.

D. Young, *Theognis*, Leipzig, 1961.

MUSIC AND ART

W. D. Anderson, *Ethos and Education in Greek Music*, Harvard, 1966.

P. E. Arias and M. Hirmer, *A History of Greek Vase Painting*, London, 1962.

J. D. Beazley, 'A hymn to Hermes', *A.J.A.* 1948, 336–40.

R. M. Cook, *Greek Painted Pottery*, London, 1960.

R. S. Folson, *Handbook of Greek Pottery*, London, 1967.

I. Henderson, 'Ancient Greek music' in *The New Oxford History of Music*, vol. 1.

H. Immerwahr, 'Book rolls on Attic vases', in *Classical, mediaeval and renaissance studies in honour of Berthold Louis Ullman*, vol. 1, 11–48.

G. M. A. Richter and M. Milne, *Shapes and Names of Athenian Vases*, New York, 1935.

M. Wegner, *Das Musikleben der Griechen*, Berlin, 1949.

Die Musensarkophage, Berlin, 1966.

R. P. Winnington-Ingram, 'Ancient Greek music' in *Lustrum* 1958, 5–57.

Index Locorum

See also entry under author's name in General Index

Italic figures show page numbers in this book.

Aeschylus, *Prometheus Vinctus* 442–506, *103*; 459–61, *19*

Aristophanes, *Acharnians* 393–489, *159–61*; 665–75, *74* f.

Wasps 1022, 1049–50, *74*

Thesmophoriazusae 49–57, *96* f.

Frogs 756–end, *148–57*

Aristotle, *Poetics* 1460a11–b5, *118* f.

Bacchylides, 5.1–6, *55*; 5.16–30, *85* f.; 12.1–4, *56* f.; 13.221–31, *57*; 19.1–14, *67* f.

Democritus, D.-K. 18, 21, *86* f.

Euripides, *Bacchae* 409–16, *21* f.

Electra 520–44, *135* f.

Hercules Furens 673–86, *73* f.

Hesiod, *Theogony* 2–8, *20* f.; 22–34, *35*; 27–8, *112* f.; 39–43, *15*; 53–65, *10*; 81–97, *117*

Homer, *Iliad* 2.485–92, *40*; 2.594–600, *27*

Odyssey, 8.489–91, *121*; 22.347–8, *92*

Parmenides, D.-K. 1.1–28, *66* ff.

Pindar, *Olympian* 6.22–6, *63* f.

Nemean 3.1–5, *54*; 7.20–4, *118*

Isthmian 2.1–11, *111* f.

Paean 6.38–45, *59* f.; 7(b).10–17, *60*

Plato, *Ion* 533D–E, *80* f.; 533E–534C, *81*, *83–6*; 535C–E, *121* f.

Phaedrus 245A, *82*; 258E–259E, *78* f.

Protagoras 339–348B, *145–8*

Simonides, *P.M.G.* 542, *144–8*

Solon, 1.1–14, *47* f.

Stesichorus, *P.M.G.* 192, *114* f.

Theognis, 769–72, *109*

Timotheus, *P.M.G.* 791.202–36, *99*

General Index

Aeschylus, 18, 19, 70, 71, 76, 80, 91, 100, 103–4, 108, 114, 124, 136, 138–9, 149, 150–7, 160
Aesthetic theory, 131, 141–4
Agalma 55–6
Agathon, 73, 75, 137, 138
Alcaeus, 100
Alcman, 11, 14, 15, 16, 18, 20, 39, 48, 100, 101, 102, 122
Allegory, 131
Anacreon, 39, 86, 89, 100, 124, 141
Anaxagoras, 131, 132
Anaximenes, 134
Antiphon, 134, 142
Apollo, 12, 13, 18, 19, 23–9 *passim*, 36, 41, 44, 50, 57, 58, 59, 61, 70, 72, 80, 84, 85, 88, 92, 99, 102, 117
Archilochus, 36–7, 39, 40, 41, 90, 93, 113, 123, 124, 135, 137–8, 140
Aretē, 67, 73, 107, 139, 144, 145–8
Aristeas, 65, 85
Aristides, 12
Aristophanes, 2, 5, 8, 13, 14, 15, 20, 23, 40–1, 71–6 *passim*, 84, 86, 88, 89, 93, 96–105 *passim*, 108–9, 111, 114, 123, 125, 127, 130, 133, 134, 136–141, 148–161
Aristotle, 1, 2, 3, 6, 17, 19, 98, 105, 112, 118–19, 120, 127, 135, 136, 138, 139, 141, 142, 144
Athyrma, 56
Auden, W. H., 49–50, 51, 158

Bacchylides, 13, 15, 16, 17, 18, 21, 23, 26, 37, 38, 39, 41, 46, 48, 52–8, 63, 67–8, 72, 75, 84, 85–6, 88, 95, 98, 100, 114, 124, 126, 127, 129, 135, 159

166

Blind poet, 28–9, 115–16
Byron, 13

Callias, 101
Callimachus, 115
Calliope, 1, 6, 17, 19, 25, 26, 27, 28, 55, 63, 79, 99, 101
Certamen, 135
Charis, Charites *see* Graces
Choerilus, 41, 47, 98
Cicero, 87
Cleobulus, 95
Clio, 17, 18, 23, 55, 56, 57, 126
Corinna, 18, 21, 135
Crates, 104
Cratinus, 37, 75, 89, 90, 94, 97, 98, 101, 104, 136, 151
Critias, 137–8, 141

Damastes, 134
Damon, 131–2
Democritus, 35, 86–7, 102, 103, 132, 134, 137
Demodocus, 37, 38, 42, 46, 64, 116, 121, 136, 143
Dionysius Chalcus, 17
Dionysus, 22, 25, 71, 76, 80, 81, 82, 83, 90
Dissoi Logoi, 116, 120, 143

Eliot, T. S., 3, 6, 8, 9, 90, 159
Emotion, 120–6
Empedocles, 16, 40, 67, 85, 110
Empson, W., 62–3
Epic Cycle, 11, 28, 46–7, 81–2
Epicharmus, 13, 15, 90
Epimenides, 35
Erato, 18, 27, 79
Eumelus, 11, 24
Eupolis, 96, 100, 101, 124, 137

Euripides, 12, 13, 15, 17, 19, 21, 29,
41, 52, 71–6, 81, 87, 97, 98, 101,
103, 108, 114, 123, 125, 126, 127,
136, 138, 139, 149, 150–7, 159–61
Euterpe, 18

Fame, 17, 55, 58, 85, 110–11, 126–9
François Vase, 12, 16, 25, 27

Glaucon, 134
Gorgias, 114, 116, 119–20, 123,
133, 138, 142
Graces, The, 12, 15, 22, 26, 68, 72,
73, 80, 83, 118, 125–6

Handbooks, 2, 132
Helicon, 20, 21, 22, 24, 26, 27, 35,
60, 110, 112–13
Heraclitus, 82, 113, 130
Hermippus, 20, 101
Herodotus, 94, 134
Hesiod, 1, 10, 11, 12–16, 18, 20, 21,
22, 24, 25, 35, 36, 37, 41, 47, 66,
67, 73, 84, 87, 93, 94, 98, 100,
102, 106, 110, 112–13, 114, 115,
117, 120, 121, 122, 123, 124, 131,
138, 151, 159
Hippias, 133, 139, 144
Hipponax, 141
Homer, 1, 12, 15, 20, 22, 24, 27,
36, 37, 40, 41–6, 49, 52, 54, 59,
61, 64–5, 66, 67, 69, 70, 72, 73,
79, 81, 83, 84, 85, 86, 87, 89, 92,
93, 95, 98, 100, 102, 106, 107,
110, 113, 114, 115, 116, 117, 118,
120, 121–6 *passim*, 131, 133, 134,
135, 136, 137, 138, 140, 149, 159
Homeric Hymns, 15, 24, 47, 72
Hymn to Apollo, 12, 15, 24, 47,
100, 110
Hymn to Hermes, 20, 24, 37, 47,
64, 65, 84, 92, 97
Horace, 22, 87, 91, 95, 138

Ibycus, 21, 49, 127, 135
Imagery,
Metaphor, 5, 62–3

Craft-metaphor, 55, 93–6, 104,
149
Muses' chariot, 26, 61, 63–4, 70,
74
Gift of song, 37, 38–9, 47, 55, 57,
60, 101, 117
Path of song, 55, 64–9, 136
Streams, etc., of song, 22–3, 81,
83, 88–90, 124
Song as garland, etc., 81, 95,
111, 128–9, 138
Song as honey, 83, 124, 138
Song as philtre, 124
Song as weapon, 69–70
Song as wine, 90, 125
Poet as interpreter of Muses, 59,
88; as their messenger, 41, 61,
109; as their pupil, 35, 37, 40;
as their servant, 41, 55; as
their son, 17, 61, 99, 101–2
Inspiration, 35, 49, 60, 78, 79–90
Invention, 60, 73, 101–2
Isocrates, 88, 139

Juvenal, 22

Lasus of Hermione, 132

Margites, 41, 110
Melpomene, 18, 27
Metagenes, 104, 136
Metre, 75, 149, 153, 154, 155
Metrodorus, 131, 134
Mimesis, 142–4
Mimnermus, 11, 47, 159
Mnemosyne, 10, 11, 18, 19, 20, 44,
47, 55, 59, 60, 74, 80, 128
Musaeus, 18, 25, 27, 102, 105, 134
Muses, The, 1–77 *passim*, 78–82,
88, 95, 96, 98, 99, 102, 103,
107–8, 109, 110, 112–13, 115,
117, 120, 122, 125, 126, 127,
128, 129, 130, 138, 141, 151,
153, 154, 160, 161
Invocations to Muses, 41–6, 48,
49, 53–4, 79, 141
Music, 99, 102, 107, 120, 131–2,
144, 151, 153

167